The Mastiff
Aristocratic Guardian

by

dee dee Andersson

Doral Publishing
1998

Published by Doral Publishing, Inc.
8560 Salish Lane #300, Wilsonville, Oregon 97070-9612
Order through National Book Network, Nashville, TN

Printed in the United States of America.

Edited by Luana Luther
Cover design by Universal Graphics

Library of Congress Number: 98-70320

ISBN: 0-944875-51-3

The Mastiff: aristocratic guardian/ by dee dee Andersson.
    302 p. cm.
  ISBN: 0-944-87551-3 (he)
  History, breeding, development and showing of a giant breed.
  1. Dog breeds—Mastiff. 2. Dogs—History. 3. Dog shows. 1. Andersson, dee dee.
SF429.M36 1998
636.7   98-70320
                                      CIP

DEDICATION

This book is dedicated to my wonderful husband, Bjorn, for your unstinting and absolute support of my "mastiff habit." When other family members thought I lost my marbles, you always had faith and stood firm by me. I also dedicate this book to Sherman and Maggie because without you two, there would be nothing to write about. You were both the best. I still miss you every single day and wish you were back here with me and we could be starting all over again together.

iv

ACKNOWLEDGMENTS

My very dear friends, Carol Mathews, Cat Angus, Irene Byrne, Nancy Hempel, Gay Jordan and Cathy Babins, thank you for encouraging and believing in me. Without you, this project may not have been started. Midway through writing the book, a man entered my life whom I fondly call my Angel (he calls himself my Devil). Let me explain. A kind and wonderful gentleman from Germany, Werner Preugschat, took my project to his own heart and through his great generosity I was put in the unique and enviable position of having access to ancient books, treatises, manuscripts, documents and artwork. Because of him, I was able to read ancient literary works dealing with Mastiffs. Thank you, Werner, for the artwork, research, hundreds of faxes, and for your caring and time. A special thanks to Professor Raymond Triquet, president of the French Dogue de Bordeaux Club, for helping me research Fidelle de Fenelon; to Ursula Muller-Naegeli for the Saint Bernard pictures; to Jim Fietsam for drawing the standard illustrations; to Mary Louise Owens and Nicki Camerra for walking me through obedience; to Dr. Steven J. Dugan and Dr. Susan Barden for providing a comprehensive explanation of hereditary eye conditions that may affect Mastiffs; to my friend Dr. Jeff Klemm for sharing your knowledge. Thanks to all the marvelous Mastiff folks who sent me articles and pictures, I wish space had allowed every picture to be included. Finally, my heartfelt thanks to Dr. Grossman, publisher of the book. Based on a few paragraphs, you took a chance on a total unknown. I hope I made you proud.

dee dee

CONTENTS

FOREWORD

Always intrigued with the past (I spent years working on family genealogy), I knew to do justice to a book about Mastiffs would require dedication and hours of tedious research. Even armed with a realistic attitude, until I started researching I did not know the magnitude of the Mastiff role in history. When humans learned to write, Mastiffs were already around, and stories about them were being recorded. They fought in wars for man, participated in cruel sports to entertain man, underwent physical mutilation to qualify as keeper of man's home and goods and, finally, in our civilized time, Mastiffs are still here—as our beloved pets, friends and companions, and, yes, our Guardians.

My goal was to tell readers why Mastiffs are the greatest animals on earth. This book is the labor of my love for them, my way of repaying them for all they have given me. I sought to tell their history, their stories, their peculiarities, their likes and dislikes. Whether stories were written in ancient times, or in the present century, the theme is always the same—Mastiffs are noble. They always commanded attention which explains why so much was written about them in history. They were always remarked upon for their fidelity, courage, mental and physical strength, their stubbornness and ability to carry a grudge—never forgetting an insult or trespass—their inborn instinct to protect any they consider their own and their willingness to risk their lives to protect ours. Out of love and respect for what they are, where they came from, what they endured, and what they mean to all of us today, I present to you, dear reader, the wonderful Mastiff.

CHAPTER 1
THE ANCIENT MASTIFF - WAR
AND GUARDIAN

Mastiffs, or dogs of true Mastiff type, have existed since the human race began recording history. There is no doubt Mastiffs, or dogs that were progenitors of today's Mastiff, were dogs of war in the forefront of battles and employed to bait bears, bulls, lions, tigers, leopards and even human gladiators.

Mastiff-type dogs were utilized as draft animals, called tinker dogs, hauling heavy-weighted tools on their backs for their masters. They were the muscle and force used to turn wheels to draw water from deep wells and called water drawers. A butcher's dog reprimanded and brought in cattle and oxen for his master. The most noteworthy task of the Mastiff throughout the ages, however, was as protector of the home and guardian of the family, a noble role that remains unchanged up to the present time.

Many breeds claim ancient heritage, however, it is an indisputable fact that dogs of Mastiff type were being bred to battle in arenas and fight side by side with the Roman Legions before Christ was born. One historian wrote the Mastiff's origin "is lost in the mist of antiquity."

Because so many different names were used for Mastiff-type dogs, the issue of whether or not the ancient dogs were true Mastiffs

A Faithful Guardian.

This drawing comes from Part I Four-Footed Beasts, of Friedrich Justin Bertuch's Picture Book for Children *published circa 1790.*

is still debated by historians. Probably, Professor Low came nearest to the truth when he said:

> We do not know of any species of canis yet existing in a natural state, which may be regarded as the parent stock of the Mastiff, though such may exist or have existed, is rendered probable by the characters of the race, which have remained constant from age to age, and distinguished the true Mastiff from every other race of dogs.

We can no more solve the question of the origin of Mastiffs than Aristotle's question which came first, the chicken or the egg? Is the Mastiff the root of the tree, the trunk, or a large branch? If the Mastiff is a branch, what is the trunk or root? If there is no single root, what combination made up the root? There just are no definitive answers. We do not know with certainty if the Mastiff is an original breed. We do not know the original birth place. We do not even know the original colors of Mastiffs. Based on information we have, we can speculate on what was probable. We know Mastiff-type dogs existed in ancient times, possibly as far back in history as 5000-2000 B.C. Colors were pied (white and black), tans, reds, blacks, and blue brindles. There were dogs with pendulous ears and truncated muzzles.

We know the word Mastiff was generically used to describe a familial or functional type rather than a particular breed and there is no doubt the dogs underwent some changes in the finer points of appearance—suitability for work being the fundamental goal. It is probable that qualities evolved in a specific direction, to develop desirable characteristics, such as strength, endurance, intelligence and courage—and those characteristics survived the processes of change and are still strong inherent traits in our Mastiffs today.

The confusion over what constituted the ancient Mastiff is compounded by the various names used to describe dogs that came down through the ages and eventually evolved into that which is now known simply as the Mastiff. In each period of history, mostly

Both Plate 19 (left), the Englische Dogge, and Plate 20 (below), showing the German Bullenbeiser, were published in Naturgetreue Darstellung des Hynd, *by Theodor Gotz, in 1853. A typical rendering of the early pied-color Mastiff and note the rear dewclaw.*

depending on the origin of or languages used by the humans ruling at the time, names were used such as pugnax, pugnaces, alan, allan, alaunt, bandog, band-dog, bandadoc, tie-dog, tydog, curre, mastin, mastif, mastive, massivus, masty, mastyf, mestyf, mastyfe, masif, mastino, Mastiff and sagina. One thing not in question is the Mastiff that exists today is a direct descendent of the hardy and powerful dogs who hunted the wolf, baited the bear and bull, defended the family and flock, and were ancient dogs of war.

The theory believed for centuries is that Phoenicians brought Mastiffs to England. The oriental scholar Bochartus who died in 1667, wrote that "Phoenicians came as far as the islands called Casseterides (Sicily Islands) which abounded in tin." In 1886,

Plates No. 1 (above), Englische Docke, and No. 2 (right), Bahrenbeisser are from 1738 by Johann Elias Ridinger and from the private collection of Werner Preugschat.

M. B. Wynn wrote they came to Cornwall and called Britain "Baractanac or Bractanack, i.e. the land of tin." George Macaulay Trevelyan (Cambridge Regius Professor of Modern History 1927-1940) about Britain wrote "from Iberian and Celtic to Saxon and Danish settlers, from prehistoric and Phoenician traders to Roman and Norman overlords, successive tides of warlike colonists, the most energetic seamen, farmers and merchants of Europe came by the wavepath to inhabit her" and "Cornwall, Wales, and the Highlands of Scotland are inhabited by the oldest stocks...they were...Iberians', coming down, traffickers'to chaffer with the Phoenician traders on the shore." He said dark Iberians had begun early stages of civilized life, explaining how hunters and users of flint learned the uses to which man can turn the dog, goat and other domesticated animals.

One of the earliest illustrations of a dog of true Mastiff type is a Babylonian bas-relief, circa 2200 B.C. The Babylonians carved hunting and war scenes in mud which Assyrians later copied in stone. Scenes show two varieties of dogs, Greyhounds and Mastiff-type dogs that are frequently depicted attacking lions or hunting wild horses, and they are featured in many ceremonial processions. Esar-Haddon's tomb is adorned by an Assyrian Mastiff put there by Assurbanipal, his son who ruled Assyria from 669 to 630 B.C., and he supposedly had Mastiffs. Five clay models are in the British Museum. Figures of terra-cotta Mastiffs were buried beneath the thresholds of Assyrian homes so their spirits would repel evil spirits that may try to enter. Dogs similar to Mastiffs were illustrated on a

belt excavated in Mesopotamia circa 4th Century B.C., approximately 1000 years after Assurbanipal.

King Pyrrhus of Epirus found a Mastiff-type dog guarding his dead master's body. Witnesses said he had not moved from his master's side for three days—not even to eat or drink. Pyrrhus saw to the man's burial, and commanded the dog be brought along and cared for well. A few days afterwards soldiers were paraded before the king who had the dog at his side. When the dog saw the murderers, "he rushed upon them incontinently with loud barks and raging fury, turning often towards Pyrrhus in such a way that not only the King but all his attendants conceived a strong suspicion that these must be the men who had killed his master." The men subsequently confessed to the deed, were tried and put to death. There is a statue of the Molossus of Olympia, Pyrrhus' daughter, and it strongly resembles a Mastiff.

Towards the end of the third "Georgic," Virgil (70-19 B.C.) advised farmers to feed swift Spartan hounds and "keen Molossian" on fat whey. Molossians, protection and watch dogs, were bred by the Molossi tribes that inhabited ancient Epirus. Gratius Faliscus, author of a Cynegeticon about 8 A.D wrote, following the discovery of Britain, that the "pugnaces of Epirus were pitted against the pugnaces of Britain, and the latter completely beat them."

The Bayeux Tapestry, a medieval embroidery preserved from the 11th Century, is a cream-colored linen fabric about 230 feet long and 20 inches wide, comprised of more than 70 panels depicting King Harold and William the Conqueror at the Battle of Hastings in 1066. The main body of the second panel has two small and three larger collared dogs running before the king. The collared dogs are rangy, show decisive tuck-up and have elongated necks with longer heads and do not appear to be of Mastiff type, although they cannot be ruled out altogether as Mastiffs. In the borders of panels seven and twelve, and in the main body of panel eight, are dogs that are of definite Mastiff type. These dogs are heavier, deeper bodied and have shorter faces.

Marco Polo wrote that the great Mogul Emperor of the Yuan Dynasty (1215-1294), Kublai Khan, conducted hunts on an enormous scale and had 5,000 Mastiffs for hunting lions and other big game. Tibetans had Mastiff-type dogs described as "large as donkeys" which were used to guard their flocks.

Drawing from **The Complete German Hunter** *by Hanns Friedrich von Fleming, Leipzig, anno 1749.* **Published by Johann Christian Martini, Book Dealer.**

The Master of the Game written circa 1402-1404 by Edward, 2nd Duke of York is the earliest English manuscript on hunting and the hunting abilities of Mastiffs and alauntes are described. Gentle Alauntes were like Greyhounds except in head "which should be great and short" with small eyes. The preferred color was white with black spots around ears which should be "standing" and "sharp above."

A veutreres Alaunte, also likened to Greyhounds, had great heads, lips and ears. This kind baited bulls and hunted wild boars and their nature was to "hold fast, but they be (heavy) and foul (ugly)" and it was not considered a great loss if this kind was killed by a bull or boar. They must have been slow because greyhounds had to slow the beast down before the Alaunte would grab and hold.

The butcher's Alaunte brought oxen in and guarded homes. They were also good at bull baiting and boar hunting "whether it be with greyhounds at the tryst or with running hounds at bay within the covert. Hounds were not efficient at getting boars out of thickets, but when men let such mastiffs run at the boar they take him in the thick spires (wood) so that any man can slay him, or they make him come out of his strength, so that he shall not remain long at bay."

The Mastiff's nature and office was to: "keep his master's house, and it is a good kind of hound, for they keep and defend with all their power all their master's goods. They be of a churlish nature and ugly shape. Nevertheless there are some that come to be

"The Danish Dog" (left) and "The Mastiff" (below) were drawn by and published by Sydenham Edwards (1800) in Cynographia Britannica.

berslettis (most likely shooting dogs) and also to bring well and fast and wanlace (range) about. Sometimes there be many good, especially for men who hunt for profit of the household to get flesh. Also of Mastiffs and alaunts there be (bred) many good for the wild boar."

More than a thousand years later Dr. Johannes Caius wrote *Of English Dogges* (1576), translated by Abraham Flemming, Student, and he called none of the dogs of Mastiff-type alauntes.

The *Mastyve* or *Bandogge*: [I]s vaste, huge, stubborne, ougly, and eager, of a hevy and burthenous body, and therfore but of litle swiftnesse, terrible, and frightfull to beholde, and more fearce and fell then any Arcadian curre (notwithstanding they are sayd to have their generation of the violent Lyon)...they are appoynted to watche and keepe farme places and countrey cotages...when there is any feare conceaved of theefes, robbers, spoylers, and nightwanderers. They are serviceable, against the Foxe and Badger, to drive wilde and tame Swyne out of Medowes, pastures, glebelands and places planted with fruite, to bayte and take the Bull by the eare, when occasion so requireth. One dogge or two at the uttermost, sufficient for that purpose be the Bull never so monstrous, never so fearce, never so furious, never so stearne, never so untameable. For it is a kinde of dogge capeable of courage, violent and valiaunt, striking could feare into the harts of men, but standing in feare of no man, in so much that no weapons wil make him shrincke, nor abridge his boldnes. Our Englishe men (to the intent that their dogges might the more fell and fearce) assist nature with arte, use, and custome, for they teach their dogges to baite the Beare, to baite the Bull and other such like cruell and bloudy beastes...without any collar to defende their throates, and oftentimes they traine them up in fighting and wrestling with any man having for the safegarde of his lyfe, eyther a Pikestaffe, a clubbe or a sword and by using them to such exercises as these, their dogges become more sturdy and strong. The force which is in them surmounteth all beleefe, the fast holde which they take with their teeth exceedeth all credit, three of them against a

Beare, fowre against a Lyon are sufficient, both
to try masteryes with them and utterly to over-
match them.

A *Butchers Dogge* was named for his use: "for his service
affordeth great benefite to the Butcher as well in the following as in
taking his cattell when neede constraineth, urgeth, and requireth."

The *Molossus* is named for the country in Epirus called
Molossia, "which harboureth many stoute, stronge, and sturdy
Dogges of this sort, for the dogges of that countrey are good in
deede."

This is a sketch from Le
Chien *by Eug. Gayot,
published 1867.*

Water Drawers were "of the greater and waighter sort, drawing water out of wels and deepe pittes, by a wheele which they turne
rounde about by the moving of their burthenous bodies."

Tynckers Curres were so named because "they beare bigge
budgettes fraught with Tinckers tooles, and mettall meete to mend
kettels, porrige pottes, skellets, and chasers, and other such like
trumpery requisite for their occupacion and loytering trade" and
"this kind of dogges hath this principall property ingrafted in them,
that they love their maisters liberally, and hate straungers
despightfully; wherupon it followeth that they are to their masters
in traveiling a singuler safgarde, defending them forceably from the
invasion of villons and theefes, preserving their lyfes from losse, and
their health from hassard, their fleshe from hacking and hewing with
such like desperate daungers."

Defending Dogges were named because "if it chaunce that the
maister bee oppressed, either by a multitude, or by the greater

violence and so be beaten downe that he lye groveling on the grounde, that this dogge forsaketh not his master, no not when he is starcke deade: But induring the force of famishment and the outragious tempestes of the weather, most vigilantly watcheth and carefully keepeth the deade carkasse many dayes, indevouring furthermore, to kil the murtherer of his master, if he may get any advantage. Or else by barcking, by howling, by furious jarring, snarring, and such like means betrayeth the malefactor as desirous to have the death of his aforesayd master rigorouslye revenged."

Barnabe Googe translated *Rei Rusticae Libri* (1570) authored by Conradus Heresbachiur (Conrade Heresbatch) who wrote of the Shepheardes Mastie and the Bandog. About the Bandog:

> [O]f the Mastie that keepeth the house: for this purpose you must provide you such a one, as hath a large and a mighty body, a great and a shrill voyce, that both with his barking he may discover, and with his sight dismay the theefe, yea being not seene, with the horror of his voyce put him to flight. His stature must neither be long, nor short, but well set, his head great, his eyes sharpe, and fierie, either browne, or gray, his lippes blackishe, neyther turning up, nor hanging too much downe, his mouth blacke and wide, his neather jawe fatte,

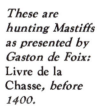

These are hunting Mastiffs as presented by Gaston de Foix: Livre de la Chasse, *before 1400.*

and comming out of it of eyther side a fang, appearing more outward then his other teeth, his upper teeth even with his neather, not hanging too much over, sharpe and hidden with his lippes, his countenance like a Lions, his brest great, and shaghard, his shoulders brode, his legges bigge, his tayle short, his feete very great, his disposition must neyther be too gentle, nor too cursit, that he neither fawne upon a theefe, nor fle upon his friends, very waking, no gadder abroade, nor lavishe of his mouth, barking without cause, neither maketh it any matter

Chevy Chace (1825/26, is etched by Charles George Lewis from the original by Sir E. Landseer, R.A. Pinxt.

to drive the deer with hound and horne
Erle Perey took his way
The chiefest harts in Chevy Chase
To kill and bear away

Engraved for the Woburn Gallery, the original picture is at Woburn, and was exhibited at the Royal Academy of Arts, Burlington House in 1826, and the British Justitation in 1827. The sketch was sold at the artist's sale, lot 119, for 250 guineas, to Messrs. Agnew, March 1874.

though he be not swift: for his is but to fight at home, and to give warning of the enimie.

The Shepheardes Mastie was:

[T]he Dogge that is for the folde, must neyther be so gaunt nor swyft as the Grayhound, nor so fatte nor heavy as the Masty of the house, but very strong, and able to fight and followe the chase, that he may be able to beate away the Woolfe, or other beastes, and to followe the theefe, and recover the praye, and therefore his body would rather be long, then short and thicke: in all other poyntes he must agree with the Bandogge. His head must be great, smoothe, and ful of braines, his eares great, and hanging, his joyntes long, his forelegges shorter then his hinder, but very strayght and great, his clawes wyde, his nayles hard, his heele neyther fleshy nor to hard, the ridge of his backe not to much appearing, nor crooked, his ribs round and well knitte, his shoulder joyntes well distant, his buttockes fatte, and broade, and in all other parts (as I sayd) of the Bandogge before. For his colour it maketh no great matter, though Varro would have him white, and so would Columella, the Dogge for the feelde, as he would have the house Dogge to be blacke: but the pyed colour is judged nought in them both. The white they commend, because he may be discerned from the Woolfe in the night, whereby they shall not strike the Dogge instede of the Woolfe. The blacke agayne for the house, is best commended, because of his terrour to the theefe in the day, and the hurt that he may doo by night, by reason of his not being seene: the Dunne, the branded, and the redde, doo not mislike me so they be well marked beside.

Topsell, in *The Historie of Fovre-Footed Beasts* (1607), said
Bandogs were named for the ligament, band or chain used to tie
them and the Tydog or Mastive (also called Sagina due to the "fatnes
of his body") were named because they are usually "tyed, are mighty,
grosse, and fat fed." He wrote that the dogs of Illyria which were
called "mastini" had upper lips hanging over the lower lips, and
"look fierce like lyons, whom they resemble in neck, eyes, face,
colour and nails, falling upon bears and boars."

Two hundred years after *Master of Game* was written, Randle
Cotgrave's *A Dictionarie of the French and English Tongues* used similar descriptions. The Allan was big, strong, thick headed and had a
short snout—"the brood whereof came first out of Albania (Epirus)."
Allan de boucherie, the butcher's dog, was still used to bring in oxen
and keep their stalls. Allan gentil was still compared to a Greyhound
except for the short, thick head. Allan vautre was still a "great and
ougly curre" with a big head, hanging lips and slouching ears, "kept
onely to bait the Beare and wild Boare." The Dogue was a "Mastiffe,
or great dog" and the Mastin was "a Mastive or Bandog, a great
(countrey) curre."

In 1615, Geruase Markeham, in *Covntrey Contentments*,
wrote there were "divers kindes (hounds), as the slow-hound, which
is a large great dogge, tall, and heavy, and are bred for the most part
in the West countreys of this Kingdome, as also in Ches-Shire, and
Lanca-Shire." Interestingly, Cheshire was where the famous Lyme
Hall Mastiffs came from and the Bold Hall line, not as famous as
Lyme Hall but bred for several centuries, was in Lancashire.

A New General English Dictionary, 1740, by Thomas Dyche/
William Pardon, said a Bandog was a large, fierce dog usually
chained in the day and loosed at night to defend against thieves and
they were used for bull or bear baiting and "mastiff fighting." The
Mastiff was said to be "of the largest breed, kept by people who have
large yards before their houses, as a defence against thieves climb-
ing over the wall."

Forest laws date from 1016 when Canutus took England's
Crown. There were probably laws before, since historically forests
were a royal prerogative, but his were the first to record such laws
and to relate to dogs. Chapter 16, pertaining to keeping dogs by and
in forest boundaries, has more than 8,000 words about Mastiffs, with

Star Constellation of the Dog - Taken from an astrological manuscript in the Staatsbibliothek Preussische Kulturbesik Berlin, Mss. Collection (Cod. fol. 244, 16th Century). The text is full of superstition in our modern times. The picture, showing a broad and short-muzzled sort of dog with a strong body, suggests a kind of dog today called molossian. This picture my not have been published since 1600.

only an occasional mention of Greyhounds, Spaniels, Mastiff-type curres and small dogs. The laws protected "wilde Goates, Hares, and Connies... wilde Horses, Bugalles, Kine, and such like. Foxes and Wolves are not accounted beasts of the Forest, nor of Venerie, and therefore the killing of them shall not yeeld any recompence. Yet notwithstanding, the killing of them within the bounds of the Forest is a breach of the kings roiall (royal) free Chase, and therefore the offender shall for the same yeeld a recompence. A wild Boare, although he bee a beast of the Forest, yet he is in no wise accounted a beast of Venerie."

Mastiffs were "lawed" or maimed by genucission, hoxing, hocksinewing, hambling, hozing, expeditation, espealtare, espeuteisoun, espelotte and footing. Genucission, done in Canutus' time, was "a kind of cutting or laming in the hammes" which foresters called hamling, hoxing and hock-synewing. Sinew cutting was unpopular as it crippled the dogs to the point they were useless.

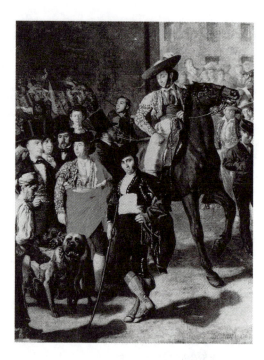

Artwork by Manual Castellano (1863), Prado, Madrid, from the private collection of Werner Preugschat.

Cutting claws off the Mastiff forefoot began under Henry II and was called "Expeditatio Mastiuorum, the expeditating of Mastives." Expeditation laws were exact: "Set one of his forefeet upon a piece of wood of eight inches thicke, and a foot square, the one with a mallet, setting a chissell of two inches broad upon the three clawes of his forefoot, at one blow both smite them cleane off, and this is the manner of Expeditating Mastives." The laws say when the word Canis is used, which might mean any dog, it meant and was intended for "Mastives onely" and no other dog. The king required Mastiffs be expeditated anywhere that "his wild beasts have a peace." Forest dwellers or inhabitants could keep Mastiffs to defend their homes provided the animals were expedited. The Charta de Foresta called for an "inquirie for the lawing and expedition of Mastives" every third year to be done "by the view and testimonie of honest men." The law recognized "Mastives doe sometimes chaunce to fasten upon a Deere" but if a deer was caught by a legally expeditated Mastiff the owner was not liable. Mastiffs were also forbidden to go to the field to "drive or feare away the kings Deere."

Some historians think Mastiffs are too slow to catch a deer, but the forest laws applied to royal stags who were merely made out of breath. My Mastiffs catch smaller, swift, wild game so I know they could easily wind a deer. Wynn pointed out John Crabtree had deer at Kirklees Hall run down and killed by his Mastiffs. It is difficult to write about the cruelty inflicted on Mastiffs, but it is part of their history. To put matters in perspective, Edward the Confessor enforced death for hunting in royal forests and any man who put a wild beast out of breath, even unintentionally, was fined or flogged, and if it was a royal deer, the sentence was two years imprisonment or deprival of all privileges and exclusion from human society (friendless man). If a serf killed a deer, his life was forfeit. William I's laws said "whoever took a stag or buck was deprived of his eyes."

Perkin Legh fought for King Edward III and The Black Prince in France and at the Battle of Cressie, and for this the Legh family received Lyme Hall. When they died, Sir Perkin served Rich-

This picture is dated by Musee d'Art et d'Histoire before 1800, drawn by Jacques-Laurent Agasse.

ard II and "left him not in his troubles, but was taken with him, and beheaded at Chester by Henry IV; and the said Sir Piers, his son, served Henry V, and was slain at the battle of Agincourt." Sir Piers was accompanied to Agincourt by his Mastiff bitch in October 1415, and she protected her fallen master where he lay undiscovered and mortally wounded in the night following the battle. When found alive he was moved to Paris where he died of his injuries. The Mastiff bitch, bred and in whelp at the time, went with Sir Peers to Paris where she subsequently whelped her litter. The Mastiff bitch and her litter returned to Lyme Hall with the body of Sir Peers. The litter was kept by the Legh family and the breed is said to have been kept up at Lyme Hall until the last of them were destroyed as an act of patriotism due to food shortages during the First World War. According to Stowe's Annual, James I (1603-1625) sent two Lyme Hall Mastiffs to King Phillip.

CHAPTER 2
LATER IN HISTORY - BAITING, FIGHTING AND GUARDIAN

Gladiatorial shows and pitting animals one against another was a favorite entertainment of the Romans. In all likelihood they brought the sport with them when they dominated in parts of early Britain, and so began the practice of pitting animals against dogs in England. Bear baiting existed as early as the time of Edward the Confessor and was popular from the time of Edward I to that of Henry VII. In the 16th Century, it was a regular national amusement. Bull baiting, which lasted for a longer period, was also practiced. In the Tudor reigns, bear baiting was very popular and rules were developed to ensure sporting treatment towards the bear and Mastiff. Henry VII hung a Mastiff for its audacity in fighting and overcoming a lion (the king of beasts) unassisted.

In 1800, Sydenham Edwards wrote "in Scotland they (Mastiffs) must have been in great perfection" and seven from there "were observed to be so fierce at the games that they universally imagined them to have been brought over in cages of iron and that provoking the mastiff to this degree of fury would naturally be a theatrical trick of the procurers to strike the spectators."

Chaucer wrote "the alan was good for baiting either the lion or the bear" and "even the horse and ass suffered, the latter animal furnishing a spirited combat." Per Stowe's Survey, under a penalty of 20 shillings, baiting the bear, bull or horse in the open streets of London was prohibited.

In the time of King John, the Lord of Stamford stood on his castle walls and watched two bulls fighting, one of which belonged to a butcher in the local town who set "a great mastiff dog" on his bull and the dog forced the bull into town. Stamford enjoyed the "sport and tumult that ensued" so much he "gave the aftermath for ever, for grazing to the butchers of the town" on condition the bull-running be repeated annually.

In the 17th Century, Aldrovandus offered a verse by Bargeus that described the Mastiff:

Let that kind of dog attack and stop huge bulls
and bears, and stay them in flight with an inflicted wound, whose ears hang broad, whose
lip from above droops loosely, and that has a
fierce aspect and a very big neck. Let his head
be flat, and his snout above all blunt, and
withal large feet, and a curved claw, and soft
pads, thigh upraised, belly not too protuber-
ant. Let his legs be straight, and also the parts
between the loins long. Let his spine be double,
his loins fat, his colour bay, his chest comely;
and let him be such as breathes fire from a wide
nostril what time he fills the woods with his
bark, and runs with sudden anger conceived in
his ample chest. Then, too, his eyes gleam, and
his neck swells up and often he twists his tail
round to his hairy back.

To the modern-day Mastiff fancier, this easily brings to mind
a Mastiff preparing to retaliate for some perceived trespass.

Three Mastiffs were considered more than the equal of a
bear and four for a lion, although lions were baited less frequently
and only with picked dogs. One story about a Mastiff's skill had to

*This portrayal shows the kennel of a dog dealer by Jaques-Laurent Agasse,
(after) 1808, Le Chenil (the kennel), Pencil, crayon, sanguine 20/25 cm,
Musee de'Art dt Histoire, Geneve (Switzerland).*

do with Lord Buckhurst who was ambassador for a few weeks in 1572 to the Court of Charles IX of France. Buckhurst had a Mastiff that pulled down a bear, a leopard and a lion and these amazing feats are said to have been accomplished unassisted. This is not an isolated case either, as there was a story of a Mastiff killing a tiger in India in single combat.

Color painting of three pied Mastiffs at bear from the private collection of Werner Preugschat.

When Alexander the Great went to India:

[T]he King of Albanie gave him a dogge of an huge and extraordinary bignesse. And Alexander taking great delight and contentment to see so goodly and so faire a dogge: let loose unto him first Beares, afterwards wild Bores; and last of all fallow Deere. But this dogge making no reckoning of all this game lay still couchant, and never stirred nor made at them. This great Commander Alexander, a man of mightie spirit, and highminded, offended at the lazynesse and cowardice of so great a bodie, commanded that he should be killed, and so he was. News hereof went presently to the King of Albanie. Whereupon he sent unto him a second dogge, with this message—That he should not make trial of this too

against such little beastes but either set a Lion
or an Elephant at him: saying moreover that
hee had in all but those two of that kind: and
if hee were killed likewise hee were like to have
no more of that race and breed. Alexander
made no stay, but presently put out a lion, and
immediately he saw his backe broken and all to
rent and torne by the dogge. Afterwards he
commanded to bring forth an Elephant, and in
no fight took he greater pleasure than in this:
for the dogge at the first with his rough,
shagged haire, that overspread his whole bodie,
came with full mouth, thundering (as it were)
and barking terribly against the Elephant.
Soon after he leapeth and flieth upon him, ris-
ing and mounting guard against the great
beast, now of one side, then of another: maintaining combate right artificially, one while as-
sailing another while avoiding his enemie: and
so nimbly he bestireth from side to side, that
with continuall turning about too and fro, the
Elephant grew giddie in the head, insomuch as
he came tumbling downe, and made the
ground to shake under him with his fall.

A Mastiff given to the Great Mogul Jehangir, son and suc-
cessor of the celebrated Akbar, by James I killed a leopard and then
a bear, which some large dogs, given him by the Shah of Persia,
would not touch. This impressed the Mogul and is why a special

*This has been published as
Reinagle's Mastiff, From the
Sportsman's Cabinet, 1805 - the
notation on the back of the picture:
A Lyme Hall Mastiff chained in a
sawpit, a view of London across the
Thames in the distance. Bought at
Sotherby, January 20, 1965,
attributed to W. Marlors.*

present of Mastiffs went with Sir Thomas Roe when he became ambassador in 1615.

After a thousand years of popularity, the sport of animal baiting was made illegal in England in 1835. Those opposed to ending it felt it "inspired courage and produced a nobleness of sentiment, and an elevation of mind." Wynn disagreed that it produced nobleness of sentiment or elevation of mind, but he felt it produced some noble Mastiffs, and elevated their muscular development. He

A pyramid of dogs.

pointed out that some writers whose knowledge and experience of the breed was limited sneered at the idea of a Mastiff attacking a lion or bear, and said it would be truly ridiculous to think any of the weak-loined, straight-hocked, short-winded London monstrosities could make any sort of fight even against a wolf, but it did not alter the fact that the breed in past times were more capable and could have been brought back to the grand old type by selection of the best specimens for breeding.

CHAPTER 3
MASTIFF TALES

Captain Thomas Brown in *Biographical Sketches and Authentic Anecdotes of Dogs* (1829) recounted the following stories:

A blacksmith of the name of Smith, at Stirches, near Hawick, had a large Mastiff, which generally lay on the smithy hearth in cold weather. One evening a farmer's servant in the neighborhood came for some plough-irons which were repairing, gave the dog a kick, and possessed himself of his place on the warm stones. The Mastiff, in the meantime, only looked sulky at him, and lay down at the door, but when the man went away with his plough-irons on his shoulders the dog followed him, and, at the distance of sixty yards from the smithy, flew upon him, and, seizing him by the collar, brought him to the ground. He offered him no personal injury, but treated him in a manner which strongly indicated his sovereign contempt for the delinquent.

Taken from **Biographical Sketches and Authenticate Anecdotes of Dogs** *by Captain Thomas Brown, Edinburgh, 1829, drawn by Captain Brown.**

A carrier of the name of Hislop, at Ferneyherst, near Stow, on Galawater, had a Mastiff which when a puppy, had been struck by a cadger. This offense he kept in mind ever afterwards, and took every opportunity of revenging himself on the traveller for the injury, and would never allow him to pass through the village, unless some of Hislop's family interposed to keep him off. One day the cadger being much annoyed at this antipathy of the dog, said to

Hislop, "I would give all the eggs which I have in my creels to make up friendship with your dog." Hislop said in reply, "he would endeavour, if possible, to obtain his favour for his friend." The carrier went towards a draw-well, and was followed by his dog and the cadger; Hislop, as if by accident, pushed the dog into the well, and allowed it to struggle a considerable time, with a vain endeavour to get out: when he seemed to be getting pretty tired, Hislop desired the cadger to pull him out, which he accordingly did. The dog, on being extricated, after shaking himself, fawned upon his deliverer, as if sensible he had saved his life, and ever afterwards refrained from molesting him as he passed through the village; nay, he uniformly received him with kindness wherever they met, and frequently would convoy him a mile or two on his way.

Mastiff and Lamb *is from the private collection of Werner Preugschat.*

About the year 1742, a lady, who resided in a lone house in Cheshire, permitted all her servants, except one female, to go to a supper and dance, at a Christmas merry-meeting, held at an inn about three miles distant, and kept by the uncle of the maid who had remained in the house with her mistress. The servants were not expected due back till the morning, consequently the doors and windows were, as usual, secured, and the lady and her servant were going to bed, when they were alarmed by the voice of some persons apparently attempting to break into the house.

Fortunately, a great Mastiff dog, named Caesar, was in the kitchen, and set up a tremendous barking, which, however, had not the effect of intimidating the robbers. The maidservant distinctly heard that the attempt to enter the house was made by the villains endeavouring to force a way through a hole under the sunk storey, in the adjoining back-kitchen or scullery. Being a young woman of courage, she went towards the spot, accompanied by the dog, and, patting him on the back, exclaimed, "At him Caesar!" The dog made a furious attack on the person who seemed to be at the hole, and gave something a violent shake, when all became quiet, and the animal returned to her with his mouth all besmeared with blood. She afterwards heard some little bustle outside of the house, which soon was stilled. The lady and servant sat up until morning, without further molestation, when, on going into the court, a quantity of blood was found on the outside of the wall.

The other servants, on their return, brought word to the maid that her uncle, the innkeeper, had died suddenly during the course of the night, they understood, of a fit of apoplexy, and was intended to be buried that day. The maid got leave to go to the funeral, and was surprised to find the coffin, on her arrival, screwed down. She insisted on taking a last view of the body, which was most unwillingly granted; when, to her great surprise and horror, she found his death had been occasioned from his throat being torn open. What had happened the evening before immediately rushed to her imagination, and it appeared too evident to her, that she had been the innocent cause of her uncle's death; and, upon further inquiry, it was proved that he and one of his servants had formed the design of robbing the house and murdering the lady, in her unprotected condition, during the absence of her servants; but, by the watchfulness and courage of her dog, their design was frustrated.

Sir Harry Lee of Ditchley, in Oxfordshire, ancestor of the Earl of Litchfield, had a Mastiff which guarded the house and yard; but had never met with any particular attention from his master, and was retained for his usefulness alone, and not at all as a favorite. One night, as Sir Harry was retiring to his chamber, attended by his faithful valet, an Italian, the Mastiff silently followed him up stairs, which he had never been known to do before, and, to his master's astonishment, presented himself in his bedroom. Being deemed an intruder, he was instantly ordered to be turned out; which being

Mastiff titled On Guard *from the private collection of Werner Preugschat.*

done, the poor animal began scratching violently at the door, and howling loudly for admission. The valet was sent to drive him away. Discouragement, however, could not check his intended labour of love, or rather providential impulse: he returned again, and was more importunate than before to be let in.

Sir Harry, weary of opposition, bade the servant open the door, that they might see what he wanted to do. This done, the Mastiff, with a wag of his tail, and a look of affection at his lord, deliberately walked up, and crawling under the bed, laid himself down, as if desirous to take up his night's lodging there. To save farther trouble, but not for any partiality for his company, the indulgence was allowed. About the solemn hour of midnight, the chamberdoor opened, and a person was heard stepping across the room: Sir Harry started from his sleep; the dog sprang from his covert, and seizing the unwelcome disturber, fixed him to the spot! All was dark: Sir Harry rang his bell in great trepidation in order to procure a light. The person was pinned to the floor by the courageous Mastiff, and roared for assistance. It was found to be the valet, who little expected such a reception. He endeavoured to apologize for his intrusion, and to make the reasons which induced him to make this step appear plausible: but the importunity of the dog, the time, the place, the manner of the valet, all raised suspicions in Sir Harry's mind, and he determined to refer the investigation of the business to a magistrate. The perfidious Italian, alternately terrified by the dread of punishment and soothed with hopes of pardon, at length confessed that it was his intention to murder his master, and then rob the house.

The diabolical design was frustrated only by the instinctive attachment of the dog to his master, which seemed to have been directed on this occasion by the interposition of Providence. How else could the poor animal have known the meditated assassination? How else could he have learnt to submit to injury and insult for his well-meant services; and, finally, seize and detain a person who, it is probable, had shown him more kindness than his owner had ever done? However this may be, still the facts are indisputable. A full-length picture of Sir Harry, with the Mastiff by his side, and the words, "More faithful than favoured," is still to be seen at the family-seat at Ditchley, and is a lasting monument of the gratitude of the master, the ingratitude and perfidy of the servant, and the fidelity of the dog.

A Mastiff dog belonging to the Honourable Peter Bold of Bold, Esq. attended his master in his chamber during the tedious sickness consequent on a pulmonary consumption. After the gentleman expired, and his corpse was removed, the dog almost every moment entered the apartment, making a mournful whining noise, and continued his

This drawing was done prior to 1900 and is from the private collection of Werner Preugschat.

researches for several days through all the rooms of the house, but in vain; he then retired to his kennel, which he could not be induced to leave, but, refusing all manner of sustenance, died. Of this fact, and his previous affection, the surgeon who attended the master was an eyewitness. Some may hesitate to call this reason, but certainly a deeper sense of sorrow and gratitude could not have been shown by any creature whatever.

A large dog of the Mastiff breed, hardly full-grown, attached himself to a very small spaniel, ill with the distemper, from which the former was himself but newly recovered. He commenced this attention to the spaniel the moment he saw it, and, for several weeks, he continued it unremittingly, licking him clean, following him everywhere, and carefully protecting him from harm. When the large dog was fed, he has been seen to save a portion, and to solicit the little one to eat; and in one instance he was observed to select a favourite morsel, and carry it to the house where the sick animal lay. When the spaniel was, from illness, unable to move, the Mastiff used to sit at the door of his kennel, where he would remain for hours, guarding him from interruption. Here was no instinct, no interest—it was wholly the action of the best qualities of the mind.

The following tale was printed by the Proprietors in *The Sportsman Cabinet or A Correct Delineation of The Canine Race* (1803):

A French Officer, more remarkable for his birth and spirit than his riches, had served the Venetian republic with great valour and fidelity for some years, but had not met with preferment by any means adequate to his merits. One day he waited on an "Illstrissimo" whom he had repeatedly solicited in vain, but on whose friendship he had still some reliance. The reception he met with was cool and mortifying; the noble turned his back on the necessitous veteran and left him to find his way to the street, through a suit of apartments magnificently furnished. He passed them in a state of philosophic rumination, casting his eyes on a sumptuous sideboard, where stood on a damask cloth, in preparation for a strong entertainment, an invaluable collection of Venice glass, formed and polished to the highest degree of perfection; he took hold of the corner of the linen, and turning to a faithful English Mastiff who always accompanied him, said to the animal, in a seeming absence of mind, "There, my poor old friend! You see how these scoundrels enjoy themselves, and yet how we are treated!" The poor dog looked up in his master's face, wagging his tail as if he understood him. The master walked on, but the mastiff slackening his pace, laid hold of the damask cloth with his teeth, and at one hearty pull brought all the sideboard in shivers to the ground, thereby depriving the insolent noble of his favourite exhibition of sublunary splendour.

Edward Jesse, Esq. published this story in *Anecdotes of Dogs* (1858):

My neighbour, Mr. Penrhyn, has two noble mastiffs of the Lyme breed, which I believe is now nearly extinct. It is probably, however, preserved by Thomas Leigh, Esq. of Lyme Park, in Cheshire, who has also the wild breed of cattle, now only, I believe, found at Lyme Park, and at Chillington, in Yorkshire, the seat of Lord Tankerville. There is a story current at Lyme Park, that some years ago a dog of the breed in question, whilst walking with the steward in the park, took offence at one of the wild bulls, and would instantly have attacked it, but was with difficulty restrained by the steward. The dog returned home, evidently bearing the offence in mind, and the next morning, the steward, seeing him covered with blood, suspected something amiss, and on going into the park, found that not only the bull, but two cows had been worried by him.

Drawing of a Mastiff published in Anecdotes of Dogs *by Edward Jesse, Esq., of London, 1858.*

CHAPTER 4
EARLY BREEDING IN ENGLAND AND
THROUGH TWO WORLD WARS

In *Dogs: Their History and Development* (1928), Edward Ash wrote that even though type had altered from the early ages, it had not altered sufficiently enough to create any doubt that Mastiffs are descended from the long ago Mastiffs. He felt the main characteristics were so strong that accidental or deliberate crosses had little or no effect. It is logical to assume some breedings were done by design to produce certain sorts of animals appropriate for the various functions: fighting dogs, baiting dogs, guarding dogs, etc. There were probably an equal number of accidental breedings occurring through sheer happenstance.

Captaine R. Whitbourne in *A Discourse and Discovery of New-Foundland* (1620) shows us how easily cross breedings could happen: "The Wolves and beastes of the Countrey (Newfoundland) came downe neere them to the Seaside, where they were labouring about their Fish, howling and making a noise: so that at each time my Mastiffe-dogge went unto them the one began to fawne and play with the other, and so went together into the Woods, and continued with them, every of these times, nine or ten dayes, and did returne unto us without any hurt. Hereof I am no way superstitious, yet it is something strange to me, that the wilde beastes, being followed by a sterne Mastiffe-dogge, should grow to a familiaritie with him, seeing their natures are repugnant."

Alpine Mastiff engraving by Landseer from a drawing by his brother, published by Sherwood Jones & Co., January 1, 1825.

With the end of fighting it was inevitable Mastiff popularity would decline. To rebuild the breed, crosses were resorted to, particularly with Bulldogs and Alpine Mastiffs. Hugh Dalziel, *The St. Bernard* (about 1879), wrote that the first authenticated case of a hospice dog going to England was in 1815, and he was more like an open-coated English Mastiff than a St. Bernard: "The dog was about a year old when he was received at Leasowe Castle in May, 1815. His length was 6 ft. 4 in. and height in middle of back 2 ft. 7 in. and he is now larger and is still growing. He saved a lady from drowning since he has been in England."

Joseph H. Fleischli, *The Saint Bernard* (1954), wrote in 1817 that "dogs from the Hospice were taken to England in order to replenish the mastiff in that country." Until 1865, Swiss dogs were called Alpine Mastiffs. When reviewing evolution of Mastiffs as a distinct breed, Alpine Mastiffs, or St. Bernards as they were named later, cannot be disregarded. Early breeders in England used Alpine Mastiffs and called the offspring Mastiffs, and the same strains were bred by the Great Saint Bernard monks but the fruits of their labor were named St. Bernards.

Barry der Menschenretter is the most famous dog in history. *The holy dog of the Great Saint Bernard* who saved 40 lives before dying in 1814. He is always called a St. Bernard, yet he lived when it was not yet a distinct breed—he was an Alpine Mastiff. If one compares his pictures to old pied-colored Mastiffs, similarities are noted as much more striking than differences.

Picture of Barry der Menschenretter.

Henrich Schumacher (1831-1893), a pioneer Saint Bernard breeder, said monks sought outside blood from Pyrenean, German Boarhound and Newfoundlands in 1830 believing long hair would protect the dogs, plus Newfoundlands were stronger, larger and not as degenerated through inbreeding. Since Alpine Mastiffs were bred in England afterwards, the Newfoundland cross, etc. made its way into Mastiffs.

Writing about St. Bernard champion "Bayard," Hugh Dalziel said there was "the clearest evidence his maternal G.G.G.G. grandsire, Pluto, was an English Mastiff" and "the grand dog Tell, whose fame was worldwide...but it certainly is a singular incident in dog-

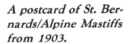

A postcard of St. Bernards/Alpine Mastiffs from 1903.

showing that Mr. Macdona should, twenty years later, be winning champion prizes with the descendant of an English Mastiff" and "whatever may be thought of the bar sinister on Bayard's escutcheon, he is a magnificent specimen of the St. Bernard, and not a whit the worse for having the one hundred and twenty-eight part of good English Mastiff blood in him." It may not be coincidence Dalziel talks of Saint breeders Miss Hale, Mr. Armitage and Miss Aglionby who bred Mastiffs at the same time.

Dalziel wrote: "The strain for which the greatest, or rather absolute purity is claimed is the Lyme Hall mastiff, which has been in the Legh family since the beginning of the fifteenth century, if not from a still earlier date; but whether the existing dogs of this strain have been kept pure by absolute in-and-in breeding, or with such merely occasional cross with some closely-allied strain as may have been found necessary to prevent deterioration, so that we may rely on it as representing the original type, I have no means of knowing."

Captain Garnier's Eve was said to be of Lyme Hall blood and part boarhound (Dane). Wynn, and other writers, alluded to Lyme Hall producing a strain lacking the short face so desirable in Mastiffs, and fine bodies showing too much Dane type. Even so, it was prestigious for a Mastiff to claim ancestry from Lyme Hall.

The earliest breeders who left lineage which can be followed were Mr. Robinson of Bold Hall, Commissioner Thompson whose line continued through the efforts of his grandson, J. W. Thompson,

T.H.V. Lukey, John Crabtree and Bill George, the latter two being reputable dog dealers. The elder Thompson had a black called Sall and a black and white named Trusty, from which came Nostal Priory Lion and Rose, who was bred to Robinson's Bold to get Holdsworths Lion. Crabtree's Duchess, found in a fox trap, bred to Lion got Bet who was bred to Watertons Tiger, a cropped, short-tail Dane, to get Scotts Tiny. Tiny to Gibsons Nero (brother to Bets) got Sir Armitages Old White-Faced Tiger. H. Crabtree's Venus (Tiny's sister), was bred to Wynn's Nostal Priory Lion to get Armitage's Duchess/Venus who was bred to Old Tiger to get the younger Thompson's Dorah.

Lukey's Old Bob Tail Countess, of Alpine blood, bred to Lord Hertford's Pluto got Yarrow who was put to Lord Waldegrave's Turk/Couchez, of Alpine blood, to get Lukey's Bruce I. Bruce I to his sister Nell got Bruce II. Lukey's Duchess, by Armitages Tiger ex Thompsons Countess, bred to Bruce II got Lukey's Countess who was bred to Garnier's Lion, by Adam and Eve, to get Lukey's Governor. Governor to Horns Jenny, of Alpine lineage, got Lukey's Rufus. Rufus to Fields Nell III, by Cautley's Quaker (of Thompson lineage) out of Guppy's Nell II (whose dam, Lord Darnley's Nell I was said from a bull sire and Mastiff dam) produced Field's Ch. King.

Edwin Nichols' Juno was bred to Ansdell's Leo of Lyme Hall blood, to produce Nichol's Duchess who was bred to Sir Domville's Oscar to get Nichols' Venus. Venus bred to Nichols' Quaker, by Raymond's Prince (who went back to Darnley's Nell I) out of Raymond's Duchess, produced Aglionby's Hilda who was bred to Ch. King to produce Ch. Turk, Ch. Wolf, Ch. Knight Templar, Ch. Emperor, Ch. Prince and Ch. Argus.

Dog shows began in England in 1859, and in 1860 six Mastiffs were benched at Birmingham. By 1871, 64 Mastiffs were at the Crystal Palace, 81 in 1872 and by 1875 the entry eclipsed at 83.

In 1873, a Mastiff Club was formed but a contrary rule was made to which members agreed whereby, under penalty of expulsion, no member would attend a show in which Mastiffs were judged by anyone other than a club member. Due to a lack of support by other breeders, the club was doomed. In 1883, breeders gathered to found the Old English Mastiff Club, a hardier and healthier club still strong today. A standard was drawn up that continues in effect with only minor changes.

Registrations went from more than 200 in 1883 to 116 in 1890. Thirty Mastiffs were entered at Birmingham in 1883, 10 in 1885 and 14 in 1886. In 1886, 51 Mastiffs were at the Crystal Palace, and, in 1888, 49 at the Agricultural Hall. In 1891, 51 Mastiffs were at the Crystal Palace, 27 at Crufts in 1894 and 37 at Leicester in 1895.

W. K. Taunton's Kathleen of Riverside and Tarquinius were donated to the British Museum of Natural History. Kathleen was by Thurlow, by Beaufort (Beau ex The Lady Isabel) out of Carshalton Hilda (Hotspur ex Carshalton Bella). Kathleen's dam was Carshalton Alice by Constable (Hotspur ex Empress of Ting) out of Lady Blodwen (Bassario ex Blanche). Tarquinius was by Hidalgo, by Plutarch (Don Juan II ex Lady Dudley) out of Stella III (Ogilvie ex Jubilee Beauty). Tarquinius' dam was Joan, by Tom Bowling (Ogilvie ex Jubilee Beauty) out of Maggie May (Sir Stafford ex Chocolate Girl). The museum also has a specimen reputed to be of Lyme Hall descent which was presented to it by Mr. Kingdon

Between mid-1800 and early 1900, some prominent breeders emerged: Mark Beaufoy, R. Cook (Ilford Kennels), Rev. Mellor, Hunter Johnson, N. Norman Higgs, Loftus Leigh Pemberton, W. H. Shackleton (whose Mastiffs, Ch. Viscount of Lidgett and Ch. Brompton Duchess, won every trophy offered and were barred from competing for the Mastiff Club's 40-guinea cups as they won them five times), Edward Hanbury (breeder of Ch. Wolsey, whose son Cardinal is credited with preserving the brindle color), Dr. Sidney Turner about whom Wynn said he should get no small credit for producing a litter containing Orlando, The Lady Ella, The Lady Gladys, Rosalind, Elaine and Vivien, Mrs. G. Willins (breeder of Ch. Minting), Robert Leadbetter (Ch. Marksman's breeder), Dr. Forbes-Winslow (bred Ch. Hotspur), Captain Piddocke, and Lt.Col. Zaccheus Walker (breeder of Ch. Stentor, Ch. Charming Duchess and Ch. Britain's Belle), Mrs. Kennett-Westcroft and Mrs. D Berry (breeder of Ch. Young Mary Bull).

There were 24 registrations in 1900, 35 in 1908 and 60 in 1913. By the end of the First World War, outcrosses were necessary again to rebuild the breed. Once more breeders surfaced when they

Ch. Wolsey was born in 1873 by Ch. Rajah out of Queen. Continuation of the ancient brindle color is thought to have been preserved through Wolsey's son, Cardinal.

were most needed, G. and H. Cook (Cleveland), Norman Haigh (Ashenhurst), H. Young (Wantley), Mr. and Mrs. Oliver (Hellingly), Miss Ianthe Bell (Withybush), Messrs. R. H. Thomas and C. R. Oliver (Menai), R. Bennett (Broomcourt), Mrs. Edger (Delaval), Mr. Taylor (Saxondale), F. J. Hawkings (Goldhawk), Mrs. Kennet (Westcroft), Mrs. N. Dicken (Goring) and Mr. and Mrs. L. Scheerboom (Havengore). Miss Bell and Mr. and Mrs. Scheerboom first acquired Mastiffs in the early 1920s; they suspended Mastiff breeding during the Second World War and resumed afterwards. Knowing the war was imminent, some Mastiffs were exported to America, but by the time peace was reached, the outlook for the breed was dismal at best and greatly at risk for survival in its hereditary homeland. In October 1946, the first meeting since 1939 of the Old English Mastiff Club convened and 15 people pledged to do what they could to save the breed.

Sally of Coldblow, registered in 1944, was the only bitch native to England successfully bred after the war. Her sire, Robin of Brunwins was by Ch. Christopher of Havengore ex Hortia and her dam, Hortia, was by Ch. Uther Penarvon ex Boadicea of Delaval. Sally's pedigree went back to prewar Mastiffs providing breeders the solitary connection of Mastiffs through the war.

A brindle dog of unknown pedigree, wearing an engraved collar with the name Taurus or Toris, was found wandering London

*A drawing of prize dogs at the National Dog Show,
Glasgow, 1871. No. 2, Mastiff, Hector, Mrs. Rawlinson,
Graythwaite, Ulverstone. Artist, Fearsoy Jr.*

during the bombing. He was registered as Templecombe Taurus and declared to be a Mastiff. Douglas Oliff has compelling correspondence that suggests Taurus was born in 1941, sired by a Bullmastiff, Burngreave Baron (Millbrook Bruce ex Lady Chita), out of a brindle Mastiff bitch, Chenda (Bayard of Delaval ex Gundreda of Delaval). Indeed, whether or not Taurus was a Mastiff, Sally conceived to him and a puppy bitch survived, born January 1947, who became Nydia of Frithend. Of 18 puppies in three litters, Nydia is the only offspring from Taurus that survived.

With the perilous survival of Mastiffs in mind, the United Kingdom Kennel Club gave approval to the Old English Mastiff Club to register Mastiffs in the club name and thus came about the unusual OEMC prefix. These special Mastiffs, overseen by the club, were entrusted into the custody of people who would carry out their selective breeding to assure continuation of the breed. By 1950, there were an estimated 50 Mastiffs in England.

Major K. Hulbert privately imported Valiant Diadem who sired Breviry of Bowers Church, Cora of Wormhill, Duchess of Moonsfield, Hadrian, Hercules, Hippolyta and Horatius of Hollesley, Jascot Fritham Grizelda, Jill of Flushdike, Valerie of Rayne, OEMC Baldur, OEMC Baroness, OEMC Beatrix, OEMC Beaufort, OEMC Beowulf, OEMC Boadicea, OEMC Cardinal, OEMC Countess, OEMC Elgiva, OEMC Governor, OEMC Lion, OEMC Prudence, Ch. OEMC Rodney of Havengore, OEMC Rowena, OEMC Turk and OEMC Wolsey.

Frederick Bowles privately brought in Sheba and Craig of Mansatta who were bred together to produce Jana of Mansatta. OEMC Heatherbelle Sterling Silver and OEMC Heatherbelle Portia of Goring were imported from Canada. Silver sired Faithful Gilliard of Sparry, Janus of Benfleet, Malita Salome, Semper Fidelis of Sparry and Withybush Magnus, Odin and Lady Welcome. Portia became dam of OEMC Baldur, OEMC Beaufort, OEMC Beowulf, OEMC Boadicea, OEMC Cardinal, OEMC Countess, OEMC Elgiva, OEMC Governor, OEMC Lion, OEMC Rowena, OEMC Turk, OEMC Wolsey and Withybush Beatrix and Katherine.

Mrs. A. B. Duke privately imported Heatherbelle Bearhill's Priscilla Amelia and Heatherbelle Bearhill's Rajah who sired Benedict, Havengore Petronella, Meps Jumbo and Ch. Vilna of

Left: Ianthe Bell; right: Masie Anderson, July 15, 1959.

Eng. Ch. Rodney of Havengore. Sire: Valiant Diadem. Dam: Nydia of Frithend. Owner: Mrs. Scheerboom. Rodney was the first champion in England after the war. He is shown here in 1951 at 18 months.

Eng. Ch. Diann of Havengore. Sire: Hugh of Havengore. Dam: OEMC Boadicea. Breeder/Owner Mrs. Scheerboom.

Three of Mrs. Scheerboom's Havengore puppies born July 1956. Shown here at 6 weeks old.

*Famous brother/sister Eng. Ch. Hollesley Rowella
and Eng. Ch. Hollesley Medicine Man (by Eng.
Ch. Copenore Rab out of Eng. Ch. Devil Dancer of
Hollesley) shown with breeders/owners Mrs. P.
Day and Miss H. Day and owner Mrs. P.
Greenwell.*

Mansatta, Fanifold Undine and Unity and Ch. Vyking Aethelwulf
of Salyng. Mrs. Mayne privately imported Fanifold Heatherbelle
Priscilla's Martha who was dam to Fanifold Undine and Unity.

Miss Bell exported Withybush Magnus to America where he
bred Peach Farm Priscilla to produce Weyacres Lincoln who was
imported by Miss Bell. He won the OEMC Progeny Award in 1960.

Other well known breeders are Mr. and Mrs. Lindley
(Copenore), Maisie Anderson (Benfleet and Bardayle), Marguerite
Perrenoud (Meps), Anne Davies (Nantymynydd), Irene Craigh
(Kisumu), W. Hanson (Blackroc), Mrs. Mather (Weatherhill), Major
and Mrs. G. Reardon (Buckhall), Mrs. P. and Miss H. Day
(Hollesley), Mrs. E. R. Degerdon (Grangemoor), Vivian Corbett
(Jakote), Mrs. Harrild (Moonsfield) Mr. and Mrs. Cowe (Forefoot),
Janet Atkinson (Honeycroft), Mr. and Mrs. G. Hicks (Jilgrajon), Mrs

M. Smith (Balclutha), Mr. and Mrs. Rice and Janet Webberley Griggs (Darkling), Peter and Anne Griffin (Domas), Messrs. R. Thomas and P. Tugwell (Bredwardine), Mr. and Mrs. D. Baxter (Lesdon and Farnaby), Mrs. C. Robson-Jones (Gildasan), David Blaxter (Namous), Raymond Boatwright (Glynpedr), Mr. and Mrs. D. Joynes (Damaria), Mr. and Mrs. D. Chidwick (Cedwalla), C. J. Coan (Luckhurst), S. Critchley (Ormondstow), Mrs. J. Critoph (Famrise), C. Eraclides (Alcama), Mr. and Mrs. Chris Say (Bulliff), Mr. L. A. McDonald (Longendale), Mr. and Mrs. Sargent (Trevabyn), Dr. and Mrs. Collinson (Dawnstar), Mrs. E. M. Davies (Cenninpedr), Mr. and Mrs. Green (Jengren), D. Norfolk (Celerity) and Douglas Oliff (Wyaston).

CHAPTER 5
MASTIFF HISTORY IN AMERICA

The first Mastiffs in America were probably those mentioned in *The Roanoke Voyages* (1584-1590) which document Sir Walter Raleigh's explorations. At a distance from their Albemarle Sound home base and concerned about food rations, Raleigh wrote, "that whiles there was left one halfe pinte of corne for a man, that we should not leave the search of that River, and that there were in the companie two mastives, upon the pottage [soup] of which with sassafras leaves (if the worst fell out) the companie would make shift to live two dayes."

Purchas His Pilgrimes (1625) reveals that Englishman Martin Pring came to Plymouth Harbor in 1603 to grow sassafras and was accompanied by "Foole" and "Gallant," "two excellent Mastives of whom the Indians were more afraid than twentie of his men. One of these Mastives would carrie a halfe Pike in his mouth."

Norman Howard Carp-Gordon's *The Making of the Modern Mastiff* states: "The first published chronicles of the Pilgrims' experiences at 'Plimouth Plantation', Mourt's Relation (London, 1622), records that the Mayflower's passengers on her first voyage to Massachusetts in 1620 included 'a great Mastiffe bitch.' She apparently belonged to Peter Browne, who survived the hardships and ordeals of that first year to participate in the original Thanksgiving."

Narratives of Early Virginia (1600-1625) describes John Smith lamenting Deputy George Thorpe's benevolence towards Indians who were afraid of Mastiffs and Thorpe denied them nothing "in so much that when they complained that our Mastives did feare them, he to content them in all things, caused some of them to be kiled in their presence, to the great displeasure of the owners, and would have had all the rest guelt to make them the milder, might he have had his will." Thorpe was killed on March 22, 1622, during an Indian raid and the colonists wanted to pursue and chase them with their "horses and blood-Hounds to draw after them, and Mastives to teare them."

New Englands Prospect (1634) by William Wood spoke of Mastiffs in colonial Massachusetts:

> The Woolves be different in some respects from
> them of other countries...these ravenous
> rangers doe most frequent our English
> habitations...they be made much like a
> Mungrell, being big boned, lanke paunched,
> deepe breasted, having a thicke necke, and
> head, pricke eares, and long snoute, with dan-
> gerous teeth, long flaring haire, and a great
> bush taile; it is thought of many, that our En-
> glish Mastiffes might be too hard for them; but
> it is no such matter, for they care no more for
> an ordinary Mastiffe, than an ordinary Mastiffe
> cares for a Curre...

In 18th Century America, from Virginia through Pennsylvania to Massachusetts, Mastiffs guarded against Indian uprisings.
They would sound early alarms and help prevent sneak attacks.
Triggered by Ben Franklin's November 2, 1755, letter recommend-
ing the army use dogs to hunt Indians, Col. H. Boquet, an English
field officer, wrote: "I wish we would make use of the Spanish
Method to hunt them with English Dogs."

Except for an occasional mention of Mastiffs, from the time
when the earliest settlers landed in America accompanied by Mastiffs until the late 1800s, there is little known about them. Show
records and early articles tell us some of the first Mastiffs being exhibited. We know Captain Garnier brought Adam and Eve to
North America and left them behind when he returned to England
with their son, Lion. Supposedly descendants of Adam ex Eve
spread from Canada to Midwestern America.

In 1885, nine Mastiffs were registered, 41 in 1886, 166 in
1887, and 239 in 1888. By 1889, 373 were registered. Of the 37
breeds registered, Mastiffs were the fifth most popular breed in
America, behind English Setters, St. Bernards, Collies and Pointers.
After this they fell from popularity and by the First World War had
practically disappeared altogether in America and remained nearly
obsolete for the next 10 to 15 years. By 1889, seven were champions,
Mr. Stevenson's Homer and Prussian Princess, E. H. Moore's Ilford
Caution and Minting, Dr. Frank Perry's Ilford Cromwell, George
and Henry Cromwell's The Lady Clare and Wacouta Nap. E. H.

Moore's Sears Monarch and W. K. Taunton's Beaufort finished in 1890. In 1891 and 1892, there were no new champions, and Moore's Lady Coleus finished in 1893. J. L. Winchell's Ch. Beauforts Black Prince and C. A. Lougest's Lady Diana finished in 1894.

Six Mastiffs finished in 1895, Edwin Kimball's Elkson, Ethel (owner unknown), Moore's Ilford Chancellor, Winchell's Merlin and Moses and Charles Bunn's Sinaloa. In 1896, 1897 and 1898, one Mastiff finished each year, respectively, Lougest's Emperor William, Lancelot Younghusband's Prince Cola and Winchell's Black Prince's Brampton. At an 1888 show, Ilford Caution and Cromwell, Homer, The Lady Clare, Bal Gal and Prussian Princess were shown in champion, Winchells Boss, Minting and Moore's Imperial Chancellor were in open dog and Idalia, Hebe, Mayflower, Winchells Bess, Stevenson's Queen II, Moore's Duchess and Daphne were in open bitch. The year 1899 had no new champions and only W. E. Meek's California Cube finished in 1900, after which there were no champions until 1914 when Morris Kinney's British Monarch finished.

There were no new champions in 1915 and only Kinney's Bernice in 1916 and in 1917 P. D. Folwell's Queen Bess II finished. From 1918 to 1922, there were no new champions. In 1904, 10 Mastiffs were shown and only four in 1910, and one in 1911. By 1930, 11 Mastiffs were registered, in 1935, there were 25, and in 1941, 42 were registered.

Anyone sharing my fetish for tracing ancestry will wish to know just how far back we can actually go with pedigrees of our dogs today to connect them in an unbroken line to the earliest

Boatswain Plavia and Eng. Ch. Archie Hazelemere (grandsire to Ch. Bernice, the first Mastiff in America to whom American Mastiffs can be traced) from the private collection of Werner Preugschat.

Mastiffs. I shall attempt to lay a trail that can be followed. There was great commerce and cooperation between English and North American breeders, so in some cases it is impossible to know whether the animals were born abroad or in North America.

We know Morris Kenney of New Jersey imported five Mastiffs in 1913, but we will concern ourselves only with the two that perpetuated the chain, Bernice (born 1907 by Eng. Ch. Ronald Widmere ex Buena Ventura) and British Monarch (born 1909 by Salisbury ex Countess Sondersburg). Bernice's dam's lineage is unknown and her sire was by Eng. Ch. Archie Hazlemere ex Lady Winifred, born 1902, which is where the pedigree stops. Salisbury was by Melinotte, born 1897, ex The Rebel Queen, and Countess Sondersburg's lineage is unknown. Monarch, who finished in 1914, was bred to Ben MaCree (lineage unknown) to produce Lady Gabrielle. Bernice was bred to Survivor (Adam ex Oscott Nora) to produce Beowulf and Minerva, born in 1912, before importation at six years to America where she earned her championship at nine years of age.

Adam was by Black Prince, born 1898 (Invicta ex Black Princess) out of Lady Curly (lineage unknown). Oscott Nora, born 1905, was by Melinotte ex Queen Ernestine (lineage unknown). Minerva, who stayed in England, was bred to Bayardo to get Princess Lie-A-Bed and Minerva and Stapleford Pedro produced Collyhurst Squire. Beowulf was bred to Jessica (King of the North ex Marwood Pride) to get Eng. Ch. Master Beowulf and Lady Kathleen. Beowulf and Lady Gabrielle produced Sunflower, born 1915, who was bred to Eng. Ch. The Scarlet Pimpernel to produce Illingworth's Eng. Ch. Boadicea. Beowulf was then imported to Canadian C. W. Dickinson and became his "first" Beowulf.

Parkgate Duchess and Priam of Wingfield, of unknown pedigrees, were owned by Dickinson who bred them together to get Princess Mary, his second Beowulf, Boadicea and Conrad of Wingfield. Princess Mary and Wodin the Saxon (Conrad ex Boadicea) got Prasagutus of Wingfield and Mary of Knollwood; Princess Mary and Weland (Adamite ex Gascoign Queen) produced Orlando of Wingfield. Adamite's sire Count Willington was by Duke of Heatherville (Eng. Ch. Felix ex Oscott Sheilah) out of Lusitania (pedigree unknown). Felix came from Nuneaton Lion ex Kitty

Marton and Oscott Sheilah's sire Salisbury who came from Melinotte and the Rebel Queen and her dam Queen Alexandra was of unknown lineage. Adamite's dam, Adam's Last was by Adam (Black Prince ex Lady Curly) out of Lady Godiva (Dick Marton ex Countess). Mary of Knollwood bred to the first Beowulf got Gwenfra of Wingfield who was bred to Weland to get Eanfleda of Wingfield. Eanfleda was bred to half-brother Orlando to produce Betty. In 1922 the second Beowulf and his daughter Cleopatra (out of Boadicea) were the only new American champions.

Some fanciers met at Westminster Kennel Club (WKC) in 1929 to form a club and, on March 13, enthusiasts organized the Mastiff Club of America, Inc., chartered as a membership corporation under New York laws. The first member meeting, September 7, was at Miss Elizabeth Stillman's Kenridge Farms, Cornwall-on-Hudson, New York, in conjunction with Storm King Kennel Club's show. Bylaws and a standard were adopted and from the incorporators officers elected were: President F. J. A. Bier, Vice-President John Barnhard, Vice-President/Treasurer Paul Chapman Jr., and Secretary C. R. Williams. Other incorporators were Miss Stillman, Mrs. Grace Williams and Chauncey Stillman. The first standard featured a picture of Oliver's Ch. Joseph of Hellingly as a typical Mastiff.

Little is known about early breeders. Joanna Chapman imported a pair of apricots to breed; Eliot Stillman imported Caractacus of Hellingly, and Stamford White got Guy Greenwood's top winner, Parsifal. Derek and Dauntless of Dervot were imported by Coy Burnett, the Hedfors imported Lady Marjorie of Beamsley and Miss Stillman's kennel was known for good Mastiffs. Beier supposedly showed Mastiffs for more than 40 years and was recognized as the breed authority with the passing of Dickinson. Beier got Betty from Dickinson in 1928 and imported Hawkeye Bruce in 1929. He imported Thor of the Isles (Ch. Prince ex Jersey Queen) who was bred to Betty to get Bayberry June and Maizie of St. Paul. June and Caractacus of Hellingly (Ch. Cleveland Premier ex Princess Bunty) produced Buddy and Wayne Alter's St. Paul Mike, who bred to Maizie got Dorothy W who was bred to Brutus of Saxondale (Ch. Arolite ex Hilda of Hellingly) to get Buster of Saxondale. Broomcourt Nell (Brigadier ex Veldicea) was bred to Roxbury Boy to produce Edward Griffins two dogs, Boss and Brian of Roxbroom.

Col. Percy Hobart Titus and William Josse owned Buzzard Pride (Comet Menai ex Judy of Hellingly) in 1931. Titus (1940 Mastiff Club president) determined there were only 35 Mastiffs in America in 1932. He imported Goldhawk Elsie (Sioux Chief ex Tess of Woodbrook) and Roxbury Boy and Millfold Lass (Ch. Ajax of Hellingly ex Sweet Memory). Lass was bred to Buddy to get Manthorne Mogul, Joy and Ch. June, who finished in 1937, the first champion in 15 years and the last until 1951. Pride was bred to Roxbury Boy to produce Merles Brunhilda of Lyme Hall.

Dr. Harry Veach owned Angeles Queen, King and Tristram, all by Brian of Roxbroom out of Goldhawk Elsie. *Queen* bred to Griffins Boss got Angeles Princess and Victoria. Princess to Buster of Saxondale produced Nero of Milton. Victoria and Buster produced Duchess of Saint Paul and Alters Big Jumbo. Nero and Duchess produced *Sheba of Mansatta, who was privately exported to England's Frederick Bowles after the war.* Big Jumbo bred to Manthorne Joy produced Byron Parker's Emblem and Joy of Parkhurst who were bred to each other to produce *Honey of Parkhurst, who was privately exported to England's Mrs. P. Day* and Big Jumbo bred to Olivia of Mansatta (Gail of Altnacraig ex Blythe of Hampton) produced Valiant Cythera. *King* bred to Rolanda got Angeles Empress and President. President and Gwendolyn of Altnacraig produced Austin of Chaseway. *Tristram* was bred to Merles Brunhilda of Lyme Hall (Roxbury Boy ex Buzzard Pride) to produce Shanno of Lyme Hall.

Patty and John Brill's Peach Farm blood stands behind all Mastiffs in the world and gives a continuous line back to the earliest strains. Both were Mastiff Club presidents—she in 1961 and he in 1967, 1968 and 1969. Their first Mastiffs, born 1935, were Manthorne Peach Farm Matilda, (Roxbury Boy ex Goldhawk Elsie) and Manthorne Mogul (Buddy ex Millfold Lass). Mogul and Matilda produced Clothilde who was bred to Baron of Altnacraig to get Huguenot who, bred back to Mogul, got Rosita who was bred to Hector of Knockrivoch to produce Cressida and Belinda. Cressida bred to Captain Richard and Ginette Patch's Donaghmore's Wahb got Donaghmore's Arthur. Belinda and Austin of Chaseway produced Dora, Priscilla, Michael and Buckley Sir Anthony. Arthur and Dora produced Lalla, Rachel, Arabella and Donough. Peach

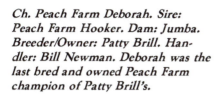

Ch. Peach Farm Deborah. Sire: Peach Farm Hooker. Dam: Jumba. Breeder/Owner: Patty Brill. Handler: Bill Newman. Deborah was the last bred and owned Peach Farm champion of Patty Brill's.

Farm Thisby came from Austin and Brinda (Siebensachen of Santa Cruz ex Ruby Star Delilah). Thisby bred to Arthur got Herman and Mamba who was bred to Timothy of Havengore (Ch. Rodney of Havengore ex OEMC Beatrix) to get Peach Farm Pandora. Notable winners of Peach Farm are Ch. Funk Farm Lulu, Katrina (BOB 1951 Mastiff Specialty), Hobo (BOB 1952 Mastiff Specialty), Ch. Maxwell, Ch. Megan O'Dare, Ch. Moira O'Dare, Ch. Oak Ridge Queen of Sheba (grandam to BOB 1985 Mastiff Specialty), and Ch. Renrock Brian O'Dare (sire to BOB 1973, 1974 and 1975 Mastiff Specialties).

The Brills were special, and left a legacy of Mastiffs and themselves. Everyone remembers them with love. Mary Moore Williams, Eve Olsen Fisher and Bill Newman all have stories about them. Mary said Patty was a character and from the first meeting was like a friend of long standing. Her daughter used to accompany the Brills to their summer home in Maine. Eve remembers Patty stopping to visit in Connecticut on the way to Maine, and puppies were always along on the trip. Old Peach Farm in Hockessin is now a development with no sign left of the big house or pool. Mary says Patty would be very unhappy to see that! They had a separate kitchen built for pots; huge pots to stir up dog food, for the 30 or more dogs always living in the house and yard.

Mr. and Mrs. James F. Clark, Altnacraig Kennels, in 1933 imported Princess Bess of Tiddicar (Ch. Ajax of Hellingly ex Break of Day) and Duke of Hellingly (Ajax ex Ch. Josephine); in 1935 Maud and Monarch of Hellingly (Ch. Marksman ex Girl of Trelyon); in 1936 King, Kathleen, Kate and Katrina of Hellingly (King Baldur of Hellingly ex Elaine); and in 1939 Frederick Bowles sent them Peter and Gyn of Hammercliffe (Ch. Christopher of Havengore ex Prunella). The Clarks imported Rolanda (Brockwell of Goring ex Boadicea of Delaval) in 1940 who they bred to Angeles King which produced Angeles President and Empress. Duke bred to Maud got Aldwin (BOB 1940 Mastiff Specialty), Alair and Annora of Altnacraig; Duke to Kathleen got Baron, Blythe and Boyce (Greenwich KC Group 4 and BOB 1941 Mastiff Specialty); King and Maud produced Eric; Boyce to Maud got Faxon; and the last Altnacraig litter, in 1944, came from Aldwin and Kathleen who produced Gail and Gwendolyn of Altnacraig, who was bred to Angeles President which produced Austin of Chaseway.

In 1942, Merle Campbell bred Merles Brunhilda of Lyme Hall to Tristram to get Shanno of Lyme Hall who was bred to his Angeles Empress to get Lady Diana who was bred to Hector of Knockrivoch to get Donaghmores Wahb. Empress and Faxon of Altnacraig (Boyce ex Maud) got Merles Tanna who was bred to Shanno to produce Canadian Champions Heatherbelle Lady Diana and Lady Hyacinthe. Merle owned Weyacres Tars and Winnie (Withybush Magnus ex Peach Farm Priscilla), postwar Mastiffs that went back to his original line. Winnie and Heatherbelle Priscilla's Leo (Parkers Jumbo of Parkhurst ex Ch. Heatherbelle Hyacinthe's Priscilla) produced Merles Princess. Tars and Princess produced Merles Alvin, Ch. Titan Tangela and Goffs Leo.

In 1959, an unusual and significant circumstance occurred that would affect Mastiffs in America and Europe. Merle bought a Dogue de Bordeaux bitch from Monsieur M. van Capel of the de Fenelon Kennels in France. The bitch, born in France on July 18, 1956, came from a litter of five puppies, two dogs registered as Fakir and Flicq and three bitches registered as Fany, Fidelle and Follette by Ch. Xohor de Fenelon (by V. Pach ex Sara) out of Erine de Fenelon (Bouddha de Bethsaida ex Dolphye de Fenelon). What made this so uncommon is Fidelle de Fenelon left France a registered

Dogue de Bordeaux Ch. Poupee, great grandam to sire of Fidelle de Fenelon. This picture was published in 1952 in France and is shown by the courtesy of Professor Raymond Triquet, president of the Dogue de Bordeaux Club, France.

Dogue de Bordeaux Ch. International Xohor de Fenelon was sire to Fidelle de Fenelon. This picture was published in 1952 in France and is shown by the courtesy of Professor Raymond Triquet, president of the Dogue de Bordeaux Club, France.

Dogue de Bordeaux and was registered with the same name as a Mastiff in America. Fidelle (see pedigree) was bred to Weyacres Tars to produce *Baron of Weyacres Tars, CDX* and *Buffnell de Finell, CD* and she was bred to Merles Alvin to produce *Merles Puello* and *Krishna.* To understand how permeated the breed is now with Dogue de Bordeaux, the grandchildren of Fidelle through *Baron* are Bowats Roar'N Rumble of Corgeen (ex Mystery Girl of Bowat) and Bowats Silver Sheik (ex Copenore Libra); through Buffnell is Cameo II, CD (by Peach Farm Amos); through Puello are Duncan of Windsor and Merles Toris (by Goffs Leo); through Krishna are Blondie of Old Mill and Heatherbelle Baby Sue (by Merles Toris) and Heatherbelle's Princess Jan (by Goffs Leo).

```
                                        Bordeaux IV R12796
                              Bonzo LOF46
                                        Beaute II R12265
                   Tim LOF121
                                        Ch. Diamant R129755
                              Zaza II LOF39756
                                        Ch. Poupee II LOF46 R2265
          V. Pach LOF 123 b. 10/24/47
                                        Bordeaux IV R12796
                              Bonzo LOF45
                                        Beaute II R12265
                   Urah LOF122
                                        Bordeaux IV R12796
                              Ch. Poupee II LOF46 R2265
                                        Olga R2803
          Ch. Xohor De Fenelon LOF1DBX149 b. 4/28/49
                                        Siguir II R2449
                              Kaid LOF2
                                        Mina R12450
                   Negus D'Hautpoul LOF55
                                        Hussard LOF20
                              Java LOF26
                                        Gamine II LOF22
          Sara LOF63
                                        Kaid LOF2
                              Negus D'Hautpoul LOF55
                                        Java LOF25
                   Ora LOF62
                                        Brutus LOF34
                              La Creole LOF44
                                        Rosy LOF41
Fidelle De Fenelon (French Import) W945019 LOF542 Born 7/18/56
                                        Sultan De Bordeaux R3886
                              Sam De Cerbere R3889
                                        Quessy Du Cerbere R3887
                   Viborg De La Ter De Pe LOF118 b. 6/22/47
                                        Sultan De Bordeaux R3886
                              S'Judith De Cerbere R4092
                                        Quessy Du Cerbere R3887
          Bouddha De Bethsaida LOF1448 b. 10/12/52
                                        Ursus R4733
                              Volean R7475
                                        Uma R4737
                   X'Venus Du Cap Maure LOF467
                                        Sam Du Cerbere R3889
                              Venus Du Cerbere LOF 422
                                        Scarlette Du Cerbere R3891
          Erine De Fenelon LOF516
                                        Tim LOF121
                              V. Pach LOF 123 b. 10/24/47
                                        Urah LOF122
                   Ch. Xohor De Fenelon LOF1DBX149 b. 4/28/49
                                        Negus D'Hautpoul LOF55
                              Sara LOF63
                                        Ora LOF62
          Dolphye De Fenelon LOF459 b. 8/26/54
                                        Sam De Cerbere  R3889
                              Urson De Fenelon LOF76
                                        Sara LOF63
                   Wlan De Fenelon LOF178 b. 10/28/48
                                        Oural LOF64
                              Ukasa De Fenelon LOF67
                                        Sara LOF63
```

Fidelle's great-grandchildren through Roar 'N Rumble are Ch. Bradleys Budget, Ch. Rumblin Ekos His Majesty Thor (BOB 1971, 1972 and 1973 Mastiff Specialties), Ch. Rumblin Ekos Sassy Sea Nymph, Ch. Windhaven Hercules and K.J. Havengore Candy (all ex Frideswide Susan), Wayside Delilah (dam to exported Eng. Ch. The Devil From Wayside) and Ch. Megan of Summitview (ex Willowledge Long Run Magda), Hercules of Coronna (ex Regal Sebrinna) and Vaskos Lord Buck (ex Blondie); through Silver Sheik are Bowats Regal Sebrinna and Bowats Royal Duke (ex Copenore Libra) and Bowats Sybil (ex Terra Twos Juno Sospita); through Cameo is Titan Topaz (by Goffs Leo); through Duncan are Ch. Windsors McTavish (BOB 1966 Mastiff Specialty), Heatherbelle Ajax II and Windsors Aurora (all ex Willowledge Evelyn); through Toris are Mystery Girl of Bowat (ex Merles Puello), Blondie of Old Mill and Heatherbelle Baby Sue (ex Krishna); through Blondie are J & C's Lord Byron (by Count Paul), Vaskos Lord Buck, J & C's Madame Princess Ann and Aldridge Shawn Roar 'N Rumble (all by Roar 'N Rumble); through Baby Sue is Heatherbelles Sues Sally (by Ajax II); through Princess Jan is Heatherbelles Princess Candy (by Ajax II).

In 1944, John Leitch had Eric and Hector of Knockrivoch (Eric of Altnacraig ex Gyn of Hammercliff). Eric with Heatherbelle Hyacinthe's Priscilla (King Rufus of Parkhurst ex Can. Ch. Heatherbelle Lady Hyacinthe) produced *Heatherbelle Bearhill's Priscilla's Amelia, born in 1949 and privately exported to England's Mrs. Duke, after the war.* Hector bred to Lady Diana produced Donaghmore's Wahb; with Peach Farm Rosita he sired Belinda and Cressida; and bred to Valiant Cythera he sired *Valiant Diadem, who was privately exported to England's K. Hulbert after the war.*

Mr. and Mrs. Frick bred Blythe of Altnacraig to Crusader of Goring (Robert of Goring ex Deidre of Delaval) to get Blythe of Hampton who was bred to Gail of Altnacraig to produce *Craig of Mansatta, also exported to Mr. Bowles in England. Craig* and *Sheba* produced Jana of Mansatta who was bred to Heatherbelle Bearhills Rajah to produce *Benedict of Mansatta, Ch. Vilna of Mansatta, Havengore Petronella of Mansatta, and Meps Jumbo of Mansatta.*

There were no Mastiff Specialties between 1942 and 1948. In 1949, the Specialty was at the Kennel Club of Philadelphia with 19 entries. Mary Pew Benson bred and owned George Strawbridge (Wilco ex Heather of Knockrivoch) who won that year. After 14 years with no new champions George Strawbridge finished in 1951. From 1950 to 1953, Specialties were in Devon, Pennsylvania. Agatha of Chaseway won BOB in 1950, Peach Farm Katrina and Hobo won in 1951 and 1952, respectively, and in 1953, Benson's Heather of Knockrivoch won Breed. No Specialty was held in 1954.

Mrs. F. L. Weyenberg's Peach Farm Priscilla bred to Withybush Magnus (OEMC Heatherbelle Sterling Silver ex OEMC Prudence) produced Weyacres Lincoln, Tars, Wanda and Winnie. Magnus and Priscilla both go back to the prewar English lines, but through Priscilla's dam there is a continuous link to those earliest American Mastiffs, via Betty to the Wingfield strain; Eanfleda to Gwenfra, to Dickinson's first Beowulf, to Morris Kenney's Ch. Bernice who came from Eng. Ch. Ronald Widmere and Buena Ventura. Lincoln was exported to England where he was bred to Boadicea of Saxondale, Guinevere and Cleo of Sparry, Ch. Withybush Bess, Clarissa, Duskie Lady and Froda.

Ch. Mooreleigh Quentin. Sire: Moorleigh Ivan. Dam: Moorleigh Katrina. Breeder/Owner: Marie Moore. This picture was taken in 1968 of Breeder-Judge Mrs. Scheerboom awarding a prize to Quentin who was owner-handled by Marie Moore.

Marie Antoinette Moore was an international all-breed judge and horse breeder who raced them in America, England and Ireland. The American Kennel Club (AKC) Dog Museum houses her donated Mastiff memorabilia. Her dog, Peach Farm Michael (Austin ex Belinda) was bred to Lady of Clearview (Valiant Dreadful ex Mattie of Clearview) to get Mooreleigh Maurice. Weyacres

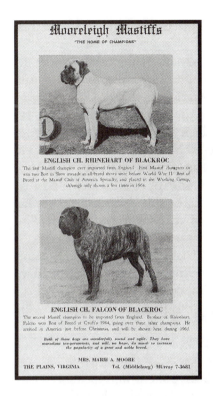

An advertisement of Marie Moore's.

Wanda was bred to Meps Bing (Ch. Vyking Aethelwulf of Salyng ex Withybush Beatrix) to produce Mooreleigh Monarch and Ch. Moby Dick (BOB 1957 and 1959 Specialties and 1959 Groups 3 and 4) and Wanda and Maurice produced Miriam who was bred to Monarch to get David. She imported Ch. Meps Berenice (Aethelwulf ex Beatrix) who won BOB in 1955 and BOS in 1956 at Mastiff Specialties and a Group 4 in 1955. Marie brought in Ariadne of Sparry and Ch. Adonis of Sparry (Faithful Gillard of Sparry ex Semper Fidelis of Sparry) who won BOB at the 1956, 1958 and 1960 Mastiff Specialties. In 1956, she imported Ch. Minerva of Zimapan (Crusader of Sparry ex Fanifold Undine).

She owned the first dual champion, Eng. Am. Ch. Rhinehart of Blackroc (Ch. Drake of Havengore ex Gipsy of Havengore) who won BOB at the 1964 and 1965 Mastiff Specialties and a Group 4 in 1964. She bred Ch. Mooreleigh Joyce (David ex Barbara) who won BOS at the 1964 Specialty. In 1961, she imported Eng. Am. Ch. Falcon of Blackroc who won Group 4 twice in 1965 and placed in group in 1966. Marie imported Ch. Beaucaris Queen of Sheba Beaucaris Marcus of Kisumu ex Mischief of Havengore). She bred Katrina to Ivan to get Ch. Mooreleigh Quentin (BOW 1968 National Specialty). In 1973, Marie was Mastiff Club president. Eve Olsen Fisher says Marie was of strong character. She had a tiny, fragile build, but her personality was huge and her love of animals inexhaustible. In her latter years, she was complimentary if she saw quality and equally outspoken when Mastiffs did not live up to her expectations.

Eve says Marie was devoted to Mastiffs and partially responsible for the breed getting more recognition. It was largely due to the combined efforts of Eve, Patty and Marie that Mastiffs came out of "miscellaneous classes" and went into the Working Group. Eve told of meeting Marie at the New York dock and boarding the ship that brought their dogs over (there were no planes for travel then and it was pointed out that one had to be sure to personally pay the ship's butcher well since it was he who took care of the dogs from port to port). Marie asked Eve why she was on the ship and learned Eve was there to pick up a dog. Marie asked "what kennel is yours from?" She had already told Eve hers was coming from Blackroc. There was a long silence. It finally became known that Marie's Mastiff was a dog while Eve was getting Raven of Blackroc who was a litter sister. There was spirited competition between these two grand ladies. Marie was Honorary OEMC Vice President in 1968 and Eve in 1969.

Marie wrote *The Mastiff* in 1978 and Eve authored *The Chinese Shar Pei* in 1979. Marie was the first Mastiff breeder/judge and Eve was the second. Marie once told Eve she would have been out of Mastiffs long ago had she not wanted and really liked the competition Eve gave her. In 1957, Marie showed Bernice to her championship and she was the only Mastiff to finish that year; there were no new champions in 1958, and in 1959 Marie finished Moby Dick, Adonis and Minerva, the only three that year; none finished in 1960, and Eve finished Beowulf in 1961, Sheba in 1962—the only champions in those years.

Stuart and Eve Olsen changed their Castle prefix to Willowledge, which was also used on the six thoroughbred horses they raced in New York, Florida and Canada. They imported Ch. Beowulf of Havengore (Hugh ex Petronella of Mansatta), BOB 1961 Mastiff Specialty, and Twinkle of Havengore (Winston ex Meps Beatrix). Beowulf and Twinkle gave them Castle Conrade and King Knight of Beardsley, who went to stud at old Peach Farm. They imported Ch. Sheba of Zimapan (Adam of Havengore ex Silver Queen) who won BOS at the 1961 Mastiff Specialty, Ch. Raven of Blackroc, Champions Geraint, Olwen and Hefina O'Nantymynydd

Eve Olsen and son, Oley, sitting with Ch. Beowulf and Ch. Sheba.

(Emrys O'Nantymynydd ex Zilgul Brigid of Frideswide), and Ch. Paul of Conturo (Farnaby Merrick ex Saxondale Rebecca).

Sheba bred to their Mooreleigh Gregory (Monarch ex Mansatta Sonja of Havengore) produced Ch. Hero who bred to Conrade produced Champions Willowledge Bathsheba, Gairheart, Grindel, Daniel, Candace, Queen Cleopatra and Catherine. Raven and Ali Kahn produced Champions Pharaoh, Melanie and Bartholomew. Bathsheba and Ali Kahn produced Ch. Willowledge Gogem and Ch. Merri Christmas, BOS Mastiff Specialty. I dare say all lines today in America are linked to old Willowledge. Stuart was Mastiff Club president in 1965 and Eve in 1970 and 1971, both served repeatedly as board members and were AKC delegates. Sadly, Stuart passed away in 1980. Eve carried on and continued breeding until her retirement nine years later. At that time, Willowledge, without interruption, had been breeding Mastiffs for 45 continuous years. Eve has been an AKC judge since 1977, judging American, Canadian and Australia's Gold Coast Specialties. Eve married Clark Fisher and they travel frequently, as she remains in great demand all over the world as an all-breed judge. Willowledge produced 66 champions including Ch. Mr. Chips (WD 1967 Mastiff Specialty and Group 2 in 1966, Group 3 in 1968) who came from their famous litter of 16. With the passing of her peers, Patty and Marie, Eve now stands alone in America, completely uncontested, as the premier former breeder and current "matriarch" of our glorious breed.

Al and Zita Deviny's Ch. Titan Tangela was the only Mastiff finished in 1963. Bred to Peach Farm Amos (Arthur ex Peach

Farm Dulcie) she produced Titan Victor who won Group 4 in 1963 and Group 3 in 1964 and was one of two Mastiffs to finish in 1964. Titan Topaz (Goffs Leo ex Cameo II, CD) bred to Ch. Ieda's Thor, CD produced Ch. Silverlace and Brunhela. Topaz bred to Titan Midas (Thor ex Tapestry) got Titan Galena. Silverlace bred to Hengist of Kisumu (Beaucaris Marcus ex Bracken) produced Ch. Blackheath Boss and Ch. Blackheath Solitaire. Brunhela and Rufus of Heatherbrook (Peach Farm Brian ex Peach Farm Lambda) produced Ed Gerace's Ch. Deer Run Maud and Ch. Deer Run Tess, Tobin Jackson's Ch. Deer Run Wellington and Titan Maeve who was bred to Midas to get Titan Gold Ducat. Galena and Deer Run Florester Bruce (Rufus of Heatherbrook ex Petite Princess Tamora) produced Deer Run Dahlia who was bred to Ducat to get Titan Saturnalia. Titan Vindicator and Titan Grendel produced the last Titan champion, Leonora, in 1977.

In 1959, Jean Greco imported Ch. Gaynor of Bardayle (Samson of Havengore ex Patricia of Bardayle) who was one of two Mastiffs to finish in 1964. She imported Withybush Edgemount Wilfred (Ch. Meps Angus ex Edgemount Elvira). Wilfred and Gaynor produced Greco's Heather and Greco's Hope of Werenhold. Heather and Henry of Havengore produced Helena of Rainbow Mountain and Heather to William Adams of Somerset produced Laurelane Eeyore. Hope and Myrddin of Parcwood (Jason of Copenore ex Bronwen of Benfleet) produced Ch. Werenhold Beatrice and Werenhold Alphea.

Two of the five Mastiffs that finished in 1966 belonged to Jean, Ch. Ginna of Havengore (Caradoc ex Delia) and Ch. Werburga (Withybush Superbus ex Dingus Mistress Ford). Werburga bred to Falcon produced Mooreleigh Undine and Ursula. Undine and Hengist of Kisumu produced Ballyherugh Dartagnan and Ch. Doire Carinthia. Ursula bred to Ch. Willowledge Clyde of Essex got Willowledge Christopher Robin. Jean owned Ch. Prince Valiant D (Bruno the Great ex Peach Farm Vanilla). Grecos Star is the first registered with the Greco prefix and her pedigree is confusing, but interesting. Peach Farm Vanilla and Dawson of Clearview (Master Brutus ex Mattie of Clearview) produced Bruno The Great. Peach Farm Vanilla to her son Bruno produced Vanilla The Great. Vanilla the Great was bred to Bruno to produce Grecos Star who was crossed out to Ch. Nelson of Hollesley (Ch. Weatherhill Thor ex Leonora) to get Ch. Grecos Bossy Boots, Ch. Rogue Jr, Born Free of Drayton, Callies Tasha, Dominic and Princess Dominic. Grecos Dominic was bred to Nelson to get Grecos Daniel who was bred to Princess Dominic to produce Ch. Misty Arrow of the Rockies, CD, Hollesley Maid, Hollesley Trixie and Ch. Hollesley Sam who sired Champions Hollesley Grizzley, Moms Midlife Crisis, Sugar Magnolia, Greenbriers Shawnda, LaGardes Pascha, Flac Big Girl of Red Bridge, Elizabeth R, Princess Andrea, Saint Anne, Saint Remne Spot and Toma Ki Hollesley. In recent years Jean imported Ch. Falmore Hall Fortescue (Ch. Hollesley Medicine Man ex Ch. Call Me Madam) and Bulliff Boom Boom (Razzermataz ex Vagabond). The Greco line was bred for more than 35 years. Jean's daughter,

Roxanne, said even in the latter stage of her illness, prior to passing away two years ago, Jean kept a beloved Mastiff at her side.

Peach Farm Cassandra. Sire: Withybush Barquest of Saxondale. Dam: Peach Farm Tweedy. Owner: Ginny Bregman. Breeder: John & Patty Brill.

Len and Ginny Bregman got Peach Farm Cassandra, by Withybush Barquest of Saxondale out of Peach Farm Tweedy (Herman ex Arabella) from Patty. Ginny became firmly established as a breeder of note with Lazy Hill Alexandra (Sandy) whose sire was War (Rufus of Heatherbrook ex Petite Princess Tamora) out of Heatherbelles Princess Candy (Ajax II ex Princess Jan). Sandy bred to Ch. Dawnwind Romulus (Ch. Gelert of Pynes Farm ex Copenore Petite) produced Lazy Hill Luath, Ch. Miss Sadie and Britains

Ginny Bregman is shown with two of Lazy Hill Louie's children: BOSS Ch. Storm Babe of Lazy Hill and Bucks BOB Ch. Autumn Rivers Big Ben.

Samantha Alexandra. Alexandra bred to Ch. Greenbriers Shambeau (Ch. Meps Tristan ex Rojondos Ramona) got Ch. Toto of Colchis Berea and Ch. Lazy Hill Athena who almost won breed in 1983 at the Specialty under English Breeder/Judge Betty Baxter.

Betty pulled out the two owner/handled brindle bitches, Ursa and Athena, and when she flipped something in the air Ursa set her head up and Athena didn't. Ginny always said Ursa won by a head. Athena bred to Toto produced Ch. Tullamore Bandit O'Lazy Hill. Athena and Louie produced Ch. Autumn River Big Ben, BOB at the Mastiff Supported Bucks County KC Show and Award of Merit 1986 Mastiff Specialty. Ginny did not breed Mastiffs on a large scale, producing only a few litters over the years, but she produces quality Mastiffs of true English type and other breeders always pay attention to her Mastiffs. I never met a more impressive Mastiff than Louie, nor one with a more generous or kinder temperament. In 1986, Ginny and I imported Ch. Damaria The Druid and Ch. Damaria The General and owned them together.

Currently, we own a youngster sired by a Greiner Hall dog out of a bitch that goes back to Louie and my Maggie.

Rodney and Charlotte Strong's Willowledge Evelyn (Beowulf ex Sheba) was bred to their Duncan of Windsor (Goffs Leo ex Merles Puello) to get Windsors Aurora and Windsors McTavish, handled by Charlotte to BOB at the 1966 Mastiff Specialty, who was one of eight Mastiffs to finish in 1967. Aurora was bred to Gunther of Windsor (Beowulf ex Willowledge Onyx) to produce Ch. Windsors Trilby Noon and Sabrina of Windsor who was bred to Ch. Ina Pauls Ben of Love Creek (Bowats Royal Duke ex Bowats Sybil) to produce Ch. Hubert of Love Creek who was bred to Ch. Thunderhills Marina (Ch. Ballyherugh's Cormac O'Conn ex Ch. Mooreleigh Yanina) to get Ch. Charbes Gypsy Rose who was bred to Ch. Ramsgate Job (Ch. Alexander of Dahlseide ex Mamas Lass Hannah) to get Ch. Windsors Prudence (Number 1 Mastiff in 1979 and 1980 and owner/handled to several group placements in 1979), Ch. Plum, Ch. Waltzing Matilda, Ch. Dahlseide Windsors Bow Belle, Ch. Adam and Ch. Dalyan of Rams Gate. Plum was bred to Tamarack Donner (Ch. Acadian Konigstiger ex Ch. Tamarack Peaches Lovecreek) to produce Ch. Windsors Harlow and Ch. Pippin, 1983 National Specialty Puppy Sweepstakes Winner.

Plum bred to Ch. Mountbatten of Colossus produced Ch. Windsors Magic Dancer. Matilda was bred to her grandsire Ch. Alexander (Master of the Woods ex Ch. Dahlseide Dame Dickens) to get Ch. Gelwils Windsors Edition who was then crossed out to Ch. Southports Prime Time (Ch. Iron Hills Warwagon ex Ch. Southports Bailey Quarters) to produce Ch. Windsors Roxy, Number 2 BOS Bitch in 1994 and Ch. Windsors Morgan, in the Top 20 Group Mastiffs and Number 13 Top BOB Dog in 1995.

Adelaide Bolte's Ch. Mooreleigh Joyce was one of the five Mastiffs to finish in 1965 and she won BOB 1963 and 1964 WKC and BOS 1962 and 1963 Mastiff Specialties. Joyce and Rhinehart produced Ch. Reveille Defender (WD 1965 Mastiff Specialty and BOB 1971 Mastiff Specialty, at 8 years of age), Ch. Sentinel (WB/BOS 1965 Mastiff Specialty), Ch. Juggernaut (BOB 1967 and 1968 Mastiff Specialties) and Ch. Tribute who was bred to Ch. Renrocks Brian O'Dare to produce Ch. Reveille Big Thunder (BOB 1974, 1975 and 1976 Mastiff Specialties), Ch. By Candlelight, Ch. Renrocks

Sean O'Dare and Ch. Lightning. Candlelight bred to Ch. Willowledge Clyde of Essex produced Ch. Reveille Twilight, Ch. Arwen Evenstar and Ch. Afterglow.

Dwayne and Judy Nash owned Friar Tuck of Havengore (Withybush Prashna of Zimapan ex Robin) and Ch. Greenbrier Rams Gate Savanah (Ch. Nelson of Hollesley ex Ch. Willowledge Candace). They owned Roco Chelsea who was bred to Ch. Ina Pauls Ben of Love Creek to produce Ch. Rachel of Rams Gate, Ch. Titus Augustus and Mamas Lass Hannah. Rachel and Rams Gate Remus produced Ch. Rams Gate Casey. Hannah to Ch. Alexander of Dahlseide produced Ch. Ramsgate Job. Savanah and Job produced Wrinkles of Rams Gate. Their bitch Rumblin Eko's Ramsgate Ariane (Ch. Willowledge Knute ex Ch. Brookmoors Taffy Jane) was bred to Rams Gate Tustin of Love Creek to produce Ch. Rams Gate Melisande and Ch. Rams Gate Keish Ohson. Ariane and Job produced Desiree de Rams Gate, Ch. Trajan and Ch. Charing. Ariane bred to Ch. Rocos Brute of Wasilla, CD (Ch. Roco Saladin ex Alecia Brandy Brown) produced Ch. Rams Gate Mandalyns Rhiannon. Desiree and Wrinkles produced Ch. Rams Gate Malise.

Gerald Danaher owned Ch. Willowledge Tammy (Beowulf ex Sheba), one of five Mastiffs to finish in 1965, who was bred to Rhinehart to produce Ballyherugh Blarney Stone, Baroness Mab, Ch. Choc-Na-Sige and Ch. Cormac O'Conn (BOB 1969 and 1970 Mastiff Specialties). Danaher owned Mooreleigh Undine who was bred to Hengist of Kisumu to get Ballyherughs Dartagnan and Ch. Doire Carinthia.

We plan breedings to get good puppies, but sometimes a breeding is not so important until years later when it takes on greater significance. Such was the case for Thurman and Mary Moore Williams. Their neighbors owned a GSD and when they rescued a Mastiff they could not keep, he, Raspberry, found a home with the Williams from 1962 until 1964. When he died, they wanted another Mastiff and were guided to the Brills who gave them the single brindle bitch puppy by King Knight of Beardsley (Beowulf ex Twinkle) out of Peach Farm Mamba (Arthur ex Thisby). The puppy was named Peach Farm Lambda. In 1965, Lamby was bred to Withybush Barquest of Saxondale (Weyacres Lincoln ex Boadicea of Saxondale) and produced a litter. It was Lamby's next litter that

Peach Farm Lambda. Sire: King Knight of Beardsley. Dam: Peach Farm Mamba. Breeder: John & Patty Brill. Owner: Mary Moore Williams.

would be providential to the breed. Peach Farm Brian (Withybush Barquest of Saxondale ex Amy) and Lamby produced 11 puppies in August 1966. The litter had three very important dogs: Heatherbrooke Keynes, Landovers Black Baron and Rufus of Heatherbrooke (placed by Patty as her stud puppy).

Keynes and Willowledge Velvet produced Copyline Eliza Doolittle who was bred to Laurelanes Eeyore to produce Ch. Bengali Tigress who was bred to Douglas' Little to get Ch. Littles Atlas of Massalane and Tigress was bred to Ch. Nemo of Massalane to produce Ch. Massalanes Dinah-Might. Tigress and Ch. Willowledge Ajaxx, CD produced Ch. My Precious of Massalane and Tigress and Atlas produced Ch. Little Ethan of Massalane. Landovers Black Baron bred to Willowledge Heidi to get Deer Run Gidget, Deer Run Gretel and Vaskos Lady Molly. Baron bred to Titan Nivea produced Somerset Atlas. Rufus of Heatherbrook bred to Petite Princess Tamora produced Ch. Deer Run Florister Bruce, Deer Run Horrendous and War and these three comprise a great portion of the foundation of Deer Run Kennels. War and Mistress Jill of Buckhall produced Ch. Deer Run Noah Massalane who is in nearly every Deer Run pedigree, and Mistress Clovia of Massalane, dam to the foundation bitch of Old School.

War bred to Heatherbelles Princess Candy produced Lazy Hill Alexandra, foundation of Lazy Hill, and War bred to Brown Ruby of Suffern produced Circe of Indian Raid. Rufus and Titan Brunhela got Ed Gerace's Ch. Deer Run Maud and Ch. Deer Run Tess, and Tobin Jackson's Ch. Deer Run Wellington. Maud is dam to the foundation bitch of Peersleigh and Wellington stands behind the start of many subsequent kennels. Conservatively, I estimate

Peach Farm Lambda's second litter sired by Peach Farm Brian. Rufus of Heatherbrooke had already been removed by his owner Dr. Tilghman when this picture was taken, however, two of these puppies were Heatherbrooke Keynes and Landover's Black Baron.

Lamby is in 85 percent of American pedigrees. She had only the two litters and one of her daughters by Brian, Wendy of Heatherbrooke, was kept by the Williams. Lamby died at 11 years and Wendy followed the year after. Heather, also from Peach Farm, joined the Williams in 1976 and when she passed on they got Punkin. Thurman and Mary do not have a Mastiff now, but they remain devoted to the breed and who knows what the future holds for them. I hope they know how grateful we are Lamby was bred to Brian those many years ago.

Robert and Marie Kross began the Werenhold line with Greco's Hope of Werenhold who was bred to Myrddin of Parcwood to produce Ch. Werenhold Beatrice and Alathea. Beatrice and Mooreleigh Viceroy (Falcon ex Reveille Mooreleigh Rachel) produced Ch. Traymatt Darci Kaki. Alathea and Hengist of Kisumu produced Dagmar and Ch. Werenhold Delilah who was bred to Viceroy to get Ch. Werenhold Faith. Dagmar and Viceroy produced Ch. Werenhold Holiday Hope, Ch. Hannibal and Harriet. Peter Gaar owned Ch. Tuppence of Blackroc (Ch. Balint of Havengore ex Berta of Copenore) and Ch. Goliath of Kisumu (Beaucaris Marcus ex Bathsheba). Tuppence and Goliath produced Deidre and Ch. Gar Stars Bravo and Tuppence and Matey of Havengore (Adamson ex Gipsy) produced Penny of Blackroc. Gaar owned Willowledge Margo (Conrade ex Hero) who was bred to Goliath to get Garstars

Alabaster, Atlas, and Attila. Penny and Garstars Attila produced the export Garstars Eric of Kisumu Canonbury.

Dr. H. L. Newbold had the remaining two Mastiffs that finished in 1965, Ch. Zilgul Silili (Ch. Balint of Havengore ex Withybush Viola) and Ch. Mooreleigh Quivira (Ivan ex Katrina). Newbold owned Ch. Justine of Rainbow Mountain (King Knight of Beardsley ex Willowledge Mistletoe) who was bred to Peach Farm Brian to get Peach Farm Ann. Newbold owned Grecos Heather who was bred to Henry of Havengore (Caradoc ex Delia) to produce Helena of Rainbow Mountain.

R. G. and Edna Mitchell owned Ch. Frideswide Hereward (Ch. Balint of Havengore ex Taddington Emma) and Peach Farm Ann (Brian ex Ch. Justine of Rainbow Mountain) who were bred to produce Ch. Berngarth Sum Queen of Clyde, Ch. Timothy, Ch. Victoria, Ch. Sum Barbie, Sum Cleopatra, Winston and Henrietta. Victoria bred to Humphrey produced Ch. Spice Hill In Honor of Jeremy. Henrietta bred to Tiberias produced Ch. Raisin Rivers Omena. Elation of Copenore was bred to Hereward to produce Ch. Berngarth Mischief. Ch. Berngarth Hereward came from the breeding of Berngarth Clarence out of a bitch named Helen.

Ed and Belva Funk owned Ch. Willowledge Candace (Conrade ex Hero) and Ch. Melanie of Willowledge (Ali Kahn ex Raven). Candace and Hereward produced Ch. Marco Polo, Ch. Rams Gate Savanah, Ch. English Toffie, and J. B. Willowledge. Candace and Ch. Paul of Conturo (Farnaby Merrick ex Saxondale Rebecca) produced Greenbrier's Lisa of Candace, Sweet Lori and Sabrina of Greenbrier. The Funks brought in Ch. Meps Tristan (Overnoons Mr Micawber of Buckhall ex Ch. Meps Portia) who was bred to Lisa to get Ch. Greenbrier Patch and Kemas Rebecca. Lisa and Admiration of Carinthia produced Petula Fouty. Lori and Admiration produced Greenbriers Bonnie Lee who was bred to Tristan to get Ch. Greenbriers Duke of Cat Walk and Ch. Nydia of Meps. Lori and Marco Polo produced Ch. Greenbriers Jody. Tristan sired such Mastiffs as Ch. Big Sky Sampson of Greenbrier, Ch. Duke Woods of Kingsborough, Ch. Columbo of Greenbrier and Ch. Greenbriers Shambeau (BOB Westminster KC and BOB 1977 Mastiff Specialty) and through Shambeau, Tristan was grandsire to Ch. Scarey Creeks Damon (1984 Top Winning Mastiff, Top Stud Dog at the 1985 and Veteran Dog 1986 Mastiff Specialties).

The Funks owned Ch. Walnut Creeks Tina (Ch. Dawnwind Romulus ex Werenhold Harriet) who was bred to Admiration to get Greenbriers Sunshine. Tina and Bredwardine Court Jester produced Westports Natalia Doll. Belva owned Ch. Greenbriers Shawnda of Greco (Hollesley Sam ex Sacha Sarele) who was bred to Ch. Groppettis Wallon to produce Ch. Greenbrier Amjo of Wallon and Shawnda bred to Ch. Grecos Hollesley Grizzley produced Ch. Greenbrier's Kiss-Me-Kate who was bred to Ch. Bredwardine Beiligwyn (Eng. Am. Ch. Arciniegas Lion of Bredwardine ex Bredwardine Berthvedw) to get Ch. Grecos Big Ben II.

Canadians Ruth and Gary Wallace owned Can. Ch. Mooreleigh Yanina (Ballyherugh's Michael ex Beaucaris Queen of Sheba) and Ch. Ballyherughs Cormac O (BOB 1969 and 1970 Mastiff Specialty) and Ch. Garstars Athena (Goliath ex Willowledge Margo). Yanina and Cormac produced Ch. Thunderhills Little Thunder, Ch. Marina and Ch. Munchkin. Cormac was bred to Ch. Chicken Little (by Falcon ex Helena of Rainbow Mountain) to produce Ch. Thunderhills Brutus, Ch. Ria of Love Creek and Ch. Bea of Love Creek and the Top Show bitch owned by Ed Gerace, Ch. Thunderhills Abbess.

Lois Savage owned Helena of Rainbow Mountain (Henry of Havengore ex Grecos Heather) who was bred to Mooreleigh Timothy to get Dahlseide Dame Puddin-Tame and Helena was bred to Falcon to get Ch. Chicken Little and Ch. Dahlseide Dame Dickens, BOB 1971 Westminster KC and BOS 1970 and 1971 Mastiff Specialties. Puddin-Tame bred to Master of the Woods (Ch. Reveille Juggernaut ex Allison of Dorevsherm) produced Ch. Odin of Dahlseide. Dickens bred to Master of the Woods produced Ch. Hannibal of Dahlseide and Ch. Alexander who sired Ch. Gulph Mills Mugger (BOB 1980 Mastiff Specialty) and Ch. Ramsgate Job (Number 1 Mastiff Stud in 1977 and 1978). Lois owned Ch. Dahlseide Windsors Bow Belle (Job ex Gypsy Rose) who was bred to Ch. Odin of Dahlseide (Master of the Woods ex Dame Puddin-Tame) to produce Dahlseide Fish N Chips, Union Jack, Ch. Dahlseide Referendum, Penny Farthing (1982 National Sweepstakes winner) and Ch. John Bull. Lois owned Dahlseide Dame Whittle (Ch. Odin ex Black Oak of the Woods) who was bred to Ch. Winterwood Wind and Tide (Shambeau ex Ch. Winterwood Hepzibah) to get Ch. Dahlseide

Tudor Rose and Ch. Crown Derby. Whittle was bred to Ch. Berengarias Drum of Reprieve (Shambeau ex Ch. Greenbranch Lovella) to get Dahlseide Sweet Melody and Ch. Dahlseide Lord Mayor, CD. Tudor Rose and Lord Mayor produced Ch. Dahlseide Bloody Mary.

Dr. William Newman owned Ch. Renrocks Brian O'Dare (Peach Farm Raynor ex Peach Farm Peaches) who was bred to Ch. Reveille Tribute to produce Ch. Reveille By Candlelight, Ch. Lightning, Ch. Renrocks Sean O'Dare and a dog owned by Judy Kessler and Bill, Ch. Big Thunder (BOB 1974, 1975 and 1976 Mastiff Specialties). Bill owned Ch. Peach Farm Moira O'Dare and Ch. Peach Farm Megan O' Dare (Warlock ex Kings Court Peach Farm Tucker), Ch. Renrock's Brendan O'Dare MS (Sean O'Dare ex Foxana of Alpenhof), Ch. Renrock's Mary Magdalene (Garlands Dominique ex Peach Farm Gruffi). He imported Ch. Nantymynydd Glenis (Cynan O'Nantymynydd ex Myfanwy O'Nantymynydd). Mary Magdalene bred to Big Thunder produced Ch. Renrocks Mariah O'Dare, Ch. Maria Linda (BOS 1976 Mastiff Speciality), Ch. Michael O'Dare and Ch. Danny O'Dare. Bill's bitch Rumblin Ekos Penny of Renrock (Ch. Windhaven Hercules ex Ch. Willowledge North Star Venus) was bred to Lightning to get Ch. Marcie and Molly O'Dare. Bill was 1978 Mastiff Club president and is currently the AKC Delegate.

Robert and Doreen Lissner owned Ch. Ina Pauls Ben of Love Creek (Bowats Royal Duke ex Bowats Sybil) and Ch. Willowledge Ann of Love Creek (Gentle Ben ex Ch. Hefina O'Nantymynydd), Ch. Thunderhills Bea and Ch. Thunderhills Ria of Love Creek. Ria and Ben produced Ch. Bens Ali of Love Creek and Ch. Bens Brymyr of Love Creek. Bea and Duke of Love Creek produced Ch. Nell of Love Creek, Ch. Finlay of Love Creek and Ch. Kingsboroughs Carmel Candy. Bea bred to Ali produced Ch. Sheffields Lovecreek Angus. Ria and Duke produced Ch. Love Creeks Silver Flo and Ch. Magnos Honorable Hatchet Man, CD. Ria bred to Finlay produced Ch. Lovecreeks Sweet Biscuit. Ria and Big Thunder produced Ch. Thunders Pride of Love Creek, Ch. Love Creeks Bronze Guard, Ch. Love Creeks Black Watch, Ch. Lovecreek Lady of the Lake and Ch. Tamarack Peaches Lovecreek (BOS Specialty Winner).

Ernest Howard owned Garstars Alabaster who was bred to Juggernaut to produce Ch. Acadian Candance Kristle, Ch. Yasmin,

Ch. Brutus and Ch. Bull Durham. Kristle bred to Thunderhills Brutus produced Ch. Molls Pride Fagin. Acadian Charlotte bred to Cecil of Alpenhof (Peach Farm Paper Tiger ex Mari of Kisumu) produced Ch. Acadian Abby of Sleepy Hollow and Çh. Boris of Kirtland. Renrocks Acadian Griselda was bred to Ch. Bull Durham to produce Ch. Acadian Konigstiger (BOW 1977 Mastiff Specialty).

Lt. Col. William and Phyllis Armstrong owned Ch. Willowledge Gregory (Knute ex Charlotte) and Caledonia Mary of Love Creek (Big Thunder ex Ria) who were bred together to get Ch. Caledonia Thurl A, Ch. Fid C and Ch. Magnus A. Mary bred to Fiddlewood Acco of Carinthia (Chancelots Vaguely Noble ex Brief of Carinthia) produced Caledonia Elsie of Carinthia and Susie Farber's great Ch. Caledonia Eric the Red (top group placing Mastiff of his day). Fid and Ch. Banyons Hymmal (Ch. Willow Points Catullus ex Ch. Willow Points Sixpence) produced Ch. Caledonia Green Mt Katrinka and Ch. Sudans Kolleen, owned by Bill and Susie. The Armstrongs owned Ch. Caledonia Elkrivers Maude (Ch. Greenbriers Shambeau ex Scarey Creeks Bambi) and Ch. Caledonia Stingers Margaret (Ch. Dawnwind Romulus ex Werenhold Harriet). After Bill passed away, Susie took the Caledonia prefix.

She owned Lady Victoria of Greenbrier (Tristan ex Bonnie Lee) who was bred to Ch. Chancelots Kilimanjaro (Ch. Plaisance Epaphus ex Ch. Buckhall Mistress Gwynne) to get Ch. Sudans Patient Abigail. More recently, Susie owned Ch. Caledonias Only Olivia (Greenbriers Duke of Cat Walk ex Ch. Grenveldt Kelly of Reese) who was bred to Ch. Grimpen of Baskerville (Ch. Banyons Fozzie Bear ex Ch. Baskervilles Agatha Christie) to get Caledonia

Ch. Deer Run Florister Bruce. Sire: Rufus of Heatherbrooke. Dam: Petite Princess Tamora. Owner: Tobin Jackson.

Cameron Pinehollow (owned with Nancy Hempel) who was bred to Ch. Pinehollows War Gator to produce Ch. Pinehollow Caledonia Jackson. Susie bred Caledonia champions Memphis Belle, Dreamer, Rumor Has It, Tempest Haven, Shelby of Ki, Sicily Tyson, Place Your Bets, Best Bet Kethry, Darkman, III, and Big Gamble, and Iron Hills champions Fixin To Start, Sara of Mellabee, Magic Bus and Color My Wagon.

Tobin Jackson started Deer Run around 1968 with Ch. Deer Run Jupiter (Olympian's Marauder ex Gynflyns Samantha). Deer Run Salome (Jupiter ex Heatherbelles Sue's Sally), Ch. Florister Bruce and Horrendous (Rufus of Heatherbrook ex Petite Princess Tamora) were born in 1969. Ch. Deer Run Wellington arrived in 1971 and Stella (Florister Bruce ex Salome) and Ch. Begoine/Beguine (Florister Bruce ex Horrendous) were born in 1972. Ch. Deer Run Noah Massalane (War ex Mistress Jill of Buckhall) was owned by Tobin's partner Donald V Gibbs. With 16 points, and after a two-year hiatus, at six Noah returned to the show ring to finish. Another of his dogs was Florister Rufus (Noah ex Ch. Nanjemoys Etasha).

Deer Run Florister Rufus. Sire: Ch. Deer Run Noah Massalane. Dam: Ch. Nanjemoy's Etasha. Breeder: Lorraine Hall. Owner: Tobin Jackson.

Although not without his critics and often surrounded by controversy, Tobin's Deer Run dogs had enviable success in the show ring and wide support in the Mastiff community. If a breeder is judged solely on the basis of wins versus losses, then Tobin surely finished far ahead—especially if consideration is given to the wins of dogs bred by other breeders whose strains were spawned by Deer Run. It would be virtually impossible to list the Deer Run Mastiffs. Probably the most famous of them all was Ch. Deer Run Wycliff (Ch. Jericho City ex Stella) who is recorded as one of the top producing sires of all time with 45 champions of record. Tobin brought imported stock from Europe (his bitch Ch. Falmore Hall Mistral, by Ch. Medicine Man ex Ch. Farnaby Fighting Faith of Falmore Hall, won BOS 1986 Mastiff Specialty) as well as shipped dogs to Europe. I do not exaggerate when I write perhaps as high as 95 percent of the Mastiffs alive today descend from Deer Run blood. Among his finest were top producers Champions Deer Run Ezekiel, Ivan, Noah Massalane, Roderick and Zachary, Sophie, Stella and Jai Bee Cleopatria. The record-holding Mastiff with 10 Best In Shows, Ch. Pinehollow Caledonia Jackson, is G.G.G. grandson to Wycliff and Ch. Deer Run William The Conqueror, record holder before Jackson with 9 Best in Shows, is a Wycliff son. Ch. Deer Run Zen, C.D. was the first Mastiff to win BIS in Puerto Rico, and Zen won BOB in 1979 at the Mastiff Specialty. Other Specialty BOB winners descending from Deer Run blood are Ch. Old Schools Ursa Major in 1983, Ch. Quellwater Deer Run Antique in 1984, Arciniegas Lion in 1986, Ch. Old Schools Primo Remo Major in 1988, Ch. Iron Hills Warwagon in 1989 and 1990, Ch. Stonehouse Country Squire in 1991, Ch. Smok'N Lads Stormy Dominic in 1992, Ch. Matts-Joshua of Dogwood Knoll in 1993, Ch. Iron Hills Earned Interest in 1994, Ch. IGuards T & T's Magic Moment in 1995, Ch. Ridgewoods Otis in 1996 and Ch. Iron Hills Into The Night in 1997.

Bruce and Marilyn Chapman owned Can. Am. Ch. Tiberias of Kisumu (Ch. Threebees Friar of Copenore ex Buckhall Hannah of Kisumu) who sired their bitch Ch. Willow Points Kristina, Ch. Imperial Frostina and Ch. Santana (all ex Ch. Berngarth Sum Queen of Clyde). Tiberias was bred to Berngarth Henrietta to produce Ch. Willow Points Sixpence, Ch. Raisin Rivers Omena, Ch. Willow Points Lyric, Ch. Delilah and Colossus. With Willowledge Imperial Aggie he sired Ch. Willow Points Catullus and Ch. Raisin Rivers Thurston. He and Willowledge Tickle produced Ch. Willow Points Abbey, Ch. Pax, and Ch. Kristina II. Tiberias bred to Landovers Sasparilla produced Ch. Willow Points Tiberia Gemini who was bred to Catullus to produce Ch. Willow Points Warwick. The Chapmans owned Ch. Rosewall Hera (Tiberias ex Willowledge Freta). Lyric was bred to Catullus produced Willow Points Shilling.

Caroline Fitzgerald owned Frideswide Susan (Matey of Havengore ex Nicolette) who was bred to Bowats Roar 'N Rumble of Corgeen to produce Ch. Windhaven Hercules, Ch. Bradleys Budget, Ch. Rumblin Ekos Sassy Sea Nymph and Ch. Rumblin Ekos His Majestys Thor. Fitzgerald bred Brookmoor Taffy Jane to Ch. Willowledge Knute to get Ch. Willowledge Sheba of R Eko, Ch. Rumblin Ekos Thojhild, and Ch. Willowledge R Eko Jim-Bill.

There is a story about Ch. Rumblin Ekos His Majestys Thor, born 1969, that will sadden Mastiff lovers, yet it needs telling. This wonderful dog was of such high quality he was able to win BOB at the 1971, 1972 and 1973 Mastiff Specialties. Then something terrible happened. Who knows what went wrong. Thor became lost or abandoned. He no longer had a family. Donald and Patricia Geil found him in a shelter April 23, 1975. He weighed 80 pounds. The Thor they found was a pathetic version of the Specialty winner; a distant reminder of the former great dog. Thor was lucky because the Geils cared so much about him. With Bill Newman's nutritional and medical guidance, and the love, patience and devotion of the Geils, Thor was carefully brought back to health. In May 1976, he attended one more Specialty and it would be his last. At 190 pounds he won Veterans. He also won the hearts of everyone there. They tell me there was not a dry eye on the show grounds. Thor died the next January and is perpetually preserved and laid to rest at the Great Valley Pet Cemetery in Frazer, Pennsylvania. I share this story for those of you who never heard it, and to remind us all of our obligation to these wonderful Mastiffs we breed.

The latter part of the 20th Century, from approximately 1965 to the present time, has been the greatest period of prosperity and security for Mastiffs in their history insofar as availability of breeding stock is concerned and the number of breeders with ongoing breeding programs. In 1971, the Mastiff Club decided the Specialty would be held every May. By 1978, the membership of the Mastiff Club had grown to include 228 members.

Jim and Mary Zellen began their Banyon line with Ch. Willow Points Sixpence, BOS 1974 Mastiff Specialty, who was bred to Ch. Willow Points Catullus to get Ch. Banyons Hymmal who was bred to Willow Points Shilling (Catullus ex Lyric) to produce Ch. Banyons Jason. Shilling and Ch. Meps Tristan produced Ch. Banyons Benson, Ch. Cassandra and Ch. Charmin (Benson and Charmin, respectively, went WB and WD 1981 Mastiff Speciality under Breeder/Judge Eve Olsen). Cassandra bred to Hymmal produced Ch. Banyons Lady Diana. Charmin and the imported Farnaby Fidelity (Ch. Parcwood W Bear ESQ of Lesdon ex Farnaby Flattering Frazes) got the beautiful brindle dog, Ch. Banyons Fozzie Bear who was bred to Banyons Hilda Sylvia (Ch. Windhavens Leontos Sayyid ex Wendy Lynn of the White House) to produce Ch. Banyons Amelia Bedelia who was put Ch. Lionsire Grizz (Ch. Deer Run Ezekiel ex Christians Bristol Cream) to produce Ch. Banyons Cosby, Ch. Swainmote Murphy Brown and Betsy. Betsy bred to Banyons Fenster (Linville Bart Too ex Linville's Chelsea) produced Ch. Banyons Oscar.

Willow Points Finale (Tiberias ex Beau Cheval's Tootsie Roll) was bred to Hymmal to get Ch. Willow Points Surrey and Banyons Meredith. Surrey bred to Benson produced Banyons Merrilee. Surry bred to her sire Hymmal produced Ch. Banyons Klara. Ch. Banyons Rumpole came from Hymmal and Brandywines Beatrice of Mega (Deer Run Zarek ex Ch. Princess Brandywine). Hilda bred to Rumpole produced Ch. Banyons Spencer and Joolie Snowsage who was bred to Cosby to get Ch. Banyons Lester and Joolie was bred to Ch. Deer Run Josh of Bull Valley (Wycliff ex Tasha Farleys First Lady) to produce Ch. Banyons Sheba Spice and Ch. Starhaven Porter. Banyons Jamie (Ch. Windhavens Leontos Sayyid ex Banyons Blacknight Trudy) bred to Ch. Twin Oaks Andrae (Sur-Wins Taxi ex Windsongs Charlotte) produced Ch. Blossom. Wendy Lynn (Hymmal ex Crooked Lake Amazon Meyers) and Leontos Sayyid (Northmoor Windhavens Onyx ex Ch. Deer Run Windhavens Hera) produced Ch. Banyons Nikka (BOS Puppy Sweepstakes 1986 Mastiff Specialty). Two-time winner of BOS at the Mastiff Supported Bucks County KC Show, Banyons Mayflower Madam (Rumpole ex Nikka) was bred to Ezekiel (Ivan ex Le MarSally) and produced Ch. Ironlions Fatal Attraction who was bred back to Banyons Marcus of Noble (Fozzie Bear ex Nikka) to get Banyons Phoebe who was bred to Cosby to produce their present bitch, Banyons Abby (named in honor of their good friend Betty Dickey's The Abby Kennel). Banyon's Mastiffs are always recognizable and of all the strains I have been privileged to view over the years, this line stands out for their consistent overall balance, heavy substance and true breed type. Jim, an AKC Mastiff judge, always handles his own dogs.

Joanne Williams owned Ch. Alexander of Dahlseide and Ch. Windsors Waltzing Matilda who was bred to Alexander to get Ch. Gelwils Alexander (Top 10 in 1985 and group placing), Meghan of Canterbury, and Ch. Special Edition (Number 1 Group Bitch in 1984; Number 4 Group Mastiff and Number 8 Mastiff in 1984). Special Edition bred to Ch. Lucas (Ch. Gulph Mills Mulcher ex Winterwoods Worth the Candle) produced Ch. Gelwils Private Dancer and Ch. Midnight Special. Special Edition was bred to Mulcher (Ch. Gulph Mills Mugger ex Ch. Greenbranch Macushla) to produce Ch. Gelwils Second Edition. Buffys Apricot Brandy (Tamarack Donner ex Ch. Rocky Hollow Lady Wookie) bred to Ch. Gelwils Alexander produced Ch. Gelwils Brandy Alexander (BOB 1987 Mastiff Specialty).

Anthony and Maxine Ficarotta owned Ch. Bengali Tigress (Laurelanes Eeyore ex Copyline Eliza Doolittle) and Ch. Nemo of Massalane (Douglas' Little ex Gasparilla Farms Margaret) who were bred together to produce Ch. Massalanes Dinah-Might (owned by Gulph Mills). Tigress and Douglas' Little produced Ch. Little George and Ch. Little Atlas of Massalane (owned by Gulph Mills) and Tigress bred to Atlas produced Massalane Grand Boulder and Ch. Little Ethan. Tigress to Willowledge Ajaxx (Ch. Willowledge Clyde of Essex ex Ch. Hefina O'Nantymynydd) got Raven, Ch. My Precious of Massalane and Massalane Tangerine. They owned War (Rufus of Heatherbrooke ex Petite Princess Tamora) who sired Mistress Clovia of Massalane and Deer Run Noah Massalane (owned by Deer Run) both out of Mistress Jill of Buckhall. War and Heatherbelle Princess Candy sired Lazy Hill Alexandra (owned by Lazy Hill). Clovia and Nemo produced Mistress Julia of Massalane (owned by Old School) and Clovia and Rajah (Douglas' Little ex Mistress Jill of Buckhall) produced Mistress Jill of Massalane. Ch. Princess Lill of Massalane (Chancelots Merely A Monarch ex Mother Natures Matilda) and Nemo produced Ch. Sasha of Massalane and Lill to Little Ethan produced Gil and Martha Rosenthal's Ch. Majestic Duchess of Ramapo Mt and Ch. Duke von Hewitt of Massalane. Jill of Massalane to Nemo produced Ch. Wyldewood Tammy of Massalane.

Mike and Dee Gensburger owned Ch. Massalanes Dinah-Might and Ch. Little Atlas of Massalane (BOW 1976 Mastiff

Specialty) and Greenbranch Ch. Dame Sybil, Ch. Dame Winifred, Ch. Cornwallis II, Ch. Macushla and Ch. Georgina. Dinah bred to Ch. Alexander of Dahlseide produced Ch. Gulph Mills Mugger (BOB 1980 Mastiff Specialty), Ch. Mischief, Ch. Flintlock T., Ch. Agamemnon and Ch. Greenbranch Molly Malone. Sybil bred to Ch. Ramsgate Job produced Ch. Gulph Mills Resounder (BOB 1982 Mastiff Specialty) and Ch. Gulph Mills Amy. Amy bred to Atlas produced Ch. Gulph Mills Dawn. Mugger and Macushla produced what is probably their best known dog, Ch. Gulph Mills Mulcher, not only a top winner in the show ring, but the second all time Top Producer with 47 champions of record. Mulcher and Dawn produced Ch. Gulph Mills Glory Be, Ch. Little Amy and Ch. Legacy who was bred to Ch. Southports Prime Time to get their Ch. Gulph Mills Bailey On The Rock (BOS 1997 Mastiff Specialty).

Dr. Roscoe and Jacqueline Guy owned Ch. Willowledge Caesar III (Willowledge Bambi ex Ch. Hefina O'Nantymynydd) and Greenbranch Lady Jane (Ch. Artifex Astronaut ex Ch. Deer Run Maud) who were bred together to get Peersleigh Lady Lorelei who when bred back to her sire, Caesar, produced Ch. Peersleigh Bridgewood Blair, Ch. Peersleigh Princess Hannah and Ch. Peersleigh Princess Carolyn (multiple group placer before Working was split nearly in half and two times BOS Westminster KC). Carolyn bred to Ch. Odin of Dahlseide produced Ch. Peersleigh Queen Heike Beta, Ch. Allison, Ch. Lady Magdelyn and my Ch. Storm Sherman. Carolyn and Ch. Berengaria's Drum of Reprieve (Ch. Greenbriers Shambeau ex Ch. Greenbranch Lovella) got Ch. Peersleigh Ingot Janus and Storm Samantha. Samantha bred to Hollesley Lord Ralegh produced Ch. Storm Banner of Peersleigh, Ch. Storm Rowena of Peersleigh, Can. Ch. Peersleigh Sergent Co-caine and Ch. Peersleigh Sudden Storm (grandsire to BOB 1992 National Specialty). It was a real loss to the breed when Jackie quit breeding to teach championship tennis.

Bill and Judy Powers owned Ch. Oak Ridges Queen of Sheba (Peach Farm Michelo ex Peach Farm Beatrix) who was bred to Ch. Reveille Lightning to produce Ch. Oak Ridge Aquila, Ch. Amber Alana, Adonis and Apollo Dook. Sheba was bred to Ch. Odin of Dahlseide to produce Ch. Oak Ridges Margaise, Morgana Le Fay and Royal of Irish Hill. Margaise was bred to Ch. Riverside

Farms Berserker (Riverside Farms Baskerville ex Cleopatra Ptolemy) to get Ch. Oak Ridges Heath Mor Galahad (BOB 1985 Mastiff Specialty), Ch. Februa Lyla, Ch. Meyers Medusa, Septem Amber, Julius Aragorn, and Maia of Irish Hill.

Terry Theriault owned Lady Martha of Apple Creek (Ch. Ina Pauls Ben of Love Creek ex Ch. Thunderhills Bea of Lovecreek) who was bred to Ch. Grand Duke O'Fern to get Buttercup who was bred to Moonshadow Nada Wildbriar to get Ch. Lady Pebbles of Apple Creek. Since then he has produced or owned such Apple Creek champions as Apricot Brandy, Beauty N A Beast, Buster Brown, Delta Dawn, Ebony Onyx, CD, Gem Dandy, Its Showtime, L Olympus Loki, Lady Cassandra, Lady Natassia, Middle Earth Oin, Priscilla Mulin, Seven Seas, Sierra, Southport Kahlua, Spirit of New Beginning and Tobius Augustus.

Mrs. Fred Bushnell Jr. owned Werenhold Harriet who was bred to Ch. Dawnwind Romulus. This breeding helped put both sire and dam in the Hall of Fame by producing nine champions: Ch. Caledonia Stingers Margaret, Ch. Walnut Creeks Atticus Finch, Ch. Tina, Ch. Dutch Master, Ch. Frederic Fonz and Ch. Shamariah, Ch. Cedric McKaye, Ch. Gemini and Ch. Baron Roscoe. There have only been a few litters that I'm aware of that have matched, but never surpassed, this breeding for producing such beautiful typey heads, heavy bone and remarkable substance. Ch. Dawnwind Romulus, Stinger, was known for passing along his great head and substance, and even in 1997, his head type still occasionally crops up in litters that breed back to him.

Nancy Hempel's Pinehollow Kennel began with Pinehollows Sadie (Ch. Paul of Conturo ex Ch. Willowledge Tallulah) who was bred to Ch. Blackheath Wild Bill (Ch. Blackheath Boss ex Mamselle of Shute) to produce Ch. Pinehollows Friar Tuck and Ch. Melton's Beau of Allendale. Ch. Feeney's Miss Meghan (Stonewall Jackson of Fouty ex Dixie Darling of Stonewall) was bred to Tuck to get Ch. Pinehollows Sabastian. Alauntes Brooke of Pinehollow (Ch. Alauntes Beauford ex Alauntes Bettilou) was bred to Gambler to get Pinehollows Kizzie. Regiments Saba (Ch. Royal Regiments Tauras ex Ch. Banyon's Bathsheba) was bred to Tuck to produce Ch. Sheriff of Nottingham and Ch. Pinehollows Lady Lizbeth who was bred to Ch. Deer Run McMunger (Wycliff ex Karema) to get Ch.

Pinehollows Chumley (Number 1 Mastiff 1985). Lizbeth and Sabastian produced The Gambler of Pinehollow and Pinehollows Sara Lee who was bred to Bredwardine Blaenpennal (Ch. Glynpedr Dom Perignon ex Zanfi Baroness of Bredwardine) to get Ch. Pinehollows Courtney (Number 1 Mastiff Bitch 1990) and Arabella. Kizzie was bred to Ch. Lionsire Ironhill Warleggen (Ezekiel ex Ch. Farleys Eledhwen Steelsheen) to produce Ch. Pinehollows War Gator (Top 10 Mastiff 1992) who was bred to Caledonia Cameron Pinehollow to produce Ch. Pinehollow Caledonia Jackson, the All Time Top Winning Mastiff who holds the record with an unprecedented 10 Best In Shows!

Jack stayed in our home for a month and I can assure you there is only one Mastiff in the world like Jack and there will never be another quite like him as he was a single-puppy litter and both his parents died. Jack not only is a splendid Mastiff, he truly has so much personality and character. He is what we breeders call a "high-flying" Mastiff. He goes air borne, lands on his feet, then flies around the ring, showing incredible reach and drive, and he never breaks stride. He has absolute confidence that nobody can take his eyes off him and the greatest presence in the ring of any Mastiff ever shown. In addition to being the happy and confident show dog, Jack is pure Mastiff and will turn into Nancy's guardian in a heartbeat!

Hal and Carol Smith Knutson owned BOS 1978 Mastiff Specialty winner Ch. Tamarack Peaches Lovecreek (Ch. Reveille Big Thunder ex Ch. Thunderhill Ria of Lovecreek) who was bred to her sire to produce Ch. Tamarack Bon Bon and Peaches was bred to Ch. Acadian Konigstiger (Ch. Acadian Bull Durham ex Renrocks Acadian Griselda) to get Ch. Tamarack Jacob of Genesis, Tamarack Donner (Hall of Fame Top Producer), Tamarack Winnifred and Ch. Tamarack Sheba (BOB 1981 Mastiff Specialty).

Irene Byrne had horses and her husband, Jerry, wanted a "horse of a dog" so they went visited Ed Gerace (Greenbranch) and Tobin Jackson (Deer Run) the same day. Their first two Mastiffs, born in 1976, were Greenbranch Beaumont (Ch. Chancelots Triple Crown ex Deer Run Maud) and Deer Run Jai Bee Sheba (Jericho City ex Bianca). Jai Bee Mastiffs was begun with the third Mastiff, Deer Run Jai Bee Cleopatria (Lancaster ex Greta). Cleo had puppies by Ch. Deer Run Ivan and Ch. Iron HIlls Rocky Hill Thor, however, it was her breedings to Wycliff that made history. These breedings not only catapulted Cleo into the position of third all-time Top Producer, but the breedings produced nine time BIS Ch. Deer Run William the Conqueror, Ch. Deer Run Countess Inez (All Time Top Producing Brood Bitch with 18 champions), Ch. Jai Bee Dixie Lass, Ch. Deer Run Jai Bee Yankee (group placer), Ch. Jai Bee Rocky Hill Trudy (Top Producer) and Ch. Jai Bee Noble Gateway (group placer). The Mastiff community lost a great friend when Jerry passed away in 1990, but Irene is continuing with the Jai Bee breeding program. Charles and Nancy Boyer owned Countess Inez, who when bred to Ezekiel produced Ch. Rocky Hill Wrightous Caesar and Ch. Rocky Hill Krystal Gail, BOB and BOS WKC.

Wrightous Caesar, owned by Jay and Ruth Winston, was Number 1 Mastiff in 1986 and 1987. I watched him show up and down the East Coast during this time and had not seen him for sev-

Ch. Rocky Hills Wrighteous Caesar. Sire: Ch. Deer Run Ezekiel. Dam: Ch. Deer Run Countess Inez. Owner: Justin & Ruth Winston. Breeder: Charles Boyer.

eral years when Jay showed him to win Veterans Class and Award of Merit at the 1992 Mastiff Specialty. Caesar had matured into one of the finest Mastiffs it has been my privilege to see. His head was gorgeous, his spring of rib incredible, his bone heavier, his front and rear superb and he was in fantastic condition for a dog just shy of eight years old. I don't know if all this is fact, but it was how it seemed to me. Caesar begged for Breed and, except for the judge and BOB and BOS winners, I doubt anybody at that show would disagree that Caesar should have won. He stood out clearly from the rest. He showed his heart out and was flawlessly shown. Neither of the judge's choices matched him for type, substance or full-blown maturity, nor was he out moved by any youngsters. Ruth told me Caesar's ashes are laid to rest with Jay. We will not be forgetting either of them.

Carol Mathews began Royal Oak in 1976 with Ch. Dawnwind Romulus Cassia, Sassy, (Ch. Dawnwind Romulus ex Arborcrest Athena) who was bred to Ch. Cedar Forests Poppy (Roling Hils Charles ex Simba Babe) to produce Ch. Royal Oaks True Admiration, Smudge. Although Smudge earned her title as a puppy and was of beautiful conformation, she had better things to do than show or make puppies. She became a star in her own television show for children.

Carol owned Castle Crest For Get Me Not, Minnow, (Ch. Camelots Mister T ex Ch. Peersleigh Allison) who was bred to my Sherman to get Ch. Royal Oaks Celtic Mercedes, Sadie, (Award of Merit 1989 Mastiff Specialty). Sadie was owned by Carol with Barb Avise and they bred her to Storm Gruffudd of Royal Oak (Ch. Damaria The General ex Ch. Storm Dixieland Delight) to produce Ch. Royal OakCeltic Maggie T, (BOS 1991 Mastiff Specialty). Carol owned Storm Gwyneira of Royal Oak (Ch. Damaria The Druid ex Ch. Storm Banner of Peersleigh) who was bred to Gruffudd to get our Ch. Storm Hammer of Royal Oak, Storm Honour of Royal Oak and Ch. Storm Shark Petrie Royal Oak. In addition to these breeder accomplishments, Carol is an excellent handler who showed Ch. Smok'N Lads Stormy Dominic to BOB 1992 Mastiff Specialty.

Lynn Urban owned Ch. Oak Ridge Aquila who was bred to Reveille Morning-star (Ch. Willowledge Clyde of Essex ex Candlelight) to produce Ch. Betelgeuse of Lyndon (1980 Top 10 Mastiffs), Ch. Reveille Lyndon Rejoice and Ch. Lady Gemini of Lyndon (RWB 1980 Mastiff Specialty). Quillie was bred to Ch. Bournewood Edwin (Bournewood Jasper ex Bourne-wood Sophie) to produce Ch. Harper of Lyndon and Ch. Mistress Carina of Lyndon. Lynn and I own 10-year-old Bredwardine Brynawelon (Bredwardine Brynawdon ex Ch. Bredwardine Beau Ide'al), Storm Pegasus of Lyndon (Sherman ex Ch. Pinewoods Dandylion of Pern) and Storm Boots of Lyndon (Hammer ex Loxley Storm Druidess).

Robert Goldblatt's kennel produces few litters, but even so he is very successful. Despite living in a remote area of Northern California which makes breeding, socializing and showing more difficult, he overcame the drawbacks. His Gulph Mills Lord Kether (Ch. Lord Mountbatten of Colossus ex Dame Winifred) was six months when he won Best Puppy and RWD at the 1978 Mastiff Specialty and he championed at 11 months. He owned Virgil, Ch. Goldleaf's Coeur de Lion (Ch. Little's Atlas of Massalane ex Ch. Gulph Mills Dame Catherine) and Ch. Greenbranch Dolly Malone who when bred together produced Ch. Goldleaf Coeur de Sol (Gail) who was bred to Mulcher to produce Ch. Goldleaf Montana (Number 3 Mastiff in 1987) and Ch. Gulph Mills D'Artagnan (Number 1 Mastiff in 1988), Ch. Goldleaf's Hope and Glory and Ch. Berengaria's False Hope and Lies. One of the best known Goldleaf Mastiffs is Ch. Blu Ridge Goldleaf of Blk Pt, Daisy (Montana ex Ch. Southports Jez of Blu Ridge). Daisy made her presence known early, finishing at nine months. She went on to become the Number 1 Bitch in 1991 and 1992, and the Number 2 Mastiff in 1992. In 1994 Ch. Gulph Mills Moonshine (Ch. Goldleaf Montana ex Ch. Gulph Mills Legacy) became Number 3 Mastiff.

John and Donna Bahlman owned Ch. Hannibal of Makar (Tiberias ex Beau Cheval's Marakesh) who was bred to their Mistress Julia of Massalane to get Old Schools Trouble who was bred to Deer Run Florister Rufus to get Ch. Old Schools Ursa Major. Trouble, a lovely brindle bitch, was on the way to her championship when a tragedy occurred and she died but her quality lived on and her legacy has been incredible. Ursa (BOB 1983 Mastiff Specialty, Number 1 Mastiff Bitch 1983 and Top Producer 1988) was bred to Ch. Deer Run McMunger (Wycliff ex Tasha Farleys First Lady) to produce Ch. Old Schools Panama Red and Ch. Von Roth's Carolina Casey.

It was the next breeding that really clicked, for when Ursa was bred to Ezekiel it produced BIS/BISS 1988 Mastiff Specialty Ch. Old Schools Primo Remo Major and BOSS 1989 Mastiff Specialty Ch. Old Schools Mitra Major. Ursa and Ch. Autumn River Big Ben (Lazy Hill Luath ex Ch. Lazy Hill Athena) produced Old School Bens Autumn Major who was bred to Ch. Old Schools Sergeant Major (Ezekiel ex Ursa) to get Ch. Old Schools Sgt Sagar. Sassys Jessie Girl was bred to Sagar to get Ch. Old Schools Woden (BOW 1996 Mastiff Specialty). The list of John and Donna's champions is long and impressive and breeders have learned never to underestimate any Old School Mastiff that enters the show ring as competition!

Scott Phoebus finished his Solomon of Iron Hills (Tiberias ex Brookmoors Star Ginger) in 1979 and his Mastiffs have been blazing a trail of glory in show rings every since. He owned Willowledge Lil Ms. Sassafras (Christopher Robin ex Nancy) who was bred to Ch. Nanjemoy Ka-Reem (Tiberias ex Ch. Beau Chevals Marakesh) to produce Ch. Rivendells Samson Viet Armis. He owned Ch. Farleys Eledhwen Steelsheen (Sheena) (Wycliff ex Tasha Farleys First Lady) and he acquired Tasha who was bred to Wycliff again to produce Ch. Iron Hills Elbereth (Tari), Ch. Deer Run Josh of Bull Valley, Ch. Deer Run Jake Enchanted Acres and Ch. Iron Hills Mithrandir. Sheena and Deer Run Caisson (Florister Rufus ex Roja Grande Dale) produced Ch. Ironhill Tobin Lev; Sheena to Chesapeake Teddy produced Ch. Deer Run Ironhills Isidore; Sheena and Ch. Deer Run McMunger produced Ch. Iron Hills Adrian; and Sheena and Ezekiel produced Ch. Warleggen and Ch. Poldark, two very well-known Mastiffs. Tari and Ch. Deer Run Zachary (Wycliff ex Surrey) got Ch. Deer Run Ahab and Ch. Iron Hills Rocky Hills Thor (1985 Number 1 Mastiff); Tari bred to Ezekiel produced Ch. Iron Hills Khan Groppetti; Tari and Warleggen produced Dave, Ch. Iron Hills Warwagon (Top Mastiff 1989 and 1990, Top Group Mastiff 1990, BOB 1989 and 1990 Mastiff Specialties).

Dave has the distinction of being the all-time Top Producing Mastiff Stud Dog with 49 champions of record. With Scott's co-owned bitch Ch. Lionsire Indigo of Pax River (Ezekiel ex Christians Bristol Cream) Dave sired eight champions, including Ch. Iron Hills Paint Your Wagon (Clarence). Scott's wife Pam persuaded him to breed Clarence to their imported German bitch Kara Stonehage (Netherlands Ch. Royal Roy van DeSaal ex Stonehage Eva) which produced Ch. Iron Hills Regal Rose, Ch. Sweet Emmaline and Ch. Iron Hills Into The Night (Butler) who is the only brindle ever to win BIS and he has done it three times and he won BOB 1997 and 1998 Mastiff Specialties.

Dave has a long and impressive list of well-known offspring, Ch. Southports Iron Maiden (1992 Top Group Bitch, 1993 Top BOB Bitch) and Ch. Southports Prime Time (3 Awards of Merit and Twice Stud Dog Winner at Mastiff Specialties, Top Producer

Collar Winner, 1994 Number 4 Group Mastiff and Number 2 Mastiff); Ch. Acorn Hill Uther Pendragon and Ch. Acorn Hill Morganna Pendragon; and Ch. Avalons Tuscon Warrior (1995 Number 5 Mastiff, Awards of Merit Mastiff Specialty and WKC). Scott's co-owned Ch. Britestar Lionsire Addition (Ch. Lionsire Grizz ex Ch. Groppetti Brite Star) bred to Dave produced Ch. Iron Hills Orpheus and Sidney, Ch. Iron Hills Earned Interest (BOB 1994 Mastiff Specialty) who is co-owned by Kevin and Julia Kriebs with Pam. Orpheus sired Ch. Ridgewoods Otis (BOB 1996 Mastiff Specialty) who is the first Mastiff to win BIS on the West Coast). Ch. Iron Hills Bet The Farm (Dave ex Lionsire Nauti-Girl) was bred to Ch. Deer Run Semper Fi Thor, CD (Ch. Deer Run Tristan ex Great Day Emeline) to produce six champions including Ch. Fixin To Start (1995 Number 2 Group Mastiff, Number 2 BOB Bitch and Number 6 BOS Bitch). Scott owned Verdunes Tolkien Dreamer (Ch. Quellwater Apollo ex Viking Valeska of Verdune) who bred to Warleggen produced Ch. Phoebus Groppetti who was bred to Sillars Lady Abigale (Ch. Deer Run Jake Enchanted Acres ex Queen Elizabeth of E Ranch) to get Ch. Sillars KO Tyson. Pam handles all of the Iron Hill Mastiffs, Dave, Butler, Posie, etc., and she showed Tyson to 1991 and 1992 Number 1 Mastiff, as well as the All Time Top Winning Mastiff up to that time.

Fred and Shirley Carnett owned Diablos Lucy Brown (Ch. Meps Tristan ex Willowledge Suzi-Q) who was bred to Ch. Gulph Mills PJ's Vulcan Deity to get Champions P-J's Silent Thunder of SH, Ch. P-J's Athena, Ch. P-J's Yarborough Hills Tabitha and Ch. Deer Run P.J. Zanzibar. Lucy bred to Mulcher produced Ch. L Olympus Hades, Ch. L Olympus Diana (1985 Number 1 Mastiff, 1987 and 1988 BOS Mastiff Specialties), Ch. L Olympus King Bruzer Dulay, Ch. L Olympus Tristanna and Ch. L Olympus Zeus (1984 BOS Mastiff Specialty). Athena and Mulcher produced Ch. L Olympus Atlas and Athena and Ch. Stonebrook Southports Byron produced Champions L Olympus Thor and Pandora and Ch. Southports Black Orpheus. Diana and Berengaria's Gulph Mills Pal produced Ch. L Olympus Sampson who was bred to Pandora to get Ch. L Olympus Nike.

Bjorn and I owned Maggie, Willowledge Meredith (Ch. Griffiths T Geronimo ex Katrina) and Ch. Peersleigh Storm

Sherman (1984 Number 3 Mastiff) who were bred together to get Ch. Storm Landmark USA Tess, CD, Ch. Suffolk Thunder, Ch. Swedish Lejon, CD, Ch. English Legacy, Ch. Swiss Berry and Scotland Magic. Maggie and Lazy Hill Louie produced Ch. Storm Babe of Lazy Hill (1985 BOS Mastiff Specialty), Ch. Trooper, Ch. Saga and Ch. Moses. Maggie won a 1985 Top Producer Collar and she was 1985 and 1986 Top Brood Bitch Mastiff Specialties. Sherman and Baby produced Ch. Storm Bounty of Lazy Hill, Ch. Dixieland Delight (WB Westminster KC), Ch. Stor Gal (twice BOS Westminster KC), Can. Ch. Yarravilles Cromwell and Treasure. Magic and Ch. Old Schools Majestic Major (Ezekiel ex Ursa) produced Ch. Storms Queen Elizabeth and Ch. Northpoint Joey (BOB Mastiff Supported Bucks County KC). Peersleigh Storm Samantha and Hollesley Lord Ralegh got Ch. Storm Banner and Ch. Storm Rowena of Peersleigh, Ch. Peersleigh Sudden Storm and Can. Ch. Peersleigh Sergent Cocaine.

With Ginny Bregman we owned Chs. Damaria The Druid and The General. Breedings of the Damaria brothers and our females produced Ch. Admiral Nelson, Ch. Faith, Ch. Hammer, Ch. Petrie, Ch. Drudwenna, Ch. Druidanna, Ch. General Lee, Ch. Ta-Tanka and Ch. Timbers Maid. Maggie, Sherman, Babe or Sam stand behind Best in Show, Group Winners and Placers, Top Ranked Mastiffs, Awards of Merit and (5) BOS Westminster KC, Awards of Merit and (4) BOS and (2) BOB Mastiff Specialties, Veteran Class and Veteran Sweepstakes Mastiff Specialties, and Hall of Fame Top Producers. Storm Mastiffs has bred and owned 41 champions and Sherman and Trooper were the first Mastiffs ever to win BIS Brace and (2) Brace Mastiff Specialties.

Patty Warfield owned 1982 and 1983 Top Mastiff Bitch and WB 1981 Mastiff Specialty and BOS Mastiff Supported Bucks County KC, Ch. Deer Run Groppetti Fawn Loni (Wycliff ex Sophie), Ch. Deer Run Groppetti Inda (Caisson ex Anita), Ch. Deer Run Groppetti Nina (Ivan ex Vanity Fair), Ch. Deer Run Roderick (Winston II ex·Emily) and Deer Run Jenny (Jupiter ex Heather). Inda bred to Ivan produced Ch. Groppetti Electra and Ch. Joynt Venture. Inda and Roderick produced Ch. Groppetti Nigel. Joynt Venture to Roderick got Ch. Groppetti Leftholz Lucy Marie, Ch. Lemon Pudding and Ch. Orderv. Jenny and Daultons Sir Henry Tizard

(Ch. Bens Ali of Love Creek ex Arwyn of Kimberlane) produced Ch. Groppetti Lambay Top Brass and Ch. Beauregaard.

Jenny and Ch. Groppettis Wallon got Ch. Groppetti Thorr and Jenny to Roderick produced Groppettis Paty of RH. Loni and Tizard produced Ch. Groppetti Valentine and Ch. Wallon (sire to 1986 BOB Mastiff National). Loni to Roderick got Ch. Groppetti Pegasus and Arciniega Saba. Pegasus and Beauregaard produced Groppetti champions Brite Star and Sir Arthur (sire of BIS, and 1991 and 1992 BOB Mastiff Specialties). Valentine put to Roderick produced Ch. Groppetti Chrissie, Ch. Humongus Pearce, Easter and Chocolate Mousse. Easter bred to Roderick produced Groppetti Carmel and Mayple Syrup. Carmel bred to Walter The Fudgeman (Deer Run Julius Caesar ex Yogie's Vanilla Fudge) got No More Rocky Road. Maple Syrup and Ch. Deer Run Tussaint produced Ch. Groppetti Razin Kain Luther, No More One For The Road and Groppetti RWR Charlotte. Mousse and One For The Road got Ch. Party Crasher. Rocky Road and Mr Nice Guy (Ch. Rocky Hollow Seacliff ex Deer Run Margo) got Ch. No More Diamond In The Ruff. Patty owns Ch. Semper Fi Groppetti Gargoyle (Semper Fi Thor, CD ex Semper Fi Kerra, CD), top ranked and BOB and Group Placing WKC.

Stephen and Leah Napotnik owned Tamarack Zada of Greiner Hall (Donner ex Maggie of Woods) and Deer Run Unger of Greiner Hall (Ivan ex Tesil). Although an accidental breeding of Unger and Zada produced a litter, it was the planned breeding of Zada to Hollesley Lord Ralegh that launched them as serious breeders of note. Saxon and Zada produced Ch. Greiner Hall Chancellor, Ch. Seton, Ch. Sauter, Ch. Chadwick, Anya and Bronwen. Anya to Bulliff Yermak (Ch. Honeycroft Danny Boy ex Bulliff Aethelflaed) got Greiner Hall Medicine Lady and Tanya. Bronwen and Ch. Grangemoor Druid (Ch. Dare Devil of Hollesley ex Kisumu Una) produced Greiner Hall Gildas of Athelney. Bronwen and Yermak got Ch. Greiner Hall Cy of Pontefract. Zada bred to Falmore Hall Fidelio (Medicine Man ex Ch. Falmorehall Call Me Madam) produced Greiner Hall Isnor, who bred to Chadwick got Ch. Greiner Hall Gipsy and Ch. Jedadiah (1992, 1993, 1994 and 1995 Top Ten Mastiffs). Medicine Lady and Greiner Hall Zechariah produced Ch. Greiner Hall Winnifred. Medicine Lady and Jedadiah produced Ch. Greiner Hall Stowaways Dawn and Ch. Aramis. Tanya and Greiner Hall Falcon (Zechariah ex Raven of Noble Hall) got Ch. Greiner's Hall Giganti Conan. The Napotniks have determinedly stayed with English imported blood, making their line rather unique as there are only a handful of us concentrating on imported lines.

David and Mary Louise Owens owned Ch. Alexander of Acorn Hill, CD (Oak Ridge Apollo Dook ex Deer Run Sweetie Pie), Deer Run Alexis of Acorn Hill (Police ex Geldas Tandy), and Ch. Lionsire Indigo of Pax River (Ezekiel ex Christians Bristol Cream). Indigo bred to Warwagon produced eight champions and bred to Ch. Acorn Hill Uther Pendragon she produced two champions, making her the fifth All Time Top Producing Bitch. She is grandam to the first brindle BIS, many group placers, 1992 and 1994 Awards of Merit WKC, 1992 BOS Jr Sweepstakes Mastiff Specialty and 1993 BOW/BOB Mastiff Supported Bucks County Kennel Cub. Arrabelle of Acorn Hills, CD (Ivan ex Lucrich) bred to Warwagon produced nine champions and three obedience champions (one CDX), two Working Dogs, two Draft Dogs and many CGC and TDI. Arrabelle is dam 1992 Best Bred by Exhibitor Bitch and BOW Sr Puppy Sweepstakes; 1992 Collar Award for High Average Score Obedience, Dog; 1993 Collar Award for BOS Bitch; 1994 Collar Award for High Schuman Point Obedience, Dog; 1995 BOS Westminster KC; 1995 Mastiff Specialty High Scoring Champion of Record, Obedience; and has a son in the Hall of Fame. It is worthy of note to mention that between them, Arrabelle and Indigo, bred to Warwagon, produced a total of 17 champions which helped put Warwagon in the position of being the All Time Top Producing Mastiff Stud Dog. In 1990, Acorn Hill's Hoof Lake Echo, CDX (Hoof Lake Farm's Brock ex Hoof Lake Farm's Penny) won the Collar Award for High Average Obedience Score, Bitch.

Puppy Sweepstakes were added to the Mastiff Specialty menu in 1982, and the Puppy Futurity was added in 1993. Independent Mastiff Specialties have been held, with the exception of 1985, since 1983. In 1989 they added Obedience Trials. Entries have grown from seven in 1941 to 568 in 1997 and the 1997 Mastiff Club membership approaches 1,000 members.

John and Carolyn Hehir owned Ch. Deer Run Sir Michael (Ivan ex Vanity Fair) and Peanut, Ch. Pinewood Dandy Lion of Pern (Ch. Calisto Give'em Hell ex Ch. Oak Ridges Februa Lyla) who was bred to Sherman to get Ch. Pinewoods Southwest Breeze (twice BOS WKC) and winner of Veterans at the 1998 Mastiff Specialty. They owned Rhoda, Ch. Windy Hills Step Aside Girls (Ch. Bankhouse Been There Before ex Ch. Windy Hills Gertrude) who was bred to Ch. Damaria The General and a single puppy survived with a complication of vision loss in one eye due to an uterine infection in the dam. That puppy became Reebok, Ch. Pinewoods One Day At A Thyme and as the name implies, they fought for her life. Reebok repaid them a thousand times over. She and Breeze were bred several times to Ch. His Majesty's Lion of Judah (Ch. Deer Run River Bull ex Ch. Deer Run Glory to God, CD) and both bitches won Collar Awards for Top Producers and are in the Top Producers Hall of Fame. A single litter of Reebok produced nine champions! (I love this story about Reebok because it demonstrates to all breeders why you never give up on a sickly puppy.) Reebok is ranked as the second all-time top producing brood bitch with 13 champions.

Joe and Carla Sanchez's top-ranked show dog Ch. Stonebrook Southports Byron (Ch. Kisumu Xavier King of Iona ex Deer Run Samantha IV) was bred to Diablo's P-J Mehitabel (Ch. Diablo's Lorenzo Salvador ex Steingers Lady Aleidea) to get Ch. Southports Bianca. They owned Southports Red Rose (Random Quest ex Tamarack Rustic Lady) and Ch. Southports Black Orpheus (Byron ex P-J's Athena). Rose and Byron produced Ch. Southport Rif Raf of Blu Ridge, Ch. Bailey Quarters, Ch. Bit O'Rose, Ch. Comstock Velvet, Ch. Maine Dream and Ch. Richelieu the Red. Rose and Orpheus produced Ch. Southports Byron Two. Bianca to Orpheus got Ch. Southports Black Grimm and Ch. Jez of Blue Ridge (1989 Number 2 BOS Bitch). Bailey and Warwagon produced Pete, Ch. Southports Prime Time (3 Awards of Merit Mastiff Specialities, Collar Award and Hall of Fame) and Maddie, Ch. Iron Maiden (1992 Top Group Bitch, 1993 Top BOB Bitch). Byron and Ch. Sturlung's Viktoria (Sturlungs Vaskr ex Sturlungs Valkyrie) produced Ch. Southports Dream Warrior (1989 Number 5 Mastiff). Several years ago, Joe and Carla got Ch. Ridgewoods Otis (Ch. Iron Hills Orpheus ex Kayla Bradee) who was 1995 Number 3 Group

Mastiff, the first Mastiff to win BIS on the West Coast, and 1996 BOB Mastiff Specialty.

Tim and Vicki Hix owned 1987 Number 1 Mastiff Bitch Ch. Hixs Scarlett Alexis (Quellwater Winston ex Markays Pecan Sandie) who was bred to BIS/BISS Ch. Old Schools Primo Remo Major to produce Ch. Oaklane Rose Bay Isis, CD, Ch. Old School Stardust, Ch. Polaris Pocahontes, CD, WD and Ch. Sir Winston Knights. Pocahontes and Ch. Argus Hill Medallion Delbert produced Ch. Oaklane Polaris Intimidator.

David and Laura Hagey owned Gulph Mills Foxglove Caelin, CD (Mulcher ex Dawn) and 1987 Number 1 BOS Bitch, 1988 Number 1 Group and BOB Bitch, (3) Collar Award winner Can. Am. Ch. Gulph Mills Marjorie, CD (Mulcher ex Ch. Lady Camelot of Hale, CD) who was bred to Ch. L Olympus Sampson (Berengaria's Gulph Mills Pal ex Diana) to get Ch. Foxglove All Rights Reserved, Ch. Double Trouble, Ch. Hales We've A Dream, CD, Ch. Moose McGillycuddy and Ariel, Can. Am. Ch. Poetry in Motion (1991 Top 10 Bitches). Marjorie and Ch. Beowulf of Wheeler's Knoll, CD (Whitakers Duke of Royalty ex Whitakers Duchess of Deer Run) produced Ch. Foxglove Hale's New Contender, Ch. Foxglove and Wheelers Praetorian and Deny, Can. Am. Int. Ch. Foxglove Won't Be Denied (1992 and 1994 Top 10 Dogs). Ch. Gulph Mills Foxglove Savanah, CD (Mulcher ex Cagney) was 1990 High in Trial Mastiff Specialty and a Top 10 BOB Bitch in 1991. Savanah and Ch. Meza's Hulk Hogan (Ch. Deer Run Sinder ex Ima Whiner T-O-O-O) produced Ch. Foxglove Singular Sensation. Poetry and Ch. Meza's Hulk Hogan produced Ch. Foxglove Avenel One For All, CD, Ch. Quite AKA Motion and Hope's Just In Time, CD, (2) All Breed High in Trials and the first Mastiff to accomplish this, and 1994 High in Trial Mastiff Specialty, and a Collar Award winner. Sensation bred to Ch. Beowulf of Wheelers Knoll got Ivy, Ch. Foxglove Seize the Moment (1995 BOW/Award of Merit Mastiff Specialty and Grand Futurity Winner).

The Hageys owned Nachtmusik Avalon Lady Annwn, CD (Barclay Carlisle Owens ex Ch. Summer In Brady Montana) who was bred to Deny to get Foxglove Classic Denial who was bred to Ch. Eldorado Rebel W/Out a Pause, CD (Ch. Wrightous Wide Body Tanker, CD ex Ch. Legendary Fanny Flaunts It, CD) to produce Can. Am. Ch. Foxglove Classic Double Take, Ch. Tyrolian

Waltzing Matilda and Ch. Tyrolian Nicolai Za Mihova (1995 WD Mastiff Specialty).

Lance and Barbara House owned Ch. Groppetti Electra (Ivan ex Inda) and Ch. Groppetti Brite Star (Beauregaard ex Pegasus). Electra became dam to Ch. Brite Stars Cassandra (1987 Best Bred-By Exhibitor Mastiff Specialty and part of the winning Brace with Phoebe), Ch. Phoebe, Ch. Crystal (1988 Bred-By Bitch Mastiff Specialty), Ch. Olivia, Ch. Tiberius, Ch. Titas (1988 Best Bred-By Exhibitor Mastiff Specialty), Ch. Delmans Thunder and Ch. Opus No Thirty. Ch. Groppetti Brite Star became dam to Ch. Brite Star Zechariah, Ch. Mirror Image, Ch. Bearly Grizz, Ch. Lionsire Addition, Ch. Nightime, Ch. Sir Winston, Ch. Warlock (1990 BOS Sweepstakes Mastiff Specialty) and Ch. Gentrys Brite Star Panda. With this foundation, they went on to produce such Brite Star champions as Apache Tears, Apache Warrior, Command Performance (1994 Reserve Best Futurity Puppy Mastiff Specialty), Devils Desiree (1992 Best In Futurity Mastiff Specialty), Fallen Angel, Grey Wolf (BOW Mastiff Supported Bucks County KC), Legacy, Limited Edition, Luck Dragon, Mariah of Wannabe, Midnite Sun, Moses of Wannabe, Mucho Grande, Opposing Force, Princess Reba, Rex, Ritterling, RR Justa Dream, Scarlet Lady, Sheena, Sir Rockofeller, Stardust, Storm Trooper, Sweet Illusion, Tristan, Voo Doo Doll, Widow Maker and Wild Thing. The Houses currently show one of the Top Dogs, Ch. Brite StarDual Image, known as Brogan, who goes back in his pedigree to Delmans Thunder and Kerry and Warwagon and Brite Star.

Mike and Karen McBee owned Ch. McBees Golden Nugget (Lochners Mighty Zeus ex Lochners Majestic Medusa) who was bred to Ch. Groppetti Sir Arthur to get Ch. Stonehouse Big Bad Bud, Ch. Country Squire (1990 Number 9 BOB Dog and Number 2 Group Mastiff, 1991 Number 4 BOB Dog and Number 2 Group Mastiff, 1991 BOB Mastiff Specialty and 1991 BIS, Number 3 Group Mastiff), Ch. Sunshine Nellie and Ch. Brazen Lady. Lady and Ch. Hedgestones Big Man (Ezekiel ex Hedgestone Roxanna) got Ch. Stonehouse Country Grey Lord and Lady bred to Warwagon got Ch. Stonehouse Country Gentleman who was bred to Ch. Lambays Stand By Me (Godfather of Oxford ex Amaretto On The Rocks) produced Ch. Drycreek Takit To The Limit (a top winning Mastiff) and Ch. Stonehouse Country Accent (1995 Number 2 BOS Bitch) who was bred to Ch. Southports Prime Time to get Ch. Stonehouse Chantilly Lace and Ch. Drycreek Bad To The Bone. Lace bred to Ch. Pinehollows Caledonia Jackson produced Ch. Stonehouse Country Vagabond.

Rich and Eva Gomez owned Hannah, Ch. Deer Run Glory to God, CD, (Durango ex Sarah of Bristol) who was in the Top 10 BOS in 1988. She earned her Working Dog Title at eight years of age. Hannah and Ch. Deer Run River Bull (Jason ex Ragtime) produced Ch. His Majestys Lion of Judah (Collar Award Top Producer with 30 champions) and Ruby, Ch. His Majestys Crown of Glory (Top Ten BOS). Judah bred to Fantasys Shaula of Creekside got Ch. Creekside Nkotb Mighty Hogan (Awards of Merit Mastiff Specialty and WKC).

Howard and Catherine Angus owned Daisy, Ch. Niniane The Enchantress (Sir William of Deer Run ex Ch. Axtell Meyers Andromeda) who was bred to Warwagon to get Ch. Avalons Tucson Warrior (Awards of Merit Mastiff Specialty and Westminster KC and Top Winning for several years), Ch. Lord Cearbhallain, CD and Ch. Iron Hill Thunder Road. Daisy bred to Ch. Storm Hammer of Royal Oak produced Ch. Avalon's Airs and Graces (Katie), Ch. Poetic Justice and Lawsamercy Ms Scarlet. Scarlet bred to Storm Bruin produced Avalon's Tapestry of Hope. Katie and Storms Limited Edition got them Maggie, Avalons Hallmark Edition.

Bobby and Robin Burns owned Ch. Thorchelseaias Noel (Rocky Hill Thor ex High Spirits Chelsea) and Ch. Night Stalker Sarah Anne (Ch. Deer Run River Bull ex Tracy) who was bred to Ezekiel to produce Burns Hall champions Avis of Ironlion (1990 WB/Award of Merit Mastiff Specialty), Jamie Lou, Mavis, Pharoh, Zackery and Zekeial. Sarah Anne and Rapscallions Sir Winston (Ch. Uther Pendragon ex Renegades Rapscallion) got Ch. Burns Hall Nicole. Jamie Lou was bred to Ch. Lionsire Grizz to get Ch. Burns Hall Goliath, Ch. Polgara and Rhoads' Chisum. Nicole was bred to Zackery to produce Ch. Matts Joshua-Dogwood Knoll (1991 WD and 1993 BOB Mastiff Specialties and BOB Mastiff Supported Bucks County Show).

CHAPTER 6
TEMPERAMENT - THE NATURAL GUARDIAN

Edward Jesse in *Anecdotes of Dogs* (1858) quotes Sir Walter Scott:

> The Almighty, who gave the dog to be the companion of our pleasures and our toils, hath invested him with a nature noble and incapable of deceit. He forgets neither friend nor foe - remembers, and with accuracy, both benefit and injury. He hath a share of man's intelligence, but no share of man's falsehood. You may bribe a soldier to slay a man with his sword, or a witness to take life by false accusation, but you cannot make a dog tear his benefactor. He is the friend of man, save when man justly incurs his enmity.

The temperament of this King of Dogdom makes it an ideal house pet and family member. Many Mastiffs are born with guilt complexes and it takes but a single harsh word to crush them. For all their great size, they are gentle, big babies at home with the humans they love. Mastiffs crave approval and affection from their families. They are very sensitive creatures. A kind word or softly spoken bit of praise means all the world to a Mastiff. The breed has an inborn dignity, an intangible presence that impresses everyone with whom they come into contact. Because of their immense dimensions and laid-back demeanor they are sometimes mistakenly thought to be slow or lazy which is a completely false impression. If motivated, they can move swiftly and decisively.

They are extremely intelligent. They may not achieve their sought after goals by conventional means, but they are certainly intelligent enough to cajole, manipulate and maneuver us poor humans into doing whatever it is they want us to do! Mastiffs can be stubborn and relentless when they require something of us. Mastiffs often sense trouble before its onset. Some are so emotionally deep, even bordering on intense, that they have the unique ability to understand and share any setback or sorrow inflicted on their families. They feel everything that affects their humans' lives. They are instinctively courageous and fearless in the face of danger, chivalrous, docile and benevolent with children and most smaller animals. Mastiffs require peace and harmony in their homes. They are the most formidable, discriminating and reliable of protection dogs and, at the same time clean, quiet and well-behaved companions that will return, doubled, all the love given to them by their humans.

The Mastiff is an honest dog that will never leave one in doubt as to his true feelings in any situation. While we have never experienced a Mastiff biting, I have often said that if a Mastiff of mine were ever to bite, it would be because he mulled it over, considered whether or not he actually wanted to bite, and then made a conscious and calculated decision to bite. The transgression would not be spontaneous or casual, but planned and executed. I would also expect the dog to look a victim in the eye coming straight at him, rather than sneaking up behind his back. The Mastiff was never intended to be a social butterfly and, indeed, such behavior would be contrary to his historical nature. It is the heritage of Mastiffs to be cautious and suspicious of strangers—after all, for centuries they were bred exclusively for this purpose. Nevertheless, the breed has endeared itself to man because it is loyal to a fault, noble and, most importantly, very peaceable. They prefer to solve discord rather than sow it. There has always been a high degree of pride associated with belonging to a well-bred Mastiff.

The extended pedigree of a true Mastiff is certainly sufficient to humble a mere human. Bill Newman, AKC delegate for the

Encore, a daughter of Ch. Pinehollow Caledonia Jackson and Storm Philly of Swede Road, owned by Bob & Jane Gurka.

breed, wrote in 1979: "It is not easy to get a four legged furry animal, who is a superior being of higher intelligence, with better breeding than you. Once that is accepted, and you can use those guidelines for a relationship with a Mastiff, you shouldn't have any trouble."

I have listened to breeders talk about how the Mastiff has been domesticated from its former nature and position in history as war and guard dog. Unquestionably, the temperament of today's Mastiff is mellowed by comparison to the temperament of the ancient Mastiff. I wonder, however, if the temperament really underwent so great a change over the centuries, or if the greater change might not have taken place in humans. Our treatment of the Mastiff, our expectations of the breed, altered. Humans no longer tied them outside during the day, only letting them loose at night to guard. Mastiffs began to spend their days as companions and friends of man. Humans no longer allowed this inherently gentle creature

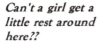

Can't a girl get a little rest around here??

to be used for cruel entertainment, such as baiting other animals. The Mastiff began to be highly regarded as a pet, and in that capacity he was socialized and allowed to be friendly with or benign to other animals. Humans no longer kept the Mastiff lean and mean to fill the role of war dog, instead he was well fed, groomed and being permitted to follow his own instincts and perform his natural chore as family guardian.

We fully understand the Mastiff now, and we treasure his noble spirit, ingrained dignity and gentle nature which was probably always present but, for the most part, unheralded or overlooked. One element of the Mastiff disposition that has remained unchanged throughout the ages is that he was always loving and good natured towards family members and always uncompromising in the presence of a threat to those he loves and protects.

One of the most famous and finest descriptions ever written about the Mastiff temperament was in *Cynographia Britannica* (1800) by Sydenham Edwards:

> What the Lion is to the Cat the Mastiff is to the Dog, the noblest of the family; he stands alone, and all others sink before him. His courage does not exceed his temper and generosity, and in attachment he equals the kindest of his race. His docility is perfect; the teazing of the smaller kinds will hardly provoke him to resent, and I have seen him down with his paw the Terrier or cur that has bit him, without offering further injury. In a family he will permit the children to play with him, and suffer all their little pranks without offence. The blind ferocity of the Bull Dog will often wound the hand of the master who assists him to combat, but the Mastiff distinguishes perfectly, enters the field with temper, and engages in the attack as if confident of success: if he overpowers, or is beaten, his master may take him immediately in his arms and fear nothing. This ancient and faithful domestic, the pride of our island, uniting the useful, the brave and the docile, though sought by foreign nations and perpetuated on the continent, is nearly extinct where he probably was an aborigine, or is bastardized by numberless crosses, everyone of which degenerate from the invaluable character of the parent,

who was deemed worthy to enter the Roman amphitheatre, and, in the presence of the masters of the world, encounter the pard, and assail even the lord of the savage tribes, whose courage was sublimed by torrid suns, and found none gallant enough to oppose him on the deserts of Zaara or the plains of Numidia.

When a Mastiff is permitted to be part of the family unit, he will put his own life on the line if that is what is required to protect his family. He always conducts himself with his own innate dignity. Because our attitudes towards the breed changed, parting company with what our ancient ancestors needed from them, we are recognizing and receiving a far gentler and kinder temperament in return.

Mastiffs need only to be given respect and kindness, nourishing food, fresh water, appropriate shelter from the cold and heat, veterinary care, and abundant affection together with consistent and sensible instruction. In return, they reward us with their undivided attention, unconditional loyalty, unbounded love, continuous protection and wonderful companionship. All this, and all we have to do is: Make them part of our family; grant them the right to lay at our feet and adore us; let them occasionally rest their impressive heads on our knees while we offer them kind words or affectionate pats; and invite them to sleep at our bedside, so we may rest secure, while they guard us through the night. So little to ask of us, for so much in return from them.

One cannot expect an immature Mastiff to have well-honed guarding or protecting instincts. Sometime around the age of two years, the Mastiff simply wakes up one morning, realizes why he was born, and, lo and behold, he becomes a "guardian." It is as though overnight someone or something whispered in his ear and instilled him with a mission in life. Upon awakening he is a totally different animal, more mature, more serious, deeper somehow, and he has total confidence in his abilities to defend and protect. The Mastiff needs absolutely no training for this mission, it comes to him naturally with age and is instinctual in the breed.

The Mastiff is no thief. With never less than four to five roaming freely in our home, none has ever trespassed by taking food off a counter or from the dining table. To do so would be terribly

*Mastiffs at play.
Both owned by the
author.*

out of character. There is always an open bag of dog food somewhere in our home and never has a bag been invaded. Many times, I have loaded our van with full bags of groceries, including fresh meat, then left those groceries in the care of the Mastiffs while I stopped here and there to perform other chores. Only once did a Mastiff get into the meat, and he was but a seven-month-old puppy (we knew who the culprit was because later that day he returned the meat wrappings to us).

Unfortunately, an occasional streak of shyness crops up in the breed. When breeding Mastiffs, one cannot always predict which litters will produce one of these truly sad and unfortunate animals. Any shy or cowardly dog is dangerous because of unpredictability. A shy Mastiff, because of its great size, can certainly be a liability and, therefore, should never be bred from and must always be carefully watched. There are two different types of shyness—hereditary and environmental. I know of nothing that can be done to improve or cure the first type of shyness. A hereditarily shy Mastiff will simply break your heart. He will belly down on the ground in fear, get a wild or frantic look in the eyes, urinate uncontrollably and possibly growl or snap at strangers. If this type is cornered, he is capable of biting just from fear. I believe this irregularity of temperament, the hereditary shyness, has lurked in the breed for centuries. While it is uncommon, still it was mentioned by Hugh Dalziel in 1889, which indicates it did not make its first appearance in modern times.

An environmentally shy Mastiff, on the other hand, has hope. This type of shyness is the result of not being taken to different places, exposed to noises, strangers and new situations. With persistence and loving patience on the part of the owner, this shyness can be greatly reduced or even overcome altogether.

Dave Hussey is shown here playing with Daisy (Ch. Blu Ridge Goldleaf of Blk Pt.). Note how athletic and powerful this bitch is with her weight completely off the ground.

There is an interesting phenomenon associated with acquiring a first Mastiff. Over the last 17 years, I have asked many people what made them get into Mastiffs? Why did they buy that first one? For me and my family, it was purely and simply for security reasons. Our home had been burglarized and we wanted a dog that would look imposing enough, without being untrustworthy or aggressive, to deter further break ins. Many I talked to acquired their first Mastiffs for similar reasons. Some people told me of a beloved pet of a different breed, such as a Great Dane, Rottweiler or Bullmastiff, that they had lost to old age or illness and how they wanted another giant dog, but not the same breed because they did not wish to be reminded of what they had lost. Another response was that some people wanted a real dog, one that they could hug. The best answer came from Jackie Guy who hesitated for a moment, then said, "Elephants don't bark."

Probably we all choose our first Mastiff partially because we want a giant dog. The problem with this is it does not stop there, the next thing that happens is we search for a bigger Mastiff and we keep searching for that elusive larger Mastiff. Together with size, another favorite reason for getting a Mastiff is temperament. The breed is well known for its wonderful disposition and a dog as large as a Mastiff must have a pleasant disposition.

When a Mastiff enters the family environment, he becomes an integral part of the family. The breed needs people the way trees need rain and sunshine. The Mastiff does not become owned by his master so much as the master becomes owned by the Mastiff. It is as though the Mastiff has some sort of magical element to its nature

Ch. Storm Hammer of Royal Oak. Sire: Storm Gruffudd of Royal Oak. Dam: Storm Gwyneira of Royal Oak. Breeder/Owner: dee dee Andersson & Carol Mathews.

and we are fascinated and mesmerized by that magic. An odd thing I have noticed over the years is one rarely meets a former owner of Mastiffs. Once a good Mastiff of true temperament is acquired, nothing else will do and eventually the first Mastiff is replaced with another Mastiff. Another aspect of the temperament is that some of them actually possess a sense of humor of sorts. I adore this element of their character. They can be quite funny and entertaining. This probably sounds ridiculous to someone who has not known a dog like this, but it really is true. A Mastiff will pick at and nag you, tease you, demand your attention, occasionally bat at your ankles with his paws while you are walking, use his head to butt you, bring his head up under your armpit and try to lift you and the moment you call him on his behavior or raise a protest, he will scrunch up his eyes and literally smile at you, showing great satisfaction to have gotten your attention with his antics. If you scold him, or if he feels you have been unreasonable with him he is quick to pout.

One of our first Mastiffs was an accomplished pouter. He would sometimes lay between the refrigerator and wall with only his huge back end facing towards the room and all our efforts to cajole him or apologize would be ignored. He would forgive us our trespass in his own time and not a moment sooner. This same Mastiff could also be quite vindictive at times. He would become so upset if we took his least favorite house mate to shows while leaving him at home, he would urinate all over that poor fellow's sleeping quarters before we returned. Without a doubt, this behavior was deliberate because at all other times he was a model of cleanliness in our home. Being avid readers, our bedroom has books covering all surfaces. This dog was confined temporarily by baby gates in the bedroom while we had dinner guests. Of all the books to which he had access and could have demolished, he found my most precious and valued *Eastern Star Bible*, given to me by my late grandmother, and he devoured most of it. How could he know the destruction of that one tiny book would be so painful to me? He just knew.

Mastiffs are extremely clever in the home, adept at turning around in tight circles and backing up while at the same time avoiding knocking over furniture or bumping things off tables. They are not the worst of droolers, as breeds go, but I have never yet met a Mastiff that did not have a fetish for coming and placing his head in my lap after drinking water and, usually, it seems as though his mouth was still filled with water. Either this is a very peculiar trait hereditary in the breed, or they are smart enough to use our laps as their towels. Despite their great dignity and noble demeanor, they are nevertheless very playful, in and out of the house. All Mastiffs are expert at the trick of standing on three legs while pawing affectionately with the fourth—they begin doing this as early as three to four weeks of age.

The breed will often use its teeth to deliver love nips in a playful manner to its adored humans, nibbling at and occasionally pinching the tiniest bit of skin. They really do not understand it sometimes hurts us and they may need to be taught to respond to a voice command such as "no teeth." Mastiffs are superb at the art of body blocking. When they desire your attention they will swing their hindquarters or the sides of their bodies directly into your path. A Mastiff that perceives danger to its human, if the animal is of true breed temperament, will quickly take control of the situation by putting himself between his human and the threat.

I worked our very first Mastiff through advanced obedience twice just to get control of her spirited temperament and, even so, I was never able to keep her on a sit-stay command when a stranger approached us. She would obey at all other times, but insisted on getting up and positioning herself in front of me when a stranger came towards us. I admit I was probably wrong to give in and let her have her way, but I remember being very impressed with her, thinking it was instinctive for her to behave that way. And, I always felt somewhat guilty when I tried to train her to do something contrary to her nature. Having since grown up in my knowledge of the breed, I now understand the value of obedience and appreciate that in most cases, like mine, it is we owners most in need of obedience lessons.

In 1858, Edward Jesse wrote:

> The Mastiff, indeed, usually shows a remarkable and peculiar warmth in his attachments; and, on the other hand, he will evince his dislike in the strongest manner. It has been observed of him, that if he is once severely corrected or insulted, it is almost impossible to eradicate the feeling from his memory, and it is no less difficult to attain a reconciliation with him. He seems conscious of his own strength, power, and authority, and will seldom condescend to lower his dignity by servile fawning; while he appears to consider his services as only befitting a trust of the highest importance. He is naturally possessed of strong instinctive sensibility, speedily obtains a knowledge of all the duties required of him, and discharges them with the most punctual assiduity. His vigilance is very striking. He makes regular rounds of the premises committed to his care, examines every part of them, and sees that everything is in a state of perfect security. During the night he will give a signal of his presence by repeated

barkings, which are increased upon the least cause of alarm. Unlike the bulldog, the Mastiff always warns before he attacks. His voice is deep and powerful in tone.

Protecting the beloved owner is the truest instinct the Mastiff possesses. We had to warn overnight guests at our home about an extraordinary trait of Sherman's in order to avoid their being awakened and alarmed. He would make the rounds of the house every night while we were sleeping. He followed a pattern of slowly going from room to room, occasionally pausing to listen, until he had covered the entire house. He had the strangest habit of standing flush to the face while you were asleep and it gave the impression he was studying your breathing. Once satisfied everything was okay he would move on to the next room and repeat the procedure with the next sleeping occupant. If could be very disconcerting feeling his hot breath on your face if you were not warned in advance and prepared.

Speaking of night habits, it would be terribly remiss of me not to advise prospective owners that Mastiffs snore. Loudly. A snoring Mastiff can cause the floor upon which he is sleeping to vibrate. An inconvenient habit that does not, I might add, prevent the Mastiff from instantly recognizing a noise in the night that is unfamiliar. In the blink of an eye, a Mastiff that is deeply asleep can bound into action to investigate and sound an alarm. Mastiffs can give every appearance of being lazy and useless, which is very deceiving because they are tuned in to everything going on around them at all times. I often think they are just saving themselves for the big missions and consequently do not bother to react to unimportant day-to-day disturbances. So, dear reader, do not let snoring put you off for it is a small price to pay for the privilege of belonging to a Gentle Giant.

Mastiffs need a lot of socialization, as already mentioned, for up to two years since they continue to grow and mature longer than most other breeds. Mastiffs can never be too friendly. They need to be exposed to as many and varied situations as possible while they are still developing mentally. Being friendly and outgoing in no way diminishes the natural guarding instinct in the breed. I have always believed that being properly socialized improves their ability to distinguish between a non-threat and a real threat. For example, if a Mastiff that is not well socialized suddenly sees a child run towards him, the child might well be perceived as a threat. A well-socialized animal, on the other hand, will know the child presents no real threat and stands his ground, wagging his tail and waiting for hugs.

We sold a Mastiff to an elderly couple who wanted a big dog because the gentleman had been robbed in broad daylight outside of a downtown department store. The man complained to us a number of times that his Mastiff was too friendly. He did not believe his dog would protect him. As the dog passed his first birthday, the man became very persistent in his efforts to gain our consent to guard train this dog. Our contract prohibited such training and we remained steadfast, telling the gentleman we would reconsider his request only after the dog reached his second birthday. When the dog was 19 months old, he accompanied the couple on vacation. They left him in their motel room when they went to breakfast. Upon returning to their room they discovered a terrified maid with an arm load of towels standing rigid with her back to the wall. She explained to the owners that each time she tried to step away from the wall the dog would stand in front of her, with hackles raised, his lip curled and he would growl. As soon as she stepped back to the wall and stood still, the dog sat down and wagged at her. That poor maid had been hugging the wall for more than 30 minutes by the time the owners returned. We were never again asked by the owners to approve guard training.

Sometimes, for no apparent reason, an even-tempered, well-socialized and totally trustworthy Mastiff will take an immediate dislike to a human. It would be well in these circumstances for the owners to remind themselves that this breed was bred for centuries as protection and guard dogs and, on occasion, they completely revert to type. That is, they will perceive something they do not like or trust about a certain person. When this occurs, generally the owner can never reconcile the Mastiff to that particular human.

One discriminating bitch of ours was remarkably perceptive in this regard and on those few occasions when she indicated she wanted nothing to do with someone, sooner or later we came to feel the same way about the person. The important thing for the owner is, whether or not you agree with your Mastiff, accept the dog's feelings and do not force the issue for you may regret it later. The Mastiff will display distinct body language to the owner such as backing away, barking or growling, and the dog's body may stiffen, hackles may rise in an effort to appear more formidable, the tail may be carried outward and curved upwards in an arc and the tip of the tail may twitch, like a cat, which should not be confused with friendly wagging. The head, instead of being carried high and proud, may be lowered and the dog will roll his eyes the slightest bit or seem to be looking out of the sides of his eyes. Even if you have never seen this type of body language from the dog before, you will not mistake it for anything but what it is.

In 1928, John Lynn Leonard, D.V.M. wrote:

> As a watchdog he is not to be ignored by any intruder and is always to be trusted in this capacity by his master. Another thing in favor of the Mastiff is that he will never, of his own accord, get his master into trouble. He strictly minds his own affairs, in relation both to people and to other dogs. Whenever he goes into action one may be certain that the cause of his doing so lies with his opponent. One may be quite certain, though, that the quarrel will end to his advantage. He never attacks suddenly with a surprise motive, but will always give full and unmistakable warning. Thus, any person or animal meeting harm from him can blame no one but himself.

I have heard it said, and believe it to be true, that the Mastiff is the only breed or non-breed of dog known to man that will only attack after all warning threats have failed. My own opinion is that anyone foolish enough to keep approaching a growling Mastiff probably deserves what he will get. The breed is not frivolous and if a Mastiff is in guard mode it would behoove anyone to take him very seriously because he assuredly has tending to business on his mind.

When our son was growing up we never had less than three Mastiffs in residence. As a toddler, our son would use our first bitch's tail to pull himself to his feet or he would keep a hand on her for balance as he toddled about. When he became of an age to sit in a bathtub of shallow water and play with his boats and ducks, we had a few scares. The door was always left open so we could listen to him playing and singing. But, several times it happened that our son screamed and we took off running only to arrive and find that Sherman was sitting in the tub with him, taking up much of the playing area. The same thing happened in the sandbox and, boy, would our son get angry when the dogs would not move out of his way! As all children will, our son would occasionally be involved in verbal disagreements and little physical altercations with his friends. The dogs would circle until our son was isolated from the other children, never at any time offering the slightest aggression to any of the

Sherman thinking of getting in the tub.

children. It seemed their goal was simply to protect the child they loved, but never to offer harm to the others. It might be well to mention the Mastiff tail if you have toddlers. When the tail swings at the child's eye level, it really causes a mighty blow and hurts. We taught our son to approach with his arm extended outward to block that wagging tail and avoid being hit in his face.

I once read that all children have nightmares or nightfrights and perhaps it's true, but, to the best of our knowledge, our son did not. Each night we would tuck him into bed the usual way and every morning we found him curled up beside Sherman at the end of the bed. We knew Sherman thought he was outsmarting us by waiting for us to retire before joining our son. Little did he know we expected and approved of him doing exactly what he was doing. Our son would tell us, with great confidence, that Sherman would not allow any monsters in his room. I do not mean, with this story, to suggest that I think Mastiffs sleeping on beds is a good thing. It is up to each individual owner which rules are set and to be adhered to by the Mastiff. I shall advise, however, that if you do not wish to have a mature Mastiff on the bed, it would be wise to prohibit the puppy from establishing the pattern. It is far easier to correct the puppy than the adult. Mastiffs are unquestionably resourceful and deceptively alert and athletic, especially if you consider their cumbersome size. They are capable of being crafty at times and quite stubborn or sly if it serves them. They have the memory of an elephant and are known to carry a grudge if crossed.

Hobart Titus told this story of a Mastiff's grudge: The dog's owner was superintendent of a construction crew and a worker threw a rock that hit the Mastiff. The dog ignored the workers but kept eyeing the stone and eventually sniffed it over carefully, then picked out the man who threw the stone and escorted him off the site. The owner was unable to reconcile the dog so that the skilled worker could return to his job.

The Mastiff memory is legendary. My husband's sister-in-law stood behind and slightly bent over our son while teaching him a karate move. I stood in the doorway watching. A Mastiff of ours interpreted the circumstances as threatening to our son. By the time I realized what was happening, the dog was preparing to launch himself into the air. He made no sound and showed no teeth, and it seemed to me that all his weight and power were centered in his chest as he started forward. It looked as though he was going to knock the poor lady through our kitchen wall. We keep no collars on the dogs at home, so I threw my arms around the dog's neck, interlocking my fingers for a firmer hold, and screamed for my husband. The dog was brought under control, calmed and the situation was diffused, however, the lady stayed with us another two days which were most uncomfortable. We were completely unable to reconcile the dog with her. He was never outwardly unkind to her, but he never stopped watching her, remaining ever ready to go into action. Even asleep, if she got up to move around the house, he would jerk his head up and monitor her every move. Nor, when she visited us two years later had he forgotten or forgiven her.

A story recently told to me by one of my associates demonstrates that "van jacking" with a Mastiff on board is not a good idea. The owner explained what happened to her while en route to a dog show. She pulled her van into a country filling station located away from the main highways. She filled her gasoline tank, situated herself back into the driver's seat and was preparing to drive away. A group of nefarious looking fellows had been hanging around the station, but she had paid no special attention to them as they were some distance away from the gasoline tanks. As she turned the key in the ignition and the van started up, she was startled to hear her side doors being opened. Even before she could react, her two-year-old Mastiff bitch, with a mighty roar and equally great lunge, dived into place positioning herself between the intruder and the owner. The owner had to get out of the van and go around in order to close the door, by which time the intruder was nearly out of sight he had moved so quickly away from the scene of the would-be crime. Typically, the Mastiff never, at any time, tried to leave the vehicle. She received much praise for a job well done.

Many Mastiff breeders and exhibitors recall an incident at the 1986 National Specialty Show. As show chairman, I had a preferential motel room at the corner overlooking the show grounds. While my husband and I attended the club's annual banquet, held off site from the show headquarters, I was paged to the telephone and informed by the motel manager we had better return at once to the room because one of our Mastiffs had broken two windows. We panicked, knowing immediately it was Sherman (the others in the

Ch. Acorn Hills Ethan, CD (owned by John Kearney, DVM and Mary-Louise Owens) shows how to cool off in hot summer weather.

room were too wise to risk injury), and we imagined him hung up in a glass window. If this were the case, we knew he would only allow me to touch him. We raced back to the motel to find an abundance of glass needing to be cleaned up, but Sherman was fine except for being in a high state of excitement.

Afterwards, we took Sherman along with us when we joined breeders socializing at the bar. Three competitors told us what had occurred in our absence. They had gone to outside our room to get a "look" at Sherman. One man told me Sherman watched him and then deliberately swung the side of his skull into the window. The man found a large garbage barrel he attempted to roll in place in front of the broken window, but the closer he came the more agitated Sherman got and before the barrel could be put in place, Sherman swung his head again and broke the second window. Sherman never attempted to leave the room through the windows. His escapades were very entertaining to exhibitors when, the next day at the Specialty, electrical cords for the show site were conveniently run through the broken windows. The judge of the show, by the way, went in and out of our room all day, having been given a key, and this was perfectly acceptable to Sherman after they were introduced to each other.

The breed is not likely to roam, being inherently territorial, however, a good-sized fenced yard is still essential if for no other reason than to keep neighboring animals out of the Mastiff's domain. Truthfully, a fence would be but a minor inconvenience to a Mastiff that is determined to get out. Thank goodness they develop tremendous respect when we establish boundaries, putting up fences outside or baby gates inside. There is an exception to every rule. One breeder we know installed electric fencing for her dog. She told me that one of her bitches completely accepts that she is going to get an electric jolt each time she goes outside of her yard. Apparently, this bitch never wanders away from her home, but she does ignore the zap to take care of whatever it is she finds interesting on the other side of the fence (which was, twice, a skunk!).

When we fenced our property, we fenced in part of a running mountain stream for the dogs' pleasure. A bitch of ours demonstrated how smart and non-confrontational she is on several occasions. When she is nearing her season and the stud dogs begin to pester her, to get away from them she will submerge herself in the water and go under the fence, then come around to the front gate and wait for us to discover she has gone missing. Neighbors have stopped by and rung up on the intercom from the gate to ask if we know one of our dogs is down there waiting to come back onto the property.

We had another great story told to us recently by a Mastiff owner. The lady listed all of the traditional characteristics of the breed that had surfaced in her dog. Then she said she was having trouble with her neighbors because of the dog. Cringing, I waited to hear something awful. It seems the neighborhood children open the gate to the fenced yard and invite the Mastiff to come out and play ball with them. Neighbors have begun telephoning the owners to ask them to please call the dog in so the children will be willing to come home for dinner!

A gentleman once told me he owned a Mastiff that would not guard him. The Mastiff lived in his back yard and was not allowed in the house. Why should the Mastiff guard him? The dog hardly knew him. In 1891, William Wade explained it perfectly: "To anyone who wishes to rear a true Mastiff, in all his perfection of utility, let me say: Begin by making a friend of your dog; let him accompany you on your walks abroad; let him come into your house and lie before your fire, and in every way connect himself with you and your welfare. If you shut him out of your house, how in the name of common sense is he to know that he has any part or interest in it? You might as well expect watching from one of a litter of black Essex pigs. Don't attempt to 'conquer' him, 'break him in,' or any of the brutalities common to the vulgar dogbreaker; a Mastiff that can be 'conquered' is not the animal you could trust were you engaged in a battle to the death with a vicious burglar or tramp; nor would such an animal be a Bayard in the protection of your wife and children in a lonely farmhouse, with you far away. Grave faults, such as killing chickens, etc., must be eradicated, but don't go at it with a club. Remember how you would treat your child in such a case, and try to follow the same lines with your dog, of course allowing for the difference in mental capacity. First love your dog, next make him love you; you will never regret having gained his love and confidence, and the day may come when you will be repaid a hundred fold."

The Clinton's Ch. His Majesty's Pinewood Samson clearly knows how to work for his dinner! Samson is also one of the top ranked Mastiffs for the last couple of years—and, yes, he is a Sherman grandson!

Many people ask which has the better temperament, dog or bitch. Both are wonderful. They are equally clean in the house and equally loving and intelligent. Males usually are a good bit larger than bitches, but any animal more than 150 pounds must be considered large, so a few pounds more or less should not make any difference. Males tend to have the more impressive heads. I have had prospective puppy buyers point to my heaviest-headed male and tell me they want a bitch with a head exactly like that! Generally, the bitch's head is a slightly more feminine version of the dog. Which sex is better really depends on personal preference. Bitches most often enter into their first heat around 9 to 12 months of age and have seasons approximately every six to seven months thereafter. There is not a single product, to my knowledge, that can be purchased to disguise the smell of a Mastiff in season, so if you live in a populated neighborhood with dogs roaming free, owning an unspayed bitch can be inconvenient.

William Shakespeare wrote "...when screech owls fly and bandogs howl," and I feel it is incumbent on me to tell the reader about a Mastiff's thunderous bark and melodious howl. A Mastiff has a deep, serious and commanding voice. In 1985, I visited a kennel that had among their Mastiffs a huge, red-eyed, white, long-haired wolf—a very evil-looking creature. I recall being told the wolf taught the Mastiffs to howl, which they regularly did each night. Eleven years later, I can tell the reader no wolf is required to teach a Mastiff to howl. Ours howl at least once every single night and they enjoy it mightily. They have different types of howls. For example, when the bitches are in season the stud dogs commiserate with each other and both sexes will howl long and low, sounding very mournful and sad. Otherwise, the nightly howl is done at high pitch—they are obviously trying to outdo one another in volume and in the length they can hold the sound. It is a joyful sound that brings warmth and laughter to the listener.

I also remember, as no doubt many others will upon being reminded, that at the 1982 Mastiff National Specialty Show, held at Trenton Kennel Club in New Jersey, all the champions were in the show ring and being examined by the judge when one veteran champion threw his magnificent head upwards and began to sing. Within seconds every Mastiff in that ring was howling. All those gorgeous heads were reaching for the sky. What a wondrous sight and sound they presented. The entire show, all breeds, judges, handlers and spectators standing around various rings, stopped what they were doing for the duration of the Mastiff sing. It was that impressive. Every year at the Nationals I hope for a repeat performance, but it has never happened again. I can only say I feel so privileged to have been in attendance and witness to the one time.

So much has been written about breed temperament it becomes challenging to portray them without becoming repetitive. That they are noble, gentle, tolerant, generous, loyal, loving and protective are known facts. What perhaps is not so well known is that by their very nature some are so devoutly dedicated and completely loyal to their owners, oftentimes to the exclusion of all people outside their family, that they have no affection left over for anyone else. This trait is worthy of our admiration yet at the same time it can create a hardship especially if a mature Mastiff must switch families. There have been instances when Mastiffs, forced by circumstances to change homes, suffered so much trauma they literally grieved themselves to death, refused to eat and gave up all interest in living. Others have been known to develop very difficult temperaments, actually becoming untrustworthy, because they were not able to transfer their trust or loyalty, nor could they bring themselves to receive affection or direction from someone new. Because the breed does not transfer well, it is even more important for them to be placed in proper homes as puppies with people willing to make a commitment for the lifetime of the dog.

When a change in families becomes necessary, the majority will make it through the transition provided new owners devote the time and energy it takes to earn their trust.

As to the cleverness of the breed, a youngster of ours lost his rawhide bone on so many occasions to a house mate bitch's cunning that as he matured he looked for ways to outmaneuver her. He would sleep with his bone safely tucked under his chin. When thirsty, he dropped the bone in the water bowl, drank his fill, then fished it back out, never once leaving it unattended. Is the Mastiff intelligent? A precise answer cannot be given. Perhaps the best answer would be to say they are selectively smart. If circumstances demand it, they can demonstrate intelligence quickly. The bitch mentioned above never came up against a baby gate she could not eventually open with her teeth, and that young male, before he matured, chewed down the middle of them. At one time, we had a garage full of baby gate halves. We had another Mastiff that refused to sit on command, but he could spell his handler's name, as well as the words cookie, bone, apple and outside. Asked if he would like to make babies, he would go from window to window looking for the arrival of a bitch requiring his attention.

Mastiffs need obedience instructions and it is a good idea to begin the lessons while the Mastiff is young. It is not a pretty sight to see a Mastiff walking its human or, worse, dragging the poor soul behind at a gallop. Seek a class in which the instructor has a gentle hand and soft method of teaching and making corrections to the dog behavior. Strong-arm tactics are simply not needed in this breed and the Mastiff temperament does not fare well if yelled at, jerked about or slapped. It does not take much to break the sensitive Mastiff spirit. There is absolutely no justification for hitting a Mastiff and the use of a rolled up newspaper is archaic. You will want your Mastiff to associate your hands with love, not fear. One of our Mastiffs would duck when we attempted to pat his head. I feared someone would think he had been beaten to behave this way. I began swinging my hand high and coming down.fast to the top of his head, stopping at the last minute without making contact. He got so used to this game he lost his fear. He would get excited and playful if it was done and he wasn't patted.

A firm voice command is usually all that is required to curtail undesirable behavior. Unprovoked aggression is the only behavior for which there should be no compromise on the part of the owner. It should be dealt with at once. A quick snap and release of a choke collar (not a pinch collar) works well. When our dogs wrestle and rough house inside the home, a bang on a counter top or wall gets their attention and suspends the activity. Mutual respect and communication need to be established before the animal attains full maturity and strength. Nearly every Mastiff born tries sooner or later to take command and run the home. They are, after all, a state of the art security system and they take their responsibility very seriously. It is imperative the human establish supremacy over the Mastiff without stomping on the gentle temperament and without diminishing the Mastiff's important role. Frankly, it would distress me if one of my grand and noble Mastiffs submitted to me. I do not want this from them. I prefer to have them respect me as their natural and accepted leader.

As youngsters they really do not comprehend their size or ability, hence they will always try to become lap dogs. When they mature, they become more aware of their power and capabilities so their behavior mellows accordingly and they are more laid back. Most of them are sedate and actually show great restraint in the company of small children without being trained for this purpose.

Any bored animal can become destructive. The more intelligent the animal, the more creative he may become in an effort to entertain himself and overcome boredom. A Mastiff that is bored can do a tremendous amount of destruction in a relatively short period of time. Years ago, a bitch we bred and sold literally ate a couch in a day while her owners were at work. After being introduced to obedience, they regularly scheduled training sessions that were fun for this bitch and she turned into a model house pet and citizen. Her owners acquired a large orange barrel, like the ones seen in winter country along the roadside filled with sand for use on snow. The barrel would be laid on its side and this bitch would put her front feet on it and push it around her property. Not only did the activity increase her athletic ability and muscle, it also exercised her mental need to be active. Such a "toy" would not be the ideal thing for a smaller breed, but it was wonderful for the Mastiff. That bitch would wander around her yard with a huge log in her mouth, bringing it with great pride to show off. Mastiffs find unique toys.

Mastiffs are not for everyone, they are expensive to purchase, raise and maintain. Due to their greater size when they need medication, they may need more and consequently incur higher costs. During the first two years of life, they may have occasional unexplained lameness, or lumps and bumps that necessitate examination to prevent overlooking something serious. This rapidly growing giant breed is prone to growth diseases and when one looks at the huge weight gains it is no wonder. To put things into perspective, we had a puppy born at eight ounces and at a year of age he weighed 175 pounds. Imagine a human baby, if you will, and if it would live at a scant eight ounces, reaching such a heavy weight in one year! Even if one takes into consideration the seven to nine years of a dog's life equaling one year of a human life, the difference in growth rate is still overwhelming.

The Mastiff requires a lot of devotion and maintenance, and if you are thinking of buying your first Mastiff, it would be wise to anticipate the costs involved to nurture him properly. Be cautioned that anyone considering buying a Mastiff with a goal of making big money from breeding litters has either been terribly mislead or has delusions of grandeur. The majority of breeders cannot sell puppies at a price elevated enough to reimburse their out-of-pocket expenses plus the time and effort expended in the breeding, whelping and raising of a litter.

If you decide you want a Mastiff, and prefer a neutered or spayed pet, please consider adoption of a rescue dog from the Mastiff Club of America. The club involves itself in relocating wonderful purebred Mastiffs who were displaced due to a variety of reasons. The dogs are carefully evaluated by knowledgeable and experienced breeders who search for appropriate homes in which new owners are environmentally and temperamentally matched with the dogs. These rescue Mastiffs are very special and bringing one into your life can be very rewarding. Just as the breed is not for everyone, nor should every Mastiff be bred. If you have come to love the breed, then love it enough to avoid harming it.

If you have decided you want to be a breeder, do the very best breeding you can, breed to make a better Mastiff and improve the breed. The AKC showed great foresight when they developed the Limited Registration for breeders. Please use it. If you recognize in one of your puppies a fault that should not be perpetuated in the progeny, sell that puppy with a Limited Registration so that the AKC will never register the offspring. Be responsible and stand behind the dogs you breed. Be prepared to take back the dogs you sell if the owners can no longer care for them. Use a written sales contract that guarantees nobody has the right to resell or give away your dogs and ensure the dogs you sell must be offered back to you. Remember, those dogs would not be out there, possibly in distress, if you had not put them out there.

If you do not plan to be a breeder, but wish to own a stud dog, your responsibility to the breed is equal to that of the breeder. Your name may not appear as breeder of record, but if you sell your dog's sperm you have a vested interest in every puppy your dog sires. Use a contract to guarantee all of your dog's offspring are protected from being resold, given away or sold for use in laboratory experiments. Refuse to breed a bitch who is not of good quality. Do not breed a bitch unless you are absolutely confident the owner is capable and willing to meet moral and financial obligations to the dam and her litter. If a Mastiff sired by your stud dog is in trouble, be prepared to rescue it. Your dog, with your consent, helped create the offspring and your obligation to the breed did not end with selling the sperm.

Mysterious Malady

There is a mysterious malady Mastiff owners suffer and this unusual ailment is hazardous to the wallet. The problem sneaks up and catches one totally off guard. Sadly, there is no known cure for the illness. You buy your first Mastiff. She is wonderful. Everyone loves her. She is beautiful, well behaved and a perfect pet. Time slips by and you worry she is lonely so you think about a canine companion and mate for her. You mention this at the veterinarian's office and people tell you about the Mastiffs they saw recently at a dog show. You make plans to go to the next show to meet breeders. The date arrives and all goes according to plan. You meet nice breeders and before you leave you reserve a puppy. You buy your second Mastiff, a show male. Maintenance and veterinary costs are now doubled, but you anticipated the increase. You were encouraged to take the puppy to fun matches so you can learn to show him yourself. He finally reaches six months of age and you enter him in his first big show. He wins over a couple of other puppy dogs and you are now bitten by the show bug. You decide you are not presenting your puppy to his best advantage. Several professional handlers complimented your puppy, so you hire one of them to show him for you. You, meanwhile, have been watching the bitches being shown and think your bitch can become a champion, too.

One problem, though, if you show two Mastiffs, the family car is not big enough. You must go and buy a van. It was a bit more expensive than you budgeted, but you really needed that generator to run the air conditioner to keep the dogs cool. It was worth it because now both Mastiffs are champions. Since they proved they are of good quality by earning their titles, you decide to breed them. You have your first litter. You keep your best puppy, naturally, and must now begin all over again at match shows. Unfortunately, the house and yard are not large enough for three Mastiffs. No problem. Sell the house. You did not like it anyway. You move to the country where houses come with five to ten acres. It was unreasonable of the bank to raise your mortgage payment so much higher, but at least the dogs have plenty of room to romp in so it was still a pretty smart move. The dumb insurance company raised your rate just because of three dogs. They refuse to listen when you explain how gentle the dogs are. You are going to shows almost every weekend and those motel rooms are expensive. It's a lot of work hauling those big crates in and out of the rooms. Meals are expensive when you travel. It would be more convenient to travel and stay in your own motor home. Undoubtedly, it would save money in the long run, plus when the family next goes on vacation the Mastiffs can go, too. Are you beginning to get the picture?

CHAPTER 7
TOP-PRODUCING MASTIFFS

There are a million thoughtless, as well as comical, jokes about us breeders floating around out there in the "real" world. Professional business people sometimes look down on us when we say we are dog breeders. They do not understand. Even our families sometimes do not understand. Normal people go to bed and count sheep. Breeders retire and in their minds they are matching up pedigrees and breeding dogs that are not even born yet, dogs they envision perhaps five years down the road. Dedicated dog breeders do what they do because they love their chosen breed. They know the world does not need more dogs, it needs better dogs. This is the true commitment of serious and honorable breeders.

A real breeder stays up night after night over-seeing fragile, perhaps sickly, puppies, trying to nourish them and give them the strength of will to live and thrive. A real breeder cries and hurts everytime a fragile puppy is lost and everytime is like the first time—you can never accustom yourself to losing a puppy. A real breeder learns to accept the loss and move on, but he learns something about why the baby was lost, and applies the knowledge to the next litter. A real breeder is thrilled to see a good stool after nasty diarrhea. Life gets temporarily put on hold while the litter needs care.

There is no feeling of achievement so great for a breeder as that of seeing a dog or bitch he bred go into a home and become a beloved pet that gives years of companionship and joy to the owners. When we breed an animal that enters the show ring and a judge finds merit and gives our baby a ribbon, we are proud because our efforts have been validated—somebody liked what we bred. When our animals lose, some of us take the loss hard although we train ourselves to be good sports; we grit our teeth, congratulate the winner and walk away determined to try again on another day.

Breeding mastiffs can be scientific, an art, or just pure dumb luck. Even if we all do everything right and breed the very best dog to the very best bitch, it is still a crap shoot. Why? Because those recessive genes we did not expect jumped forward and surfaced. *All Mastiffs, only 45 years or so back, are related to the same nine dogs.*

While most breeds will breed back to the grandsire and grandam generation, I believe Mastiffs pull from as far back as the sixth and seventh generations. Mastiffs breed true, only they breed true much further back than we expect, going back to ancestors long since dead and forgotten, or if the breeder is fairly new to the breed, going back to dogs that are total unknowns. Breeders talk about outcrossing to a different line with nothing in common—it is virtually impossible. There was so much in- and in- and inbreeding, followed by line- and line- and linebreeding, after the war that Mastiffs continue to share all the same faults, no matter the line or strain.

Any breed of dog, and any dog of any breed, is only as good or as bad as what it collectively comes from. Those famous Mastiffs that were used to revive the breed undoubtedly had hereditary faults in them. The dedicated breeders who fought so valiantly to save the breed did not have the luxury of being able to discard any Mastiff because of faults. They went to heroic lengths just to save a breed from dying out in its historical homeland, and they did not have time to worry about straight stifles, poor fronts, bad elbows, weak hindquarters or faulty eyes. Their only priority was to keep this magnificent breed from extinction. They set their goals and they accomplished their mission.

I am a breeder who believes that everything is hereditary— from the thickness of the toenails to the size of the tongue. Some traits unquestionably carry a greater degree of inheritableness than others. Genetics and nature, in the end, will have their way and determine which genes will be passed along to live again. There is a battle on right now to fight hereditary thyroid disorders, elbow and hip dysplasia, eye problems, heart problems, etc. Some people might try to lay blame at the door of a particular breeder, a specific strain, or an individual Mastiff.

If you think your own beloved Mastiff, albeit tested and cleared of all genetic disorders, does not carry those same recessive genes, then take the time to trace your own dog back to the 1950s. I guarantee your Mastiff will track backwards to the same gene pool. The Mastiff is, quite logically, a small breed in terms of numbers of registered dogs when compared to other breeds. We still do not have the resources of other breeds in that we can not lose some of the hereditary problems by outcrossing. This concept needs to be accepted by all breeders and all breeders need to work together to improve things.

Stud dogs and brood bitches bred yesterday determined the quality of Mastiffs we have today. Stud dogs and brood bitches we breed today will, likewise, fix the quality of Mastiffs tomorrow. It, therefore, follows that careful selection of breeding stock cannot be over emphasized. Our mission is to improve our breed. The Mastiff is a head breed. True Mastiff type must be retained at all costs. If it does not look like, move like, sound like, think like and behave like a Mastiff then, very simply, it is not a Mastiff. That is the bottom line. No matter how pretty, or how sound, or how genetically clear of problems, it still must look like what it is supposed to be.

Listed in this chapter are stud dogs and brood bitches that left their mark of distinction on the Mastiff breed as a whole. They are the Mastiffs that stand out because of the exceptional quality of the offspring they produced. Did, or do, these stud dogs and brood bitches have faults? Of course they do. They have also passed along recessive genes. We can only hope that the generations that will follow them have inherited or will inherit those special good qualities from them and carry them forward to future Mastiffs long after we, and they, have departed this earth. As a lover and breeder of Mastiffs, I honor these Mastiffs and pay them tribute. They earned it. I compliment the breeders of these mastiffs for their skill and success.

TOP-PRODUCING MASTIFF STUD DOGS

The name of the stud dog is followed by the total number of champion offspring, his own sire and dam, 15 and above, the names of their champion offspring:

CH. IRON HILLS WARWAGON (49)
(CH. LIONSIRE IRONHILL WARLEGGEN X CH. IRON HILLS ELBERETH)

CH. ACORN HILL MORGANA PENDRAGON

CH. ACORN HILL RUFF N'READY

CH. ACORN HILL UTHER PENDRAGON

CH. GULPH MILLS MULCHER (47)
(CH. GULPH MILLS MUGGER X CH. GREENBRANCH MACUSHLA)

CH. APPLE CREEKS GEM DANDY

CH. BERENGARIA'S FALSE HOPE & LIES

CH. GELWILS SECOND EDITION

CH. ACORN HILL'S PRINCESS NIKA

CH. ACORN HILLS ASTER

CH. ACORN HILLS DIABLO DEL SOL

CH. ACORN HILLS ETHAN, CD

CH. ACORN HILLS HOGAN, CDX

CH. ACORN HILLS MOUNTAIN LAUREL

CH. ACORN HILLS THE JOY OF CYRUS

CH. AVALON IRON HILL THUNDER ROAD

CH. AVALON'S LORD CEARBHALLAIN, CD

CH. AVALONS TUCSON WARRIOR

CH. BRITE STAR SIR WINSTON

CH. BRITE STAR'S WARLOCK

CH. CALEDONIA'S RUMOR HAS IT

CH. CALEDONIAS MEMPHIS BELLE

CH. DAME EDITH OF ACORN HILLS

CH. GENTRY'S BRITE STAR PANDA

CH. HUDSON WARDANCER

CH. HUDSONS HOME RUN WYSTAN

CH. HUDSONS ON THE WARPATH

CH. IRON HILL TEN STONE NTSTALKER

CH. IRON HILLS BET THE FARM

CH. IRON HILLS CHUCKWAGON

CH. IRON HILLS EARNED INTEREST

CH. IRON HILLS GRZATHEART LLMIKI

CH. IRON HILLS ONCE UPON A WAGON

CH. IRON HILLS ORPHEUS

CH. IRON HILLS PAINT YOUR WAGON

CH. GELWILS WINDSORS EDITION

CH. GOLDLEAF ALWAYS FAITHFUL

CH. GOLDLEAF LITTLE MULCH

CH. GOLDLEAF MONTANA

CH. GOLDLEAFS HOPE AND GLORY

CH. GULPH MILLS AJAX III

CH. GULPH MILLS AURORA BOREALIS

CH. GULPH MILLS BENTLEY

CH. GULPH MILLS BLACKPOINT ZACK P

CH. GULPH MILLS CHELSEA

CH. GULPH MILLS D'ARTAGNAN

CH. GULPH MILLS DAWNS EARLY LIGHT

CH. GULPH MILLS FOXGLOVE SAVANAH

CH. GULPH MILLS GLORY BE

CH. GULPH MILLS GOLDMINER

CH. GULPH MILLS GREYSTONE HILARY

CH. GULPH MILLS HEIDI TO MT OAKS

CH. GULPH MILLS JAKE JACOBI

CH. GULPH MILLS KELLY

CH. GULPH MILLS LEGACY

CH. GULPH MILLS LEGENDARY CAESAR, CD

CH. GULPH MILLS LITTLE AMY

CH. GULPH MILLS MAGICIAN

CH. GULPH MILLS MAGNUM

CH. GULPH MILLS MANDY

CH. GULPH MILLS MARCUS

CH. GULPH MILLS MARJORIE, CD

CH. IRON HILLS PELUSA

CH. IRON HILLS RANI DEMANN

CH. IRON HILLS SOUTHERN
GENTLEMAN

CH. IRON HILLS SPILL THE WINE

CH. IRON HILLS STORM'IN
NORMAN

CH. IRON HILLSSERIOUS RIP
HOMBRE

CH. IRONHILLS PAX RIVER
INTREPID

CH. NIGHT STALKER FANTASY
FIVE

CH. PALADIN'S CHUCKWAGON

CH. PINEHOLLOW BEANSI
BUFFAMATIC

CH. PINEHOLLOW RUN
AROUND SUE

CH. SILLARS GODDESS ATHENA

CH. SOUTHPORTS IRON MAIDEN

CH. SOUTHPORTS PRIME TIME

CH. STONEHOUSE COUNTRY
GENTLEMAN

CH. TEJAS ACE IN THE HOLE

CH. TEJAS MISS TUFFY VALLEY
VIEW

CH. TREOWE AETHELWEARD OF

CH. WHITTIER OF ACORN HILLS
HUDSON

CH. GULPH MILLS MASQUERADE

CH. GULPH MILLS MATHEW

CH. GULPH MILLS MAXWEL WINCHESTER

CH. GULPH MILLS PLATO

CH. GULPH MILLS TEJAS BOGART

CH. GULPH MILLS TEJAS SOPHIE

CH. GULPH MILLS TUPPENCE

CH. L OLYMPUS ATLAS

CH. L OLYMPUS DIANA

CH. L OLYMPUS HADES

CH. L OLYMPUS KING BRUZER DULAY

CH. L OLYMPUS TRISTANNA

CH. L OLYMPUS ZEUS

CH. LUCAS

CH. MULCHERS LA RAIDER OF HALE

CH. PENELOPE P OF BLACK POINT

CH. TASHA OF IRONGATE

CH. DEER RUN WYCLIFF (45)
**(CH. DEER RUN JERICHO CITY
X DEER RUN STELLA)**

CH. DEER RUN EZEKIEL (43)
**(CH. DEER RUN IVAN X LE MAR'S
SALLY)**

CH. CAMELOT"S LADY GUINEVERE

CH. CAMELOT'S MYSTICAL
MAGON

CH. DEER RUN BRANDY WINE

CH. DEER RUN BUCKSKIN COCHISE

CH. BRITE STAR'S GREY WOLF

CH. BURNS HALL AVIS OF IRONLION

CH. BURNS HALL JAMIE LOU

CH. BURNS HALL MAVIS

CH. DEER RUN CAMELOT'S KUJO

CH. DEER RUN CASTLEKEEP LEGEND

CH. DEER RUN CLEARLIGHT PANSIE

CH. DEER RUN COUNTESS INEZ

CH. DEER RUN DELTA LADY LY

CH. DEER RUN DESIREE

CH. DEER RUN DURANGO

CH. DEER RUN GELDA

CH. DEER RUN GROPPETTI FAWN LONI

CH. DEER RUN IVAN

CH. DEER RUN JAI BEE YANKEE

CH. DEER RUN JAKE ENCHANTED ACRES

CH. DEER RUN JOSH OF BULL VALLEY

CH. DEER RUN MAX A MILLION III

CH. DEER RUN MAYER'S LOYAL GIANT

CH. DEER RUN MCMUNGER

CH. DEER RUN MISTRES THISTLEHAIR, CD

CH. DEER RUN OSCAR BUDHOLLOW

CH. DEER RUN PANDORA'S FANTASY

CH. DEER RUN SHASTA

CH. DEER RUN SINDER

CH. DEER RUN TONKA GRANITE T

CH. DEER RUN WILLIAM THE CONQUEROR

CH. DEER RUN WINDHAVEN'S HERA

CH. DEER RUN WOODLEIGH'S ODEGAARD

CH. BURNS HALL PHAROH

CH. BURNS HALL ZACKERY

CH. BURNS HALL ZEKEIAL

CH. COLERIDGE'S BRADSTON TRINKET

CH. DEER RUN DELILAH

CH. DEER RUN SAMSON OF LIDO

CH. GROPPETTI HERE'S MAXWELL

CH. GROPPETTI NICADEMUS

CH. GROPPETTI'S B H ELLY PHANTS

CH. HEDGESTONES BIG MAN

CH. IRON HILLS KHAN GROPPETTI

CH. IRON HILLS TANIS

CH. IRONHILL LIONSIRE POLDARK

CH. IRONHILL SUDDEN JUSTICE

CH. IRONLION MOSES OF DONACHY

CH. IRONLION'S FATAL ATTRACTION

CH. LIONSIRE CANTANKEROUS EARL

CH. LIONSIRE DIVA OF EASTLAND

CH. LIONSIRE GRIZZ

CH. LIONSIRE INDIGO OF PAX RIVER

CH. LIONSIRE IRONHILL WARLEGGEN

CH. LIONSIRE KERRY OF BRITE STAR

CH. LIONSIRE MADAME DEFARGE

CH. LIONSIRE QUEEN OF SHEBA

CH. LIONSIRE ROCKEFELLER

CH. DEER RUN ZACHARY

CH. DEER RUN ZIRAH

CH. DEER RUN MAX A MILLION II

CH. DEER RUN TOUSSAINT

CH. FARLEYS ELEDHWEN
STEELSHEEN

CH. IRON HILLS ELBERETH

CH. IRON HILLS MITHRANDIR

CH. JAI BEE CALOOSA'S
ALEXANDRIA

CH. JAI BEE DEER RUN REBEL

CH. JAI BEE DIXIE LASS

CH. JAI BEE ROCKY HILL TRUDY

CH. JAI BEE WYMON OF OAKHILLS

CH. JAI BEES NOBLE GATEWAY

CH. LIONSIRE GUINEVERE

CH. WINDAMOHR'S ROCK OF

CH. WYEBIRCH MICHAEL MACKEY
LIONSIRE

CH. MORNING'S WILLOW OF ROCKYHILL

CH. NIGHT STALKER KRYSTAL

CH. NIGHT STALKER WELLINGTON

CH. OLD SCHOOL'S MAJESTIC MAJOR

CH. OLD SCHOOL'S MITRA MAJOR

CH. OLD SCHOOL'S OSA MAJOR

CH. OLD SCHOOL'S PRIMO REMO MAJOR

CH. OLD SCHOOL'S SERGEANT MAJOR

CH. OLD SCHOOLS LORD MAVRICK

CH. ROCKY HILL ALEXIS

CH. ROCKY HILL HILDA

CH. ROCKY HILL KRYSTAL GAIL

CH. ROCKY HILL WELLINGTON OF LOH

CH. ROCKY HILL WRIGHTOUS CAESAR

*CH. SEMPER FI GROPPETTI
GARGOYLE (36)*
(CH. DEER RUN SEMPER
FI THOR, CD X DEER RUN
SEMPER FI KERRA, CD)

CH. BOWSPRIT BARD'S SONG OF
THE SEA

CH. DANDYLION BAILEYS NALA
OF CHAMPAIGN

CH. DANDYLION CAVELL
ARTORIUS REX

CH. DANDYLION EVEREADY
TEDDY

CH. DANDYLION GARELLIE
DREAMTEAM

CH. DANDYLION JODIE ODIE

CH. DANDYLION LIONSIRE CAVELL

CH. GROPPETTI'S WALLON (33)

(DAULTON'S SIR HENRY TIZARD

X DEER RUN GROPPETTI FAWN LONI)

CH. ARCINIEGA'S ABRA

CH. ARCINIEGA'S LOLLY VON KILLION

CH. ARCINIEGA'S MOONSTONE ARGUS

CH. CAESAR'S ELWOOD YARDLEY

CH. CAESAR'S LEO OF FORTUNE

CH. CAESAR'S SAMURAI SUMO

CH. CAESAR'S SULTRY SUKI

CH. DANDYLION WINE AT GROPPETTIS

CH. DANDYLION'S WALTZIN MATILDA

CH. GROPETI RUFUS GRIZLEY GROPER

CH. GROPPETTI BAMA GIRL

CH. GROPPETTI BODIN MOOR'S EDWINA

CH. GROPPETTI DIXIE OF LAZY D

CH. GROPPETTI EAGLE NEST GOLIATH

CH. GROPPETTI GAR HANNAH E

CH. GROPPETTI GRECO'S SIMBA

CH. GROPPETTI LEROY

CH. GROPPETTI ROSE V MASTIFF COVE

CH. GROPPETTI THORG OF WINDSOR

CH. GROPPETTI WHISPKNGHTS ANNA

CH. GROPPETTI'S LORD HENRY OF MMRB

CH. LIONSIRE CELESTIAL SERAPHIM

CH. LIONSIRE KEATON

CH. LIONSIRE'S ANGUS OG

CH. MASTIFF COVE BELL VAL GOCHEN

CH. MASTIFF COVE ROCKNROLL HEAVN

CH. MASTIFF COVE SAVANNAH

CH. MASTIFF COVE TULLYSU V HIMMEL

CH. MASTIFF COVE'S ONE MANS LOSS

CH. MASTIFF COVES SOUTHERN GRACE

CH. COLONEL JOHNSTON OF SHILOHE

CH. GREENBRIER AMJO OF WALLON

CH. GROPPETTI THORR

CH. HAUS HUMBOLDT KEMAH DREAM

CH. HAUS HUMBOLDT WRIGHTOUS BEA

CH. MACHIAVELLI OF OLD RIVER

CH. PETROSEC ANSHEL'S ECHO

CH. PETROSEC CHATO OF CHALET

CH. PETROSEC CUATRITA

CH. PETROSEC GANNAWAYS GUNTHER

CH. PETROSEC GOLIATH

CH. PETROSEC MUY GRANDE BEXAR

CH. PETROSEC MUY GRANDE HOUSTON

CH. QUAIL HILL'S HUMONGO CHONGO

CH. SIR WILLIAM CHUMLEY

CH. T JS BELOVED DAVID

CH. TEJAS BOADICEA OF SYLMAR

CH. TEJAS IRONMAN TYSON

CH. TEJAS MIDAS

CH. TEJAS PAL OF MY HEART

CH. VON KILLION'S 'WALLETTE'

CH. WARLORDS SIR J D DAMONE

CH. WRIGHTOUS BLIND FAITH

CH. PRAIRIE BUFFALO
THUNDERCLOUD

CH. WRIGHTOUS SAM THE MAN

CH. RL'S GRIZZY JEAN OF
DANDYLION, CD

CH. WRIGHTOUS WIDE BODY TANKER,
CD

CH. SEMPER FI BELL OF THE WOODS ENG.AM.CH. ARCINIEGA'S LION OF
BREDWARDINE

CH. SEMPER FI CHARMED NO
DOUBT

CH. SEMPER FI THE BARD'S TALE

CH. SEMPER FI THE BARD'S TALE

CH. SEMPER FI TRULY IMPRESSIVE

*CH. SOUTHPORTS PRIME
TIME (32)*
**(CH. IRON HILLS WARWAGON
X CH. SOUTHPORTS BAILEY
QUARTERS)**

CH. GROPPETTI SIR ARTHUR (30)

**(CH. GROPPETTI'S BEAUREGAARD
X CH. GROPPETTI'S PEGASUS)**

CH. APPLE CREEKS IT'S SHOWTIME

CH. ALTOMS-HARWOOD WORK OF ART

CH. CC EMERALD ISLE O FERGIE

CH. CASTLE MOUNT HEATHER

CH. CC GIGANTI NAPOLEON

CH. CASTLE MOUNT MAXIMUS

CH. CC KING SIMBA O FERGIE

CH. CASTLE MOUNT'S MEGAN

CH. CC SIR MICHAEL O FERGIE

CH. CASTLE MOUNTS ATLAS

CH. GULPH MILLS BAILEY ON THE
ROCKS

CH. CGC ARABIAN'S JUST JOEY

CH. GULPH MILLS TEDDY BEAR

CH. CGC BLACK POINT'S CLASS ACT

CH. HIGH COUNTRY MEADOW
STAR

CH. CGC BLUE ANGEL OF BRITE STAR

CH. HIGH COUNTRY
STONECASTLE SIERRA

CH. CGC THUNDERPAWS HOT ROCKS

CH. HIGHCOUNTRY RUFFIANS
CALLIOPE

CH. CLUNY AT BANDA START US UP

CH. MEZA JORDAN'S JUDGEMENT

CH. CLUNY'S CROWN JEWEL OF ARTHUR

CH. MEZA'S EQUAL TIME

CH. DUKE OF HIGH PLAINS

CH. MEZA'S IN THE NICK OF TIME

CH. HURRY UP JOE'S DREAM KEEPER

CH. MIDDLE EARTH SONG O'THE
SOUTH

CH. MASTIFF COVE'S RAGING BULL

CH. RANCHO COPPER DESERT
VALLEY

CH. MASTIFF COVE'S TALK TO ME

CH. RANCHO IN THE NICK OF TIME

CH. MISTY MEADOW MERCEDES

CH. RANCHO LADY SADIE SUNSHINE

CH. MISTY MEADOW'S DUSTY MILLER

CH. RR LADY CHRISTINE

CH. MOONDANCE GUARDIAN ANGEL

CH. SOUTHPORT SEVILLE FRANGELICA

CH. MOONDANCE'S EXCALIBER

CH. SOUTHPORTS GARRISON G DAWG

CH. MOOSEHEAD'S LADY LIZABETH

CH. SOUTHPORTS MAJOR BAERRON

CH. NANJEMOY'S MAXWELL

CH. SOUTHPORTS PRIMA BELLA

CH. SILVER'S MORGAN LE FAY

CH. SOUTHPORTS PRIME WITNESS

CH. SILVER'S SHADOW OF CAMELOT

CH. SOUTHPORTS-TALAMASCA-MATRIARCH

CH. SMOK'N LAD STORMY DOMINIC

CH. STONEHOUSE CHANTILLY LACE

CH. SMOK'N LAD'S MIGHTY QUINN

CH. STONHS DRYCK BAD TO THE BONE

CH. STONEHOUSE BIG BAD BUD

CH. SUNNY VISTA'S ARGUS OF ALBION

CH. STONEHOUSE BRAZEN LADY

CH. SUNNYVISTA WARFORCE PRESENCE

CH. STONEHOUSE COUNTRY SQUIRE

CH. THUNDERPAWS BRUSCO TUGNBARGE

CH. STONEHOUSE SUNSHINE NELLI

CH. THUNDERPAWS SAY GNITE GRACIE

CH. TEJAS SONRISE DAKOTA, CD

CH. WINDSOR'S ROXY

CH. WINDSOR'S MORGAN

CH. HIS MAJESTY'S LION OF JUDAH (30)
(CH. DEER RUN RIVER BULL X CH. DEER RUN GLORY TO GOD, CD)

CH. STONEBROOK SOUTHPORTS BYRON (28)
(CH. KISUMU XAVIER KING OF IONA X DEER RUN SAMANTHA IV)

CH. BEOWULFS KODIAK PRIDE

CH. A SHOW BIZ HIPPOLYTA

CH. CASSIOPEIA OF CREEKSIDE

CH. ALBION'S BOSWORTH FIELD

CH. CREEKSIDE'S NKOTB MIGHTY HOGAN

CH. ALBION'S CHARMING CHARLES

CH. HIS MAJESTY AGINCOURT JESTER

CH. ALBION'S MAVERICK

CH. HIS MAJESTY EMANUEL BENJUDAH

CH. HIS MAJESTY GLORY HOLLY LUIA

CH. HIS MAJESTY MAPLECREEK EMILY

CH. HIS MAJESTY'S ADAM BEN JUDAH

CH. HIS MAJESTY'S AUGUSTUS DAVID

CH. HIS MAJESTY'S BRUNA LEA

CH. HIS MAJESTY'S GEORGICS POET

CH. HIS MAJESTY'S GINGER BREAD

CH. HIS MAJESTY'S JIREH BEN JUDAH

CH. HIS MAJESTY'S PINEWOOD SAMSON

CH. HIS MAJESTY'S PINEWOOD AZEKIEL

CH. HIS MAJESTY'S PINEWOOD MISSY

CH. JG'S MC HIS MAJESTY'S TANNAH

CH. PINEWOOD A CHANCE OF MISCHIEF

CH. PINEWOOD BLACK TIE AFFAIR

CH. PINEWOOD CAESAR AUGUSTUS

CH. PINEWOOD FOXGLOVE WIN-SWEPT

CH. PINEWOOD GOOD VIBRATIONS

CH. PINEWOOD HIS MAJ HOLY MOSES

CH. PINEWOOD HIS MAJESTY AMOS

CH. PINEWOODS BUMPER BURKE

CH. PINEWOODS COVER GIRL

CH. PINEWOODS MIGHTY QUINN

CH. ROBBINS HIS MAJESTY SIR OLIVER

CH. BLACK POINTS LILY OF GOLDLEAF

CH. BYRON'S HUBBA BUBBA

CH. JOSEPH OF DAKOTA

CH. KNIGHTSENS SOPHIES CHOICE

CH. L OLYMPUS PANDORA

CH. L OLYMPUS THOR

CH. MEADOWRUN DICKENS

CH. MQH KENWORTH OF ASHLEY FARMS

CH. SOUTHPORT RIF RAF OF BLU RIDGE

CH. SOUTHPORTS AUGUSTUS SEES HER

CH. SOUTHPORTS BAILEY QUARTERS

CH. SOUTHPORTS BIANCA

CH. SOUTHPORTS BIT O'ROSE

CH. SOUTHPORTS BLACK ORPHEUS

CH. SOUTHPORTS COMSTOCK CLANCY

CH. SOUTHPORTS COMSTOCK VELVET

CH. SOUTHPORTS DREAM WARRIOR

CH. SOUTHPORTS JENNA KARLEK

CH. SOUTHPORTS MAINE DREAM

CH. SOUTHPORTS RICHLIEU THE RED

CH. STABLEMATE MQH EMERALD

CH. STABLEMATE'S LADY LUCY

CH. STABLEMATES MQH AHZMAT

CH. STURLUNG'S MIA OF STABLEMATE

CH. VICTORY'S DONCASTER
ISABELLA

CH. VICTORY'S SHOWER OF BLESSINGS

CAN. AM. CH. TIBERIAS OF KISUMU (28) (ENG. CH. THREEBEES FRIAR OF COPENORE X BUCKHALL HANNAH OF KISUMU)	*CH. DEER RUN RODERICK (22)* (DEER RUN WINSTON II X DEER RUN EMILY)
CH. ADMIRATION OF CARINTHIA	CH. ADONIA OF STRATOS
CH. AGNES OF CARINTHIA	CH. BRITE STAR'S CASSANDRA
CH. BRUGH'S SINBAD OF CARLISLE	CH. BRITE STAR'S PHOEBE
CH. HANNIBAL OF MAKAR	CH. GROPPETTI CHRISSIE
CH. IMPERIAL FROSTINA	CH. GROPPETTI GOOD STUFF MAYNARD
CH. IMPERIAL HONEY BEE	CH. GROPPETTI LAKESIDE'S ELLA
CH. KING JESTER	CH. GROPPETTI LEFHOLZ LUCY MARIE
CH. LADY BOADICEA OF ELSINORE	CH. GROPPETTI LEMON PUDDING
CH. MS MAGGIE	CH. GROPPETTI MASTIFF BUSTER
CH. NANJEMOY'S ETASHA	CH. GROPPETTI NIGEL
CH. NANJEMOY'S KA-REEM	CH. GROPPETTI OF QUAIL HILL
CH. RAISIN RIVERS OMENA	CH. GROPPETTI ORDERV
CH. RAISIN RIVERS THURSTON	CH. GROPPETTI'S AREATHA
CH. ROSEWALL HERA	CH. GROPPETTI'S BUZZ SAW, CD
CH. SABU	CH. GROPPETTI'S HUMONGUS PEARCE
CH. SOLOMON OF IRON HILLS	CH. GROPPETTI'S PEGASUS
CH. VERDUNE'S JESSICA	CH. GROPPETTIS ZENA OF HALE
CH. WILLOW POINT'S ABBEY	CH. LAMBAY PHOENIX
CH. WILLOW POINT'S CATULLUS	CH. PANMARIC GROPPETTI CHANCES ARE
CH. WILLOW POINT'S DELILAH	CH. PANMARIC SECOND TIME AROUND
CH. WILLOW POINT'S KRISTINA	CH. STURLUNG'S VALFREKR
CH. WILLOW POINT'S KRISTINA II	CH. WEST POINTER'S BYRON BUDDY
CH. WILLOW POINT'S LYRIC	
CH. WILLOW POINT'S PAX	
CH. WILLOW POINT'S SANTANA	
CH. WILLOW POINT'S SIXPENCE	

CH. WILLOW POINT'S TIBERIA
GEMINI

CH. WOLVERTON OF WILLOW POINT II

CH. ACORN HILL UTHER PENDRAGON (19)
(CH. IRON HILLS WARWAGON X ARRABELLE OF ACORN HILL, CD)

CH. DEER RUN SEMPER FI THOR, CD (19)
(CH. DEER RUN TRISTAN X GREAT DAY EMALINE)

CH. ACORN HILLS SILENT KNIGHT	CH. BIG HOUSE MISTRESS LILY
CH. ACORN HILLS WIND CHIME	CH. CALEDONIA III
CH. AGAPE ALLSHOOKUP AT NEWGATE	CH. CALEDONIA PLACE YOUR BETS
CH. AGAPE APOLLO LOVES ME TENDER	CH. CALEDONIA'S BEST BET KETHRY
CH. AGAPE'S VISION UNFOLDS	CH. CALEDONIA'S BIG GAMBLE
CH. CEE-CEE'S MISTER BENTLEY	CH. IRON HILLS BIG EASY OF SEMPER FI
CH. CRYSTAL MTN BOCEEFUS GA	CH. IRON HILLS FIXIN TO START
CH. CRYSTAL MTN LADY AMBER	CH. IRON HILLS PORTFOLIO
CH. CRYSTAL MTN RED STAR	CH. IRON HILLS PRIME DIRECTIVE
CH. GUARDIA'S DREAM OF MT. ROYAL	CH. IRON HILLS SIR GARRETT
CH. GUARDIA'S ROLL OF THE DICE	CH. NYAL'S DEFERRED ANNUITY
CH. PENDRAGON BAILIFFS FARLOUGH	CH. NYAL'S MAXIMUM YIELD
CH. PENDRAGON CARA DEL SOL	CH. NYAL'S PREFERRED STOCK
CH. PENDRAGON LEONA DILLAREZ	CH. OWENS' SEMPER FI THORS' THRUD
CH. PENDRAGON'S SIR EINSTEIN	CH. SEMPER FI GROPPETTI GARGOYLE
CH. PENDRAGONS WYSIWYG WUHF-GUDE	CH. SEMPER FI THOR'S BOLD
CH. SONRISE KAY NE TAH	CH. SEMPER FI THUNDER UNDER FOOT
CH. SONRISE'S CHEYENNE NELLIE	CH. SEMPER FI'S JARHEAD
CH. SUGARFOOT'S MERRIE MADELINE	CH. SEMPER FI'S SWEET EMOTION

CH. MATTS JOSHUA-DOGWOOD KNOLL (19)
(CH. BURNS HALL ZACKERY X CH. BURNS HALL NICOLE)

CH. CLUNY'S ENCHANTED BLOSSOM

CH. CLUNY'S MECCA OF IRONCLAD

CH. CLUNYS SILVERS RAGS TO RICHES

CH. CREEKVIEW PLANTATION BOOBEAR

CH. CREEKVIEW'S MAJOR MONTGOMERY, CD

CH. DANDYLION BUTKAS

CH. DANDYLION'S MAGGIE MAGEE

CH. IRON HILLS JUST JOSHIN

CH. IRON HILLS MAGIC BUS

CH. IRON HILLS RAINDANCER

CH. CH. IRONLION PEANUT BUTTER

CH. LIONS DEN AUALANCHE

CH. LIONS DEN COUNTRY CINNAMON

CH. LIONSIRE POETRY IN MOTION

CH. LIONSIRE ROSIE OF CLUNY

CH. LIONSIRE RUN'N BEAR'S SAMSON

CH. QUEEN ELIZABETH HEAVENSGATE

CH. RL'S RAGTIME JAZZ OF CLUNY

CH. SPITFIRE'S LADY ASHLEY

CH. ELDORADO REBEL W OUT A PAUSE, CD (18)
(CH. WRIGHTOUS WIDE BODY TANKER, CD X CH. LEGENDARY FANNIE FLAUNTS IT, CD)

CH. CRESTWOOD RIGHTEOUS REBELLION

CH. ELDORADO SIMPLY IRRESTIBLE

CH. ELDORADO'S REBEL DRIFTER

CH. FARPOINT REBEL'S RAZZMATAZZ

CH. FOXGLOVE CLASSIC DOUBLE-TAKE

CH. FOXGLOVE WINDSONG'S HARLEY D

CH. HIGH COUNTRY AGAPE SCARLETT

CH. HIGH COUNTRY BROWN EYED GIRL

CH. HIGHCOUNTRY HAVENS GALORE

CH. LAZY DAZ ELDORADO MOQUI

CH. LAZY DAZ LADY RACHEL

CH. LAZY DAZ REBEL'S RAIDER

CH. LAZY DAZ TYRONE V BRAE TJARN

CH. MISTY MEADOW'S REBEL REBELION

CH. MISTY MEADOWS MLADY CASANDRA, CD

CH. NEWGATE REBEL'S JACKSON LEA

CH. TYROLIAN NICOLAI ZA MIHOVA

CH. TYROLIAN WALTZING MATILDA

CH. MEPS TRISTAN (18)

(ENG.CH. OVERNOONS MR MICAWBER O BUCKHALL X

CH. OLD SCHOOL'S PRIMO REMO MAJOR (18)
(CH. DEER RUN EZEKIEL X CH. OLD SCHOOLS' URSA MAJOR)

ENG.CH. MEPS PORTIA)
CH. ACORN HILLS ENCORE', CD

CH. ADVOCATE'S JURISPRUDENCE

CH. BANYON'S BENSON

CH. BANYON'S CASSANDRA

CH. BANYON'S CHARMIN

CH. BIG SKY SAMPSON OF
GREENBRIER

CH. BROOKMOOR'S JINGLE BELL
OF GB

CH. COLUMBO OF GREENBRIER

CH. DIABLO'S BLACK MAJIC

CH. DIABLO'S LORENZO SALVADOR

CH. DUKE WOODS OF
KINGSBOROUGH

CH. GREATGATSBY OF
RAMBLEWOOD

CH. GREENBRIER NYDIA OF MEPS

CH. GREENBRIER PATCH

CH. GREENBRIER'S SHAMBEAU

CH. RAMBLEWOODS BIG MISS PRISS

CH. RAMBLEWOODS VICTORIAN
IMAGE, CD

CH. REGIMENT'S TITANIA OF
VERDUNE

CH. ADVOCATE'S EBONY MIST

CH. BERYSTEDE LADY WOKINGHAM

CH. CHAMPAYNE LORD DARBY

CH. DE VINE BRONWYN LLEWELYN

CH. IRONLION MISS SAS QUATCH

CH. IRONLION PRIMO CLIFFORD

CH. IRONLION'S OUTRAGEOUS RAMA

CH. LIONSIRE JODI JORDAN

CH. LIONSIRE PROMISES PROMISES

CH. NIGHT STALKER HUGGY BEAR

CH. NIGHT STALKER KD BRANDYBUCK

CH. NIGHT STALKER MYSTIC LADY

CH. OAK LANE ROSE BAY ISIS, CD

CH. OAKLANE OLD SCHOOL STARDUST

CH. OAKLANE POLARIS POCAHONTES, CD

CH. OAKLANE SIR WINSTON KNIGHTS

CH. TYGER HALL MARILYN MONROE

CH. WARLORDS MS M J'S KAHLUA

*CH. PEERSLEIGH STORM
SHERMAN (18)*
**(CH. ODIN OF DAHLSEIDE X
CH. PEERSLEIGH PRINCESS
CAROLYN)**

CH. IRON HILLS ROCKY HILL THOR (17)

**(CH. DEER RUN ZACHARY X CH. IRON
HILLS ELBERETH)**

CH. CHETAKA BARROW OF STORM

CH. CHETAKA MAG BLUE
OF STORM

CH. MERCEDES' BRANDY

CH. NANJEMOY'S HANNAH
LORENJAZ

CH. IRON HILL ELENTARI STARQUEEN

CH. IRON HILLS NARSIL

CH. JAI BEE SCHEHEREZADE

CH. NIGHT STALKER A J SIMON

CH. PINEWOODS SOUTHWEST
BREEZE

CH. NIGHT STALKER RAMBO

CH. ROYAL OAK'S CELTIC
MERCEDES

CH. NIGHT STALKER RIVER VICTORY

CH. STORM BOUNTY OF LAZY HILL

CH. ROCKY HILL BIG GUN

CH. STORM DIXIELAND DELIGHT

CH. ROCKY HILL BIGSY MCGEE

CH. STORM DRESDEN OF GROVE

CH. ROCKY HILL BRIARWOOD DELIGHT

CH. STORM LANDMARK'S USA
TESS, CD

CH. ROCKY HILL GRENDEL

CH. STORM QUIET REBELLION
OF BH, CD

CH. ROCKY HILL GREYSTONE GENESIS

CH. STORM TA-TANKA
O'APPLEWHAITES

CH. ROCKY HILL ODIN

CH. STORM'S ENGLISH LEGACY

CH. ROCKY HILL'S GABE OF WINDAMOHR

CH. STORM'S MUCH GOODER

CH. ROCKY HILLS DEER RUN ZIPPORAH

CH. STORM'S STOR GAL

CH. SIDETRACK FARM DUNCAN

CH. STORM'S SUFFOLK THUNDER

CH. THORCHELSEAIAS NOEL

CH. STORM'S SWEDISH LEJON, CD

CH. VICTORIA OF SIDETRACK FARM'

CH. STORM'S SWISS BERRY

CH. DEER RUN IVAN (16)
(CH. DEER RUN WYCLIFF
X TASHA FARLEY'S FIRST LADY)

CH. DEER RUN ZACHARY (16
(CH. DEER RUN WYCLIFF
X DEER RUN SURRY)

CH. BAUM'S AUGUSTUS REX

CH. DEER RUN BRADSTON'S PHOEBE

CH. BERTWICK'S BOOMER OF
DEERRUN

CH. DEER RUN CRISSY OF BERTWICK

CH. DEER RUN BASHEBA
SUNSTREAM

CH. DEER RUN DERVISH

CH. DEER RUN EZEKIEL

CH. DEER RUN ELECTRA

CH. DEER RUN GROPPETTI NINA

CH. DEER RUN NATHAN

CH. DEER RUIN IVY LIDO

CH. DEER RUN PETROSEC HANA

CH. DEER RUN JAY BEE BRYNMORE

CH. DEER RUN QUELLWATER SERENA

CH. DEER RUN MAXINE

CH. DEER RUN SAMURAI

CH. DEER RUN MAXYHILL TOBE

CH. DEER RUN ZACHARYS CALEB

CH. DEER RUN NIKITA

CH. IRON HILLS ROCKY HILL THOR

CH. DEER RUN POLICE

CH. OAK LAIR'S GINA

CH. DEER RUN SIR MICHAEL

CH. DEER RUN VICTORIA OF
B AND V'S

CH. GROPPETTI ELECTRA

CH. GROPPETTI JOYNT VENTURE

CH. LAMBAY BATHSHEBA ATHENA

CH. OLDE ESTATE ANASTASIA

CH. QUELLWATER BRITANIA

CH. QUELLWATER DEER RUN ANTIQUE

CH. RUSLAN OF NANJEMOY

CH. ZACHARY'S LADY TITAN

CH. LIONSIRE GRIZZ (16)
**(CH. DEER RUN EZEKIEL X
CHRISTIANS BRISTOL
CREAM)**

CH. BANYON'S COSBY

CH. BANYON'S SWAINMOTE
MURPHY BROWN

CH. BEAUTIFUL BABE OF BELAIR

CH. BRITE STAR'S DREAMSMOKE

CH. BRITESTAR LIONSIRES
ADDITION

CH. BRITESTAR NIGHTTIME

CH. BRITESTAR'S BEARLY GRIZZ

CH. BRITESTARS SIR ROCKOFELLER

CH. BURNS HALL GOLIATH

CH. BURNS HALL POLGARA

CH. DUJONS HILLEREY

CH. LIONSIRE DINAH OF
BROOKSIDE

CH. LIONSIRE DUELING SISTERS

CH. LIONSIRE SIR NIGEL BEWARE,
CD

CH. LIONSIRES ELLIE OF DEER RUN

CH. MERIWETHER'S MY GAL SAL

CH. SOUTHPORTS BLACK ORPHEUS (16)
**(CH. STONEBROOK SOUTHPORTS
BYRON X CH. P-J'S ATHENA)**

CH. APPLE CREEKS SOUTHPORT KAHLUA

CH. COMSTOCKS MAIDEN VOYAGE

CH. GROPPETTI MOONSHADOW EXIDOR

CH. KNIGHTSENS ORPHEUS TOO

CH. MOONSHADOW BLOOD SWEAT AND
TEARS

CH. MT OAKS HANNIBAL

CH. MT OAKS RAPUNZEL

CH. PEARCES EMPRESSIVE BIG JAKE

CH. SOUTHPORTS BLACK GRIMM

CH. SOUTHPORTS BYRON TWO

CH. SOUTHPORTS JEZ OF BLUE RIDGE

CH. SOUTHPORTS KING SOLOMON

CH. SOUTHPORTS OH VERONICA

CH. SOUTHPORTS SIR GEORGE

CH. TEJAS HARTLEY'S SCARLETT

CH. VILLA STURLAS LADY GUINEVERE

CH. DAWNWIND ROMULUS (15)
**(ENG.CH. GELERT OF PYNES FARM
X COPENORE PETITE)**

CH. APOLLO'S DISTANT IMAGE

CH. ABORCREST BLYTHE SPIRIT

CH. ABORCREST BURGESS MEREDITH

CH. CALEDONIA STINGERS MARGARET

CH. DAWNWIND ROMULUS CASSIA

CH. GILL'S BONNIE BELLE

CH. LAZY HILL MISS SADIE

CH. WALNUT CREEK'S ATTICUS FINCH

CH. WALNUT CREEK'S BARON ROSCOE

CH. WALNUT CREEK'S CEDRIC MCKAYE

CH. WALNUT CREEK'S DUTCH MASTER

CH. WALNUT CREEK'S FREDERIC FONZ

CH. WALNUT CREEK'S GEMINI

CH. WALNUT CREEK'S SHAMARIAH

CH. WALNUT CREEK'S TINA

CH. GILDASAN ROMAN WARRIOR (14)

CH. ROCKY HILL ALEXANDER (14)

CH. SILLARS KO TYSON (14)

CH. DEER RUN DURANGO (13)

CH. GREENBRIER'S SHAMBEAU (13)

CH. LIONSIRE IRONHILL WARLEGGEN (13)

CH. RAMSGATE JOB (13)

CH. REVEILLE BIG THUNDER (13)

CH. SOUTHPORTS DREAM WARRIOR (13)

CH. BURNS HALL ZACKERY (12)

CH. DEER RUN NOAH MASSALANE (12)

CH. DEER RUN SINDER (12)

CH. PAX RIVER DOZER BY SIDETRACK (12)

TAMARACK DONNER (12)

CH. ALTOM'S PAULAS PRIDE (11)

CH. APPLE CREEKS SIERRA (11)

CH. DEER RUN RIVER BULL (11)

CH. GREINER HALL JEDADIAH (11)

CH. MCKAYES OLIVER WINGATE (11)

CH. TAMARACK WARLORD (11)

CH. WILLOWLEDGE KNUTE (11)

CH. ALEXANDER OF DAHLSEIDE (10)

CH. COLTONS BEAUREGARD (10)

CH. DUKE WOODS OF KINGSBOROUGH (10)

This litter of puppies was sired by Ch. His Majesty's Lion of Judah out of Ch. Pinewoods One Day At A Thyme—and this produced a record 9 champions from a single litter.

Above: Ch. Peersleigh Storm Sherman at 9 years with his baby son, Ch. Storm Ta-Tanka O'Applewhates. Below: Ch. Deer Run Wycliff. Sire: Ch. Deer Run Jericho City; Dam: Deer Run Stella; Breeder/Owner: D.V. Gibbs & Tobin Jackson.

Above: BISS Ch. Iron Hills Warwagon. Sire: Ch. Lionsire Ironhill Warleggen; Dam: Ch. Iron Hills Elbereth; Breeder: Scott Phoebus; Owner: Roger Barkley. Below: Ch. Gulph Mills Mulcher. Sire: Ch. Gulph Mills Mugger; Dam: Ch. Greenbranch Macushla; Breeder/Owner: Michael Gensburger.

Ch. Deer Run Ezekiel. Sire: Ch. Deer Run Ivan; Dam: LeMar's Sally; Owner: Michael Hoffman.

Ch. Groppetti Sir Arthur. Sire: Ch. Groppetti Beauregaard; Dam: Ch. Groppetti Pegasus; Breeder: Patty Groppetti; Owner: Jenny Aber & Betty Isserstadt.

Ch. His Majesty's Lion of Judah. Sire: Ch. Deer Run River Bull; Dam: Ch. Deer Run Glory To God, CD; Breeder/Owner: Eva Gomez.

Ch. Southports Prime Time. Sire: Ch. Iron Hills Warwagon; Dam: Ch. Southports Bailey Quarters; Breeder/Owner: Joe & Carla Sanchez. Pete was the #2 Mastiff in 1994; he is a 3-time Award of Merit Winner, 2-time Stud Dog Winner and in 1996, the Best Veteran Winner at Mastiff Specialties.

Ch. Stonebrook Southports Byron. Sire: Ch. Kisumu Xavier King of Iona; Dam: Deer Run Samantha IV; Owner: Joe & Carla Sanchez; Breeder: John Mechling.

Can. Am. Ch. Tiberias of Kisumu. Sire: Eng. Ch. Threebees Friar of Copenore; Dam: Buckhall Hannah of Kisumu.

Ch. Semper Fi Groppetti Gargoyle. Sire: Ch. Deer Run Semper Fi Thor, CD; Dam: Deer Run Semper Fi Kerra, CD; Breeder: Samuel & Linda Owens; Owner: Patty Warfield.

Left: Ch. Peersleigh Storm Sherman. Sire: Ch. Odin of Dahlseide; Dam: Ch. Peersleigh Princess Carolyn; Breeder: Bruce & Jackie Guy; Owner: Bjorn & dee dee Andersson. Sherman is shown winning BOB the day after the 1986 Mastiff National Specialty over the same dogs. Below: Ch. Deer Run Ivan. Sire: Ch. Deer Run Wycliff; Dam: Tasha Farley's First Lady; Breeder: Michael & Debra Farley; Owner: Tobin Jackson.

Above: Ch. Deer Run Zachary. Sire: Ch. Deer Run Wycliff; Dam: Deer Run Surry; Owner/Breeder: Tobin Jackson. Right: Ch. Southports Black Orpheus. Sire: Ch. Stonebrook Southport's Byron; Dam: Ch. P-J's Athena; Breeder: Fred & Shirley Carnett; Owner: Joe & Carla Sanchez.

Ch. Dawnwind Romulus. Sire: Eng. Ch. Gelert of Pynes Farm; Dam: Copenore Petite. Stinger won BOW at a Mastiff National Specialty Show. This Mastiff had a great influence on the breed in America and he was known for passing along his sweet temperament, enormous bone and gorgeous head.

BIS/BISS Ch. Old Schools Primo Remo Major. Sire: Ch. Deer Run Ezekiel; Dam: Ch. Old Schools' Ursa Major; Breeder/Owner: John & Donna Bahlman.

Ch. Iron Hills Rocky Hill Thor. Sire: Ch. Deer Run Zachary; Dam: Ch. Iron Hills Elbereth; Breeder: Scott Phoebus; Owner: Charles Boyer.

Ch. Groppetti's Wallon. Sire: Daulton's Sir Henry Tizard; Dam: Ch. Deer Run Groppetti Fawn Loni; Breeder: Patty Groppetti; Owner: Mario Arciniega.

BISS Ch. Matts Joshua-Dogwood Knoll. Sire: Ch. Burns Hall Zackery; Dam: Ch. Burns Hall Nicole; Breeder: Joe Spears.

BISS Ch. Reveille Big Thunder. Sire: Ch. Renrock's Brian O' Dare; Dam: Ch. Reveille Tribute; Breeder: Adelaide Bolte; Owner: Mrs. Kessler & Dr. Bill Newman.

Ch. Sillars KO Tyson. Sire: Ch. Iron Hills Phoebus Groppetti; Dam: Sillars Lady Abigale; Breeder: Jeb Sillar; Owner: Scott Phoebus.

Above: Ch. Southports Dream Warrior. Sire: Ch. Stonebrook Southports Byron; Dam: Ch. Sturlung's Viktoria; Breeder: George & Dorothy Sturla; Owner: Joe & Carla Sanchez. Left: Ch. Deer Run Noah Massalane. Sire: War; Dam: Mistress Jill of Buckhall; Breeder: Anthony Ficarotta; Owner: D.V. Gibbs & Tobin Jackson.

Above: Ch. Lionsire Ironhill Warleggen. Sire: Ch. Deer Run Ezekiel; Dam: Ch. Farleys Eledhwen Steelsheen; Breeder: Scott Phoebus. Below: Ch. Willowledge Caesar III. Sire: Willowledge Bambi; Dam: Ch. Hefina O'Nantymynydd; Breeder: Stuart & Eve Olsen; Owner: Bruce & Jackie Guy. Caesar is shown here with Jackie Guy.

Tamarack Donner. Sire: Ch. Acadian Konigstiger; Dam: Ch. Tamarack Peaches Lovecreek; Breeder/Owner/Handler: Carol Knutson.

CH. GULPH MILLS MUGGER (10)

CH. HEDGESTONES BIG MAN (10)

CH. HIS MAJESTY EMANUEL
BENJUDAH (10)

CH. IRON HILLS PORTFOLIO (10)

CH. LITTLE ATLAS OF
MASSALANE (10)

CH. WILLOWLEDGE CAESAR III (10)

TOP-PRODUCING MASTIFF BROOD BITCHES

The name of the brood bitch is followed by the total number of champion offspring in brackets, her own sire and dam, 8 and above, by the names of their champion offspring:

CH. DEER RUN COUNTESS INEZ (18)
(CH. DEER RUN WYCLIFF X DEER RUN JAI BEE CLEOPATRIA)

CH. PINEWOODS ONE DAY AT A THYME (13)
(CH. DAMARIA THE GENERAL- UK IMPORT X CH. WINDY HILLS STEP ASIDE GIRLS)

CH. MORNING'S WILLOW OF ROCKYHILL

CH. HIS MAJESTY AGINCOURT JESTER

CH. ROCKY HILL ALEXIS

CH. HIS MAJESTY'S ADAM BEN JUDAH

CH. ROCKY HILL BIG GUN

CH. HIS MAJESTY'S BRUNA LEA

CH. ROCKY HILL BIGSY MCGEE

CH. HIS MAJESTY'S GEORGICS POET

CH. ROCKY HILL BRIARWOOD DELIGHT

CH. HIS MAJESTY'S GINGER BREAD

CH. ROCKY HILL CALOOSA ALLIANCE

CH. HIS MAJESTY'S JIREH BEN JUDAH

CH. ROCKY HILL GRENDEL

CH. HIS MAJESTY'S PINEWOOD AZEKIEL

CH. ROCKY HILL GREYSTONE GENESIS

CH. HIS MAJESTY'S PINEWOOD MISSY

CH. ROCKY HILL HILDA

CH. PINEWOOD CAESAR AUGUSTUS

CH. ROCKY HILL JAI BEE SAMANTHA

CH. PINEWOOD HIS MAJ HOLY MOSES

CH. ROCKY HILL KRYSTAL GAIL

CH. PINEWOODS COVER GIRL

CH. ROCKY HILL ODIN

CH. PINEWOODS GOOD VIBRATIONS

CH. ROCKY HILL WELLINGTON OF LOH

CH. PINEWOODS MIGHTY QUINN

CH. ROCKY HILL WRIGHTOUS CAESAR

CH. ROCKY HILL ZORBA

CH. ROCKY HILL DEER RUN ZIPPORAH

CH. ROCKY HILL'S GABE OF WINDAMOHR

CH. ROCKY HILLS RUGBY QUEEN

DEER RUN JAI BEE CLEOPATRIA (12)
(CH. DEER RUN LANCASTER
X DEER RUN GRETA)

CH. BAUM'S AUGUSTUS REX

CH. DEER RUN CLEARLIGHT PANSIE

CH. DEER RUN COUNTESS INEZ

CH. DEER RUN JAI BEE YANKEE

CH. DEER RUN JAI BEE BRYNMORE

CH. DEER RUN WILLIAM THE
CONQUEROR

CH. JAI BEE CALOOSA'S
ALEXANDRIA

CH. JAI BEE DEER RUN REBEL

CH. JAI BEE DIXIE LASS

CH. JAI BEE ROCKY HILL TRUDY

CH. JAI BEE WYMON OF OAKHILLS

CH. JAI BEES NOBEL GATEWAY

CH. GULPH MILLS DAWN (11)
(CH. LITTLE'S ATLAS OF MASSALANE
X CH. GULPH MILLS AMY)

CH. GULPH MILLS AURORA BOREALIS

CH. GULPH MILLS DAWNS EARLY LIGHT

CH. GULPH MILLS DAWNY BROOKE

CH. GULPH MILLS GLORY BE

CH. GULPH MILLS GOLDMINER

CH. GULPH MILLS GREYSTONE HILARY

CH. GULPH MILLS LEGACY

CH. GULPH MILLS LITTLE AMY

CH. GULPH MILLS MAGNUM

CH. GULPH MILLS MASQUERADE

CH. GULPH MILLS MATHEW

**CH. GULPH MILLS HEIDI TO MT
OAKS (10)**
(CH. GULPH MILLS MULCHER
X CH. GULPH MILLS SARAH)

CH. APPLE CREEKS SOUTHPORT
KAHLUA

CH. HEADLEY'S MTN OAKS BIG
SUEDE

CH. HEADLEYS ADONIS OF
MT OAKS

CH. L OLYMPUS HERCULES TOO

CH. MT OAKS BRANDY
ALEXANDRIA

CH. MT OAKS GRETA

CH. MT OAKS GUNNER

CH. MT OAKS HANNIBAL

CH. MT OAKS RAGNAR

CH. MT OAKS RAPUNZEL

CH. LIONSIRE INDIGO OF PAX RIVER (10)
(CH. DEER RUN EZEKIEL
X CHRISTIANS BRISTOL CREAM)

CH. ACORN HILL RUFF N'READY

CH. ACORN HILLS SILENT KNIGHT

CH. ACORNHILLS WIND CHIME

CH. DAME EDITH OF ACORN HILLS

CH. IRON HILLS CHUCKWKAGON

CH. IRON HILLS GRZATHEART LLMIKI

CH. IRON HILLS ONCE UPON A WAGON

CH. IRON HILLS PAINT YOUR WAGON

CH. IRON HILLS SPILL THE WINE

CH. WHITTIER OF ACORN HILLS

**ARRABELLE OF ACORN HILL,
CD (9)**
(CH. DEER RUN IVAN
X DEER RUN LUCRICH)

CH. ACORN HILL MORGANA
PENDRAGON

CH. ACORN HILL THE JOY OF
CYRUS

CH. ACORN HILL UTHER
PENDRAGON

CH. ACORN HILL'S PRINCESS NIKA

CH. ACORN HILLS ASTER

CH. ACORN HILLS DIABLO DEL SOL

CH. ACORN HILLS ETHAN, CD

CH. ACORN HILLS HOGAN, CDX

CH. ACORN HILLS MOUNTAIN
LAUREL

DIABLO'S LUCY BROWN (9)
(CH. MEPS TRISTAN
X WILLOWLEDGE SUZI-Q)

CH. DEER RUN PJ'S ZANZIBAR

CH. L OLYMPUS DIANA

CH. L OLYMPUS HADES

CH. L OLYMPUS TRISTANNA

CH. L OLYMPUS ZEUS

CH. OLYMPUS KING BRUZER DULAY

CH. PJ'S ATHENA

CH. PJ'S SILENT THUNDER OF SH

CH. PJ'S YARBOROUGH HILLS TABITHA

**CH. IRON HILLS BET THE FARM
(9)**
(CH. IRON HILLS WARWAGON
X LIONSIRE NAUTI-GIRL)

CH. CALEDONIA III

CH. CALEDODNIA KC
MASTERPIECE

CH. CALEDONIA PLACE YOUR BETS

CH. CALEDONIA'S BEST BET
KETHRY

CH. CALEDONIA'S BIG GAMBLE

CH. CALEDONIA'S BLIND AMBITION

CH. IRON HILLS FIXIN TO START

CH. IRON HILLS MO MONEY MO
MONEY

CH. IRON HILLS SIR GARRETT

**CH. THUNDERHILLS RIA OF LOVECREEK
(9)**
(CH. BALLYHERUGH'S CORMAC O'CONN
X CH. CHICKEN LITTLE)

CH. BEN'S ALI OF LOVE CREEK

CH. BEN'S BRYMYR OF LOVE CREEK

CH. LOVE CREEK'S SILVER FLO

CH. LOVECREEK'S BLACK WATCH

CH. LOVECREEK'S BRONZE GUARD

CH. LOVECREEKS LADY OF THE LAKE

CH. LOVECREEKS SWEET BISCUIT

CH. MAGNO'S HONORABLE HATCHET
MAN

CH. TAMARACK PEACHES LOVECREEK

CH. WERENHOLD HARRIET (9)
(CH. MOORELEIGH VICEROY
X WERENHOLD DAGMAR)

CH. CALEDONIA STINGERS
MARGARET

CH. WALNUT CREEK'S ATTICUS
FINCH

CH. WILLOWLEDGE HERO (9)
(MOORELEIGH GREGORY
X SHEBA OF ZIMAPAN)

CH. WILLOWLEDGE BATHSHEBA

CH. WILLOWLEDGE CANDACE

CH. WALNUT CREEK'S BARON ROSCOE

CH. WALNUT CREEK'S CEDRIC MCKAYE

CH. WALNUT CREEK'S DUTCH MASTER

CH. WALNUT CREEK'S FREDERIC FONZ

CH. WALNUT CREEK'S GEMINI

CH. WALNUT CREEK'S SHAMARIAH

CH. WALNUT CREEK'S TINA

CH. WILLOWLEDGE CATHERINE

CH. WILLOWLEDGE DANIEL

CH. WILLOWLEDGE ELOISE

CH. WILLOWLEDGE GAIRHEART

CH. WILLOWLEDGE GRINDEL

CH. WILLOWLEDGE MR CHIPS

CH. WILLOWLEDGE QUEEN CLEOPATRA

WILLOWLEDGE MEREDITH (9)
(CH. GRIFFITH'S T GERONIMO
X CH. WILLOWLEDGE KATRINA)

CH. ALTOM'S MISCHEVIOUS MOLLY (8)
(CH. OAK RIDGE'S JANUS
X CH. PEERSLEIGH BRIDGEWOOD
BLAIR)

CH. STORM BABE OF LAZY HILL

CH. STORM LANDMARK'S USA TESS, CD

CH. STORM MOSES OF LAZY HILL

CH. STORM SAGA OF LAZY HILL

CH. STORM TROOPER OF LAZY HILL

CH. STORM'S ENGLISH LEGACY

CH. STORM'S SUFFOLK THUNDER

CH. STORM'S SWEDISH LEJON, CD

CH. STORM'S SWISS BERRY

CH. ALTOM TIMBER GEORGIA PEACH

CH. ALTOM'S APPALONIA OF HARWOOD

CH. ALTOM'S BURNING HEART

CH. ALTOM'S EMILY

CH. ALTOM'S HARWOOD GAGE

CH. ALTOM'S LADY WAVERLY FAENA

CH. FOOLE'S MADD MAXX

CH. SIR LOUIS OF ALTOM'S

CH. APPLE CREEKS SIERRA (8)
(CH. L OLYMPUS HADES
X APPLE CREEK'S NUTMEG'N
SPICE)

CH. BURDETTES SWEET MAGGIE MAE (8)
(CH. WINSTON VAN MARK
MERIWETHER X RIPPLING WATERS
SHANNON)

CH. APPLE CREEKS SPIRIT NEW BEGINNING

CH. APPLE CREEKS BUSTER BROWN

CH. APPLE CREEKS DELTA DAWN

CH. MIDDLE EARTH FLOWER DUMPLIN

CH. MIDDLE-EARTH LUTHLEN TINUVIL

CH. MASTIFF COVE BELL VAL GOCHEN

CH. MASTIFF COVE ROCKNROLL HEAVN

CH. MASTIFF COVE SAVANNAH

CH. MASTIFF COVE TULLYSU V HIMMEL

CH. MASTIFF COVE'S ONE MANS LOSS

CH. MIDDLE-EARTH PATTY LUMPKIN

CH. MIDDLE-EARTH WINSTON

CH. PARKHILLS LADY HILLARY

CH. GREENBRANCH LADY CHELSEA (8)
(CH. CHANCELOT'S TRIPLE CROWN X THUNDERHILL'S ABBESS)

CH. BANBURY WINTERWOOD ERCILDOUN

CH. BANKHOUSE CRYSTAL

CH. BANKHOUSE PEARL

CH. ORANSHIRES HIPPOCRATES MISS

CH. WINTERWOOD BLUE SKIES

CH. WINTERWOOD FLOOD AND FIRE

CH. WINTERWOOD HEPZIBAH

CH. WINTERWOOD THE GOOD LIFE

CH. GROPPETTI ELECTRA (8)
(CH. DEER RUN IVAN X CH. DEER RUN GROPPETTI INDA)

CH. BRITE STAR DELMAN'S THUNDER

CH. BRITE STAR TIBERIUS

CH. BRITE STAR'S CASSANDRA

CH. BRITE STAR'S CRYSTAL

CH. BRITE STAR'S OLIVIA

CH. BRITE STAR'S PHOEBE

CH. BRITE STAR'S TITAS

CH. BRITE STAR'S OPUS NO THIRTY

CH. MASTIFF COVE'S RAGING BULL

CH. MASTIFF COVE'S TALK TO ME

CH. MASTIFF COVE'S SOUTHERN GRACE

CH. GROPPETTI BRITE STAR (8)

(CH. GROPPETTI'S BEAUREGAARD X CH. GROPPETTI'S PEGASUS)

CH. BRITE STAR MIRROR IMAGE

CH. BRITE STAR SIR WINSTON

CH. BRITE STAR'S WARLOCK

CH. BRITE STAR'S ZECHARIAH

CH. BRITESTAR LIONSIRES ADDITION

CH. BRITESTAR'S BEARLY GRIZZ

CH. BRITESTAR'S NIGHTIME

CH. GENTRY'S BRITE STAR PANDA

CH. GULPH MILLS MARJORIE, CD (8)
(CH. GULPH MILLS MULCHER X CH. LADY CAMELOT OF HALE, CD)

CH. FOXGLOVE ALL RIGHTS RESERVED

CH. FOXGLOVE AND WHEELERS PRAETORIAN

CH. FOXGLOVE DOUBLE TROUBLE

CH. FOXGLOVE HALES NEW CONTENDER

CH. FOXGLOVE HALES WE'VE A DREAM, CD

CH. FOXGLOVES MOOSE MCGILLY CUDDY

CH. FOXGLOVE POETRY IN MOTION

CH. FOXGLOVE WON'T BE DENIED

CH. OLD SCHOOL'S URSA MAJOR (8)
(DEER RUN FLORISTER RUFUS X OLD SCHOOL'S TROUBLE)

CH. OLD SCHOOLS LORD MAVRICK

CH. OLD SCHOOLS MAJESTIC MAJOR

CH. OLD SCHOOLS MITRA MAJOR

CH. OLD SCHOOLS OSA MAJOR

CH. OLD SCHOOLS PANAMA RED

CH. OLD SCHOOLS PRIMO REMO MAJOR

CH. OLD SCHOOLS SERGEANT MAJOR

CH. VON ROTH'S CAROLINA CASEY

CH. BRANDYDWIND RAGAMUFFIN (7)

DEER RUN SEMPER FI EBONY, CD (7)

CH. GOLDLEAF'S COEUR DE SOL (7)

CH. JAI BEE DIXIE LASS (7)

CH. LEGENDARY FANNIE FLAUNTS IT, CD (7)

CH. MASSALANE'S DINAH-MIGHT (7)

SOUTHPORTS RED ROSE (7)

ALJAC RAZZLING ROXANNE (6)

CH. CHARBE'S GYPSY ROSE (6)

CH. GREENBRANCH DAME WINIFRED (6)

CH. JAI BEE ROCKY HILL TRUDY (6)

MEZA'S ROSEANNE ROSEANN-ADANNA (6)

NIGHT STALKER TRACY (6)

TASHA FARLEY'S FIRST LADY (8)
(WALNUT CREEK'S GRAND DUKE X LADY JENIFER OF E RANCH)

CH. DEER RUN IVAN

CH. DEER RUN JAKE ENCHANTED ACRES

CH. DEER RUN JOSH OF BULL VALLEY

CH. FARLEYS ELEDHWEN STEELSHEEN

CH. IRON HILLS ELBERETH

CH. IRON HILLS MITHRANDIR

CH. LIONSIRE GUINEVERE

CH. WINDAMOHR'S ROCK OF LIONSIRE

CH. BROOKSIDE'S EMILY (7)

DEER RUN SOPHIE (7)

GRECO'S LITTLE MISS MUFFET (7)

CH. KNIGHTSENS SOPHIES CHOICE (7)

CH. LIONSIRES ELLIE OF DEER RUN (7)

SHILOH (7)

CH. ACORN HILL MORGANA PENDRAGON (6)

CH. BRITE STAR'S CRYSTAL (6)

CHRISTIANS BRISTOL CREAM (6)

CH. GULPH MILLS SARAH (6)

MEYERS BUTTONS AND BOWS (6)

NIGHT STALKER ABBY (6)

CH. OZARKS MISTY, CDX (6)

CH. PINEWOODS SOUTHWEST BREEZE (6)

CH. RAVEN OF BLACKROC (6)

ROSE BAY HALLUCINATION (6)

CH. SIDETRACK FARM MIGHTY MAG (6)

CH. SMOK'N LAD STORMY DOMINIC (6)

CH. SOUTHPORTS MAINE DREAM (6)

CH. THORCHELSEAIAS NOEL (6)

WATSON BASSART (6)

CH. APPLE CREEKS SOUTHPORT KAHLUA (5)

CH. ARCINIEGA'S LOLLY VON KILLION (5)

CH. ASGARD'S COPPER PENNY (5)

CH. BANYON'S SHEBA SPICE (5)

CH. BLU RIDGE GOLDLEAF OF BLK PT (5)

CH. BRITE STAR'S APACHE TEARS (5)

CAESAR'S JOVIAL JUNO (5)

CH. CALEDONIA FID C (5)

CH. CASTLE MOUNT LEA DE NANJEMOY (5)

CH. CEE-CEE SHARMAINE (5)

CH. CLEARVIEWS VIRGINIA DARE (5)

CH. DAME SYBIL OF GREENBRANCH (5)

DEER RUN JENNY (5)

DEER RUN STELLA (5)

CH. FARLEY'S ELEDHWEN STEELSHEEN (5)

CH. GULPH MILLS AMY (5)

CH. GULPH MILLS LEGACY (5)

CH. HIX'S SCARLET ALEXIS (5)

CH. I-GUARDS PEACH BLOSSOM (5)

CH. I-GUARDS TINKER BELLE (5)

CH. IRON HILLS EARNED INTEREST (5)

CH. LADY JENNIFER OF HANOVER (5)

LADY LINDSAY OF WYNDEHAVEN (5)

CH. LAMAR'S LITTLE ERICA JILL (5)

MAJESTIC SHEBA OF MAPLEWOOD (5)

CH. MERIWETHER TAJ OF BLACKHAVEN (5)

CH. MEZA'S LIZABETH OF SALEM (5)

MIDDLE-EARTH TOUCH OF CLASS (5)

CH. MONTY'S DIXIE DERBY, CD (5)

NAVONOD'S FULLERTON, CD (5)

CH. NINIANE THE ENCHANTRESS (5)

CH. OAK LAIR'S FANTINE (5)

CH. OAK RIDGE AQUILLA (5)

CH. OLD SCHOOLS MITRA MAJOR (5)

CH. PAX RIVER GENOA (5)

CH. PEERSLEIGH BRIDGEWOOD BLAIR (5)

CH. PEERSLEIGH PRINCESS CAROLYN (5)

CH. RR KR'S LADY DIANA, CD (5)

RUMBLIN EKO'S RAMSGATE ARIANE (5)	SHANNON OF IVEY WOODS (5)
CH. SHEENA OF DAKOTA (5)	CH. SIDETRACKS SASSY SADIE, CD (5)
TALLULAH BIGFOOT (5)	TONY'S TEQUILA SUNRISE (5)
CH. WALNUT CREEK'S GEMINI (5)	CH. WALNUT HILL REMINISCENCE (5)
WILLOWLEDGE POLLYANNA (5)	WINTERWOOD EGLANTINE (5)

Deer Run Jai Bee Cleopatria and son Danté. Sire: Ch. Deer Run Lancaster; Dam: Deer Run Greta; Breeder: Tobin Jackson; Owner: Jerry & Irene Byrne.

Ch. Deer Run Countess Inez. Sire: Ch. Deer Run Wycliff; Dam: Deer Run Jai Bee Cleopatria; Breeder: Jerry & Irene Byrne; Owner: Charles Boyer.

Ch. Lionsire Indigo of Pax River. Sire: Ch. Deer Run Ezekiel; Dam: Christians Bristol Cream; Owner: Mary-Louise Owens.

Ch. Pinewoods One Day at a Thyme. Sire: Ch. Damaria The General; Dam: Ch. Windy Hills Step Aside Girls; Breeder/Owner: Carolyn Hehir.

Considering the fact that these animals do not all live together, here is a statement of Mastiff temperament! From left to right: Arrabelle of Acorn Hill, CD, TDI, Ch. Acorn Hills Ethan, CD, CGC, DD, WD (son), Ch. Acorn Hills Hogan, CDX, CGC, DD, WD (son), Ch. Pendragons WYSIWYG Wuhfgude, CGC (grandson), Ch. Acorn Hills Uther Pendragon, CGC, TDI (son), Ch. Acorn Hills Morgana Pendragon, CGC, TDI (daughter).

Right: Ch. Jai Bee Dixie Lass. Sire: Ch. Deer Run Wycliff; Dam: Deer Run Jai Bee Cleopatria; Breeder/Owner: Jerry & Irene Byrne. Below: Willowledge Meredith at 9 years. Sire: Ch. Griffith's T Geronimo; Dam: Ch. Willowledge Katrina; Breeder: Stuart & Eve Olsen; Owner: Bjorn & dee dee Andersson.

Ch. Groppetti Electra. Sire: Ch. Deer Run Ivan; Dam: Ch. Deer Run Groppetti Inda; Breeder: Alvin & Patty Groppetti; Owner: Lance & Barbara House.

Ch. Groppetti Brite Star. Sire: Ch. Groppetti Beauregaard; Dam: Ch. Groppetti Pegasus; Breeder: Alvin & Patty Groppetti; Owner: Lance & Barbara House. Brite Star is shown here winning the Veteran Bitch Sweepstakes at the 1991 Mastiff Specialty.

Ch. Gulph Mills Majorie, CD. Sire: Ch. Gulph Mills Mulcher; Dam: Ch. Lady Camelot of Hale, CD; Breeder: Mike Gensburger; Owner: Laura & David Hagey.

BISS Ch. Old Schools' Ursa Major. Sire: Deer Run Florister Rufus; Dam: Old School's Trouble; Breeder/ Owner: John & Donna Bahlman.

Ch. Southports Red Rose. Sire: Random Quest; Dam: Tamarack Rustic Lady; Breeder: G. & L. Whitson; Owner: Joe & Carla Sanchez.

Ch. Iron Hills Bet The
Farm. Sire: Ch. Iron Hills
Warwagon; Dam: Ch.
Lionsire Nauti Girl;
Breeder: Diane Tribby &
Scott Phoebus; Owner:
Danny & Susie Farber &
Pam Phoebus.

Above: Ch. Jai Bee Rocky Hill
Trudy. Sire: Ch. Deer Run Wycliff;
Dam: Deer Run Jai Bee Cleopatria;
Breeder/Owner: Jerry & Irene
Byrne. Right: Ch. Southports Maine
Dream. Sire: Ch. Stonebrook
Southports Byron; Dam: Ch.
Southports Red Rose; Breeder/
Owner: Joe & Carla Sanchez.

Left: Ch. Brite Stars Apache Tears. Sire: Ch. Brite Star's Titas; Dam: Ch. Lionsire Kerry of Brite Star; Breeder/Owner: Lance & Barbara House. Above: Ch. Farley's Eledhwen Steelsheen. Sire: Ch. Deer Run Wycliff; Dam: Tasha Farleys First Lady; Breeder: M. & D. Farley; Owner: Scott Phoebus.

Ch. Goldleaf Coeur de Sol. Sire: Ch. Goldleaf Coeur de Lion; Dam: Ch. Greenbranch Molly Malone; Breeder/Owner: Bob Goldblatt. "Gail" is shown winning Brood Bitch at the 1987 Mastiff Specialty with her get. On the left is Ch. Gulph Mills D'Artagnan and on her right is Ch. Goldleaf Montana.

Ch. Hix's Scarlet Alexis. Sire: Quellwater Winston; Dam: Markay's Pecan Sandie; Breeder: Marty & Kathy Otto; Owner: Tim & Vicki Hix.

BISS Ch. Iron Hills Earned Interest. Sire: Ch. Iron Hills Warwagon; Dam: Ch. Britestar Lionsires Addition; Breeder: Scott Phoebus & Diane Tribby; Owner: Julia & Kevin Kriebs & Pam Mosesian.

Ch. Monty's Dixie Derby, CD, TT, TDI, WD. Sire: Monty Son of Jericho; Dam: Deer Run Bourbon Derby; Breeder: Leslie Yeager; Owner: Wennona Brown.

Above: Ch. Niniane The Enchantress. Sire: Sir William of Deer Run; Dam: Ch. Axtell Meyer's Andromeda; Breeder: Kelly & Don Meyer & S.A. Robbins; Owner: Cat Angus. Left: Ch. Oak Ridge Aquila. Sire: Ch. Reveille Lightening; Dam: Ch. Oak Ridge's Queen of Sheba; Breeder: Bill & Judy Powers; Owner: Lynn Urban.

BOSS Ch. Old Schools Mitra
Major. Sire: Ch. Deer Run
Ezekiel; Dam: Ch. Old Schools'
Ursa Major; Breeder/Owner:
John & Donna Bahlman.

Ch. Peersleigh Princess Carolyn.
Sire: Ch. Willowledge Caesar III;
Dam: Peersleigh Lady Lorelei;
Breeder/Owner: Bruce & Jackie
Guy.

Ch. Pinewoods Southwest Breeze.
Sire: Ch. Peersleigh Storm
Sherman; Dam: Ch. Pinewoods
Dandylion of Pern; Breeder/
Owner: Carolyn Hehir.

BISS Ch. Smok'n Lad's Stormy
Dominic. Sire: Ch. Groppetti Sir
Arthur; Dam: Smok'n Lad's
Stormy Bernadette. "Dilly" won
Best of Breed at the 1992 Mastiff
National Specialty.

Right: Ch. Brite Star Crystal. Sire:
Ch. Groppetti Beauregaard; Dam:
Ch. Groppetti Electra; Breeder:
Lance & Barbara House; Owner: L.
& B. House & P. Steele.

CHAPTER 8
THE STANDARD - THEN AND NOW

First and foremost, what is a standard? A standard is the detailed written description of the ideal purebred animal of a particular breed of dog. Standards are written by parent national breed clubs and, following approval of the majority of the breed club membership, standards are submitted to The American Kennel Club (AKC) for approval. Upon acceptance by this body the standard becomes official. Once officially accepted by the breed club membership and the AKC, breeders strive to breed animals that are as close to the standard of perfection as possible, and dog show judges evaluate animals based on the written standard. Those animals that conform most closely to the written standard are considered the best specimens of the breed.

Greiner Hall Falcon. Sire: Greiner Hall Zechariah; Dam: Greiner Hall Raven Noblehall. This Mastiff has exquisite type. Although he is 32 inches at the shoulder, he gives the impression of not being that tall because of the optical illusion caused by his heavy substance, depth and width. Based on this picture, the only fault would be the lack of pigment on the ears—note that they are brindled rather than black.

Long before the advent of dog shows in Europe, the Mastiff (or dogs of true Mastiff type) existed and, as discussed in ancient history, they were being written about and described in early versions of standards. Hugh Dalziel in *British Dogs* (1880) said: "The great evil to be guarded against is that the standard should not be varied at the caprice of judges or societies, whose position gives them an adventitious influence in forming public taste and opinion."

The Mastiff was described in 1800 by Frank Adcock, Esq., a respected bulldog breeder: "Of a very powerful make, twenty-eight to thirty inches high, broad chest, head large, lips pendulous and thick ears small and hanging down, coat short and smooth, color all tanned or brindle, with a black muzzle, a dark spot over each eye, and these colors varied with white. I have examined several, and I have found them invariably a little underhung, the lower jaw beyond the upper."

Seventy-three years later, J. W. Thompson, an early breeder of Mastiffs, put many of his convictions of what constituted a Mastiff to paper. If this gentleman were alive today, I am convinced he would breed Mastiffs that would command ring attention. He had a real knack for describing a Mastiff with what we, in modern days, call balance.

BISS Ch. Matts Joshua-Dogwood Knoll. Sire: Ch. Burns Hall Zackery; Dam: Ch. Burns Hall Nicole.

Thompson did not care for tall, leggy Mastiffs, despite their popularity with some judges. He wanted substance, coat and good head over long heads or legs and light bodies. He was an advocate of proportion and good gait. He wrote that "if you can obtain great size without sacrificing stamina, courage, activity, and a well balanced proportionate head, you are right, but if you realize great size at the expense of these attributes, you are wrong." He pointed out deformity, deficiency of muscular power, narrow muzzles and poor heads needed to be eradicated. He knew Mastiffs and described the same dog most of us breed for today. He said:

> The breeder will do well to mark and sustain the
> ample forehead, the full prominent cheeks, small ears,
> the thick broad muzzle and pendulous lips, nor should

he forget to note the stout muscular legs and thighs, the brawny shoulders, deep and massive frame, and short glossy coat. I have no doubt by judicious care in breeding it is possible to produce a Mastiff large in size, massive in build, strikingly grand in head, the muscles hard and sharply developed, and the skin nearly approaching in quality the beautiful coat of the greyhound. I have a strong predilection for quality and select breeding.

M. B. Wynn wrote a detailed standard in his 1886 book that differs little in concept compared to today's standard. His ideal standard allowed for, and indeed, asked for the undershot bite; dewclaws were permissible; height at the shoulder of dogs was 27 inches and bitches 24 inches; colors considered equal for purity were fawn, good brindle and all blacks, reds, blue brindles and pieds. With a 100-point scale, he gave 40 points to the head, 40 to the body, 10 to size, general appearance of massiveness and 5 points each to coat and color. Wynn said that "vast dogs long on the legs, somewhat light in bone for their size, are not in reality Mastiffs, whatever their owners may think." Prophetic words, in 1886 or in 1996.

Castle Mount Godzilla. Sire: Ch. Groppetti Sir Arthur; Dam: Ch. Castle Mounts Lea de Nanjemoy.

The AKC approved a standard July 8, 1941, that governed the breed over the next 50 years. This ideal used a 100-point scale, allotting 32 points to the head, 53 to the body, 10 to character and symmetry and 5 to coat and color. On July 14, 1981, gait was added to the standard although the scale of points remained unchanged. This seemingly innocent addition was to have far-reaching consequences. Judges were finally able to evaluate Mastiffs on head, structure, substance, color, temperament and movement. Breeders began to strive to produce Mastiffs that could move. Where before a Mastiff could win breed almost on a head alone, if the head was affixed to an unsound body the Mastiff was overlooked in Group. It took only a few years to make a big difference.

A standard revision December 31, 1991, brought it into compliance with how other breed standards are written: The Mastiff is a large, massive, symmetrical dog with a well-knit frame. The impression is one of grandeur and dignity. Dogs are more massive throughout. Bitches should not be faulted for being somewhat smaller in all dimensions while maintaining a proportionally powerful structure. A good evaluation considers positive qualities of type and soundness with equal weight. Dogs are to be a minimum 30 inches at the shoulder and bitches are to be a minimum 27-1/2 inches at the shoulder. Dogs or bitches below the minimum standard should be faulted. The farther below standard, the greater the fault.

Ch. Deer Run Ivan. Sire: Ch. Deer Run Wycliff; Dam: Tasha Farley's First Lady.

In proportion, the dog is rectangular, the length of the dog from forechest to rump is somewhat longer than the height at the withers. The height of the dog should come from depth of body rather than length of leg. The Mastiff is massive, heavy boned and with a powerful muscle structure. Great depth and breadth is desirable. Lack of substance or slab sided is a fault.

In general outline, the head gives a massive appearance when viewed from any angle. Breadth greatly desired. Eyes are set wide apart, medium in size and never too prominent. The expression is alert but kindly. The color of eyes is brown—the darker the better

Head and Jaws of the Mastiff
Artwork by James O. Fietsam

Too undershot.

*Overdone, too much wrinkle,
neck too wet.*

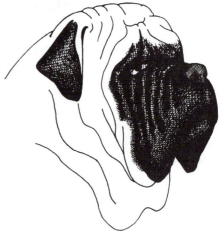

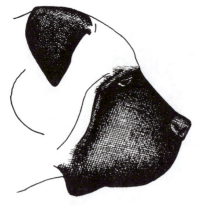

Untypical head: plain, no wrinkle, no stop, muzzle too long.

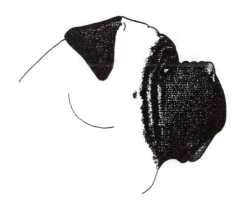

Muzzle too short.

"Round" prominent eyes showing "haw."

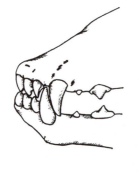

Level bite—desired.

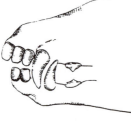

Overshot.

Slightly undershot.

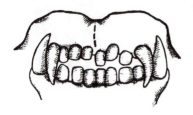

Teeth out of alignment.

and showing no haw. Light eyes or a predatory expression is undesirable. Ears are small in proportion to the skull, V-shaped, rounded at the tips, the leather moderately thin, set widely apart at the highest points on the sides of the skull continuing the outline across the summit. They should lie close to the cheeks when in repose. The ears are dark in color—the blacker the better, conforming to the color of the muzzle. The skull is broad and somewhat flattened between the ears; the forehead slightly curved, showing marked wrinkles that are particularly distinctive when at attention. The brows (superciliary ridges) are moderately raised. Muscles of the temples are well developed, those of the cheeks extremely powerful. The arch across the skull is a flattened curve with a furrow up the center of the forehead. This extends from between the eyes to halfway up the skull. The stop between the eyes is well marked but not too abrupt. The muzzle should be half the length of the skull, thus dividing the head into three parts—one for the foreface and two for the skull. In other words, the distance from the tip of the nose to stop is equal to one-half the distance between the stop and the occiput. Circumference of the muzzle (measured midway between the eyes and nose) to that of the head (measured before the ears) is a 3 to 5.

Ch. Avalon's Lord Cearbhallain, CD.
(Ch. Iron Hills Warwagon X Ch. Ninane
The Enchantress)

The muzzle should be short, broad under the eyes and running nearly equal in width to the end of the nose. It is truncated, i.e. blunt and cut off square, thus forming a right angle with the upper line of the face and of great depth from the point of the nose to the underjaw. The underjaw is broad to the end and slightly rounded. The muzzle is dark in color—the blacker the better. Snipiness of the muzzle is a fault. The nose is broad and always dark in color, the blacker the better, with spread flat nostrils (not pointed or turned up) in profile. The lips diverge at obtuse angles with the septum and sufficiently pendulous so as to show a modified square profile. Canine teeth are healthy and wide apart. The jaws are powerful. Scissors bite is preferred, but a moderately undershot jaw should not be faulted providing the teeth are not visible when the mouth is closed.

The neck is powerful, very muscular, slightly arched, and of medium length. The neck gradually increases in circumference as it approaches the shoulder. The neck is moderately "dry" (not showing an excess of loose skin). In profile, the topline should be straight, level and firm, not swaybacked, roached, or dropping off sharply behind the high point of the rump. The chest is wide, deep, rounded, and well let-down between the forelegs, extending at least

Am. Can. Ch. Genghis Khan of Swainmote. Sire: Caledonia MacGregory Dawg; Dam: Brandywines Sally.

to the elbow. The forechest should be deep and well defined with the breastbone extending in front of the foremost point of the shoulders. The ribs are well rounded. False ribs are deep and well set back. There should be a reasonable, but not exaggerated, tuck-up. The back is muscular, powerful, and straight. When viewed from the rear, there should be a slight rounding over the rump. Loins are wide and muscular. The tail is set on moderately high and reaching to the hocks or a little below; it is wide at the root, tapering to the end, hanging straight in repose, forming a slight curve, but never over the back when the dog is in motion. The shoulders are moderately sloping, powerful and muscular, with no tendency to looseness. Degree of front angulation is to match correct rear angulation. Legs are straight, strong and set wide apart, heavy boned.

The elbows are parallel to body. Pasterns are strong and bent only slightly. The feet are large, round, and compact with well-arched toes. Black nails are preferred. Hindquarters are broad, wide and muscular. Second thighs are well developed, leading to a strong hock joint. The stifle joint is moderately angulated matching the front. Rear legs are wide apart and parallel when viewed from the rear. When the portion of the leg below the hock is correctly "set back" and stands perpendicular to the ground, a plumb line dropped from the rearmost point of the hindquarters will pass in front of the foot. This rules out straight hocks, and since stifle angulation varies with hock angulation, it also rules out insufficiently angulated stifles. Straight stifles are a fault.

The outer coat is straight, coarse, and of moderately short length. The undercoat is dense, short and close lying. The coat should not be so long as to produce "fringe" on the belly, tail or hind

Applewhaite's Adam, CD. Sire: Ch. Storm Ta-Tanka O'Applewhaites; Dam: Applewhaite's Skya.

legs. The coat is long or wavy—fawn, apricot, or brindle in color. Brindle should have fawn or apricot as a background color which should be completely covered with very dark stripes. Muzzle, ears, and nose must be dark in color, the blacker the better, with similar color tone around the eye orbits and extending upward between them. A small patch of white on the chest is permitted. Excessive white on the chest or white on any other part of the body is a fault. Mask, ears, or nose lacking dark pigment is a fault.

The gait denotes power and strength. The rear legs should have drive, while the forelegs should track smoothly with good reach. In motion, the legs move straight forward; as the dog's speed increases from a walk to a trot, the feet move in toward the center line of the body to maintain balance.

Body of the Mastiff
Artwork by James O. Fietsam

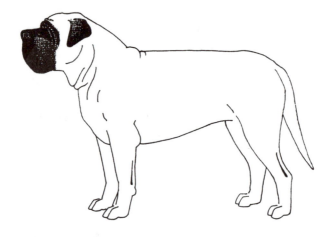

Correct.

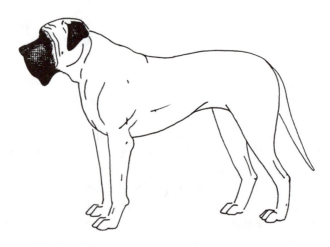

Too much tuck-up. Not enough depth of body.

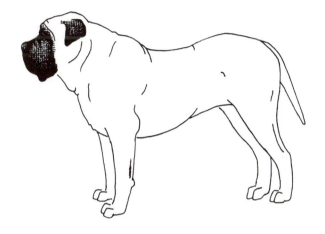

High in the rear, tail too short.

Short-coupled.

Correct upper arm and shoulder.   *Shoulder too straight.*

Correct front.

Incorrect front: too narrow and feet east/west.

Incorrect front: feet toe in, elbows incorrect.

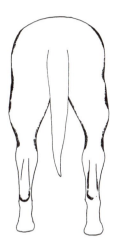

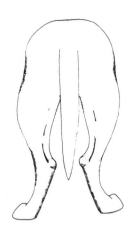

Correct hindquarters, set squarely.

Incorrect rear, cow-hocked.

Not enough bend of stifle.
Low tail set.

Moderate bend of stifle.
Correct tail set.

Ch. Foxglove Singular Sensation. Sire: Ch. Meza's Hulk Hogan; Dam: Ch. Gulph Mills Foxglove Savanah, CD. Note the high tail set and width of this bitch's second thighs.

The temperament should be a combination of grandeur and good nature, courage and docility. Dignity, rather than gaiety, is the Mastiff's correct demeanor. Judges should not condone shyness or viciousness. Conversely, judges should also beware of putting a premium on showiness.

When the standard was altered in 1991, the Mastiff Club clarified some of the points. In the 1980s, many short-coupled Mastiffs were seen. Hereditarily, Mastiffs are long backed. This trait always distinguished Mastiffs from Bullmastiffs. The standard now calls for the Mastiff to be rectangular. Femininity of bitches is now recognized, stating they should not be faulted for being somewhat smaller overall than dogs. There are still no disqualifications, but faults are more stressed. I am more forgiving of a fault historical in the breed than a fault new to the breed. Anyone wanting to know where today's faults come from needs only review pictures of yesterday's dogs. Earlier Mastiffs show poor toplines, soft in the middle or hind quarters higher than the front, often due to poor bend of stifle. Anything other than a straight topline is a fault, but I prefer the old fault known in the breed to a newer fault in which the topline slopes downward from the withers towards the back such as is called for in German Shepherds.

In 1880, Dalziel described faults he saw:

> First, I think, the ungainliness of motion caused by weak legs, particularly shown in the knee joints and the development of cow hocks; with this there is generally flat, lean, wasted

Right: Ch. Greiner Hall Chadwick. Sire: Hollesley Lord Ralegh; Dam: Tamarack Zada of Greiner hall. Below: BIS/BISS Ch. Old Schools Primo Remo Major. Sire: Ch. Deer Run Ezekiel; Dam: Ch. Old Schools' Ursa Major.

Ch. Storm Hammer of Royal Oak. Sire: Storm Gruffudd of Royal Oak; Dam: Storm Gwyneira of Royal Oak. This is a Mastiff moving with purpose, reaching and driving.

Above: Ch. Acorn Hills Ethan, CD. Sire: Ch. Iron Hills Warwagon; Dam: Arrabelle of Acorn Hill. Right: Ch. Iron Hills Spill The Wine. Sire: Ch. Iron Hills Warwagon; Dam: Ch. Lionsire Indigo of Pax River.

hams, and sometimes light, weak loins, and all these or the cow hocks alone give a shambling gait that is most objectionable. These defects are often caused by bad rearing, inferior or insufficient food, want of room or dampness in the kennel. The faults alluded to are very common, and it should be the endeavor of breeders and also of judges to get rid of them—the latter by refusing prizes to all dogs that show the faults, and the former by judicious selection and careful rearing.

The greatest fault I see in the breed today is too many champions that lack breed type. They are not what the standard describes; many males are too bitchy and many bitches are too refined; there is not enough to them, they lack size and have insufficient bone and substance. It is imperative we keep our breed type, over and above all else, or the day will arrive when they no longer resemble Mastiffs. How sad to see a Mastiff that can be mistaken for a Bullmastiff because the Mastiff is too small or a Mastiff that stands level with a Dane, but the Mastiff is without enough substance to qualify as massive. Mastiffs should stand apart from these breeds and there should never be doubt in anyone's mind what breed the animal represents.

Faults still seen are poor toplines, straight shoulders and straight stifles, not necessarily matching in the same animal, popping hocks, cow hocks, east/west fronts, overloaded shoulders, elbows set out from the body and too many low-set tails. Poor toplines often result from lack of angulation. When the dog is too straight behind and his legs placed well under the body, it pushes the rear higher than the front. If the animal is over angulated, the rear may be elevated too high unless the dog is deliberately placed with the rear legs set well back, thus bringing the topline down and level. Mastiffs are meant to have moderate angulation. Either extreme, too straight or too much bend of stifle, is incorrect and makes the Mastiff vulnerable to knee injuries.

There is still confusion about what constitutes correct movement. A number of Mastiffs have a very flashy movement; it is pretty to watch and is being consistently rewarded in the show ring. The animals almost appear to be "dancing" happily around the ring. Indeed, this movement may be eye catching, and it certainly demonstrates a showy attitude, but it is also incorrect movement. These animals are not reaching in front or driving behind, as called for in the standard. A Mastiff should give an impression of strength, power and determination when moving at a full-out gait. No Mastiff worth his name and weight ever danced towards an intruder or pranced after a deer and he did not shamble along after them. They moved with great force, the front reached, the rear drove and the earth trembled.

The most glaring fault lingering in the breed continues to be poor heads. I feel qualified to discuss this as I had to battle in my own breeding program to lose the snipey muzzle and narrow skull, caused by recessive genes that crop up unexpectedly. We actually nicknamed one of our Mastiffs "hose nose." There are still too many snipey heads as well as a few "Bullmastiffy" heads. Some Mastiffs are so overdone with wrinkle I defy anyone to know if they are at attention. From a breeder's perspective, the overdone head may be excellent in an appropriate breeding program—to get more head in the offspring—but in the show ring it should not be rewarded. Throughout this chapter Mastiff heads are shown and I daresay no judge would mistake these animals for any other breed. Breeders need to continue efforts to improve heads on breeding stock and judges could assist our breed by not rewarding incorrect types. In recent years, we have had animals that, despite incorrect head types, were impressive winners in the show ring, unfortunately leading newcomers to the breed to think those head types are what should be strived for when breeding. If you study other breeds at shows, you cannot help but be struck by the consistency of head types. Watch a Mastiff ring and you will note many different head types. As we are all breeding to the same standard, at the very least, the animals should appear to be members of the same breed. Our work as breeders is assuredly not done.

Another misconception in the breed is appropriate size. All things being equal, the larger dog should be favored over the smaller dog. Throughout the standard, words such as massive, wide and deep are used. Height is mentioned only to provide minimums for dogs and bitches and to say it should come from depth of body rather than length of leg. This is incredibly important. It means the taller Mastiff, lacking in other substance qualities, is to be faulted. What sets the Mastiff apart from other breeds is the overwhelming appearance of power. Every Mastiff should give an impression of physical strength and athletic ability. Mastiffs are not supposed to stand in a doorway and reach the top, they should fill the doorway. They were never meant to be tall, refined or elegant. They were guardians, baiting and war dogs.

One hundred years ago, Mastiffs were deliberately mutilated to prevent them from killing forest game. Because such a repulsive thing was done to them, we must assume they were capable of killing the beasts in the first place. They must have been athletic. Mastiffs today should still be capable of such athletic feats even if they are domesticated to the extent they no longer perform such actions. Old literature repeatedly tells us of Mastiffs baiting lions, bears and bulls. To have done this they had endurance, courage, were brave of heart and were very muscular and strong. The standard does not compromise, it still describes the same type of animal today.

Mastiff feet should be large, round and compact with well-arched toes. There are too many Mastiffs with splayed feet, and long, flat toes. If the foundation is weak, what does it say about the rest of the structure? Those feet must carry awesome weight for many years and they need to be up to the task or the whole dog will suffer.

I guarantee those knights in former times did not carry the Mastiff up on horseback to get to the site where there was to be a battle. The Mastiff had to run alongside the horse the whole way and then have the energy to fight when he arrived. The Mastiff was not pretty, he was not built for speed, nor was he a sight hound. He was built for endurance, economy of movement, sheer strength, great courage and heart. The Mastiffs today should retain these same characteristics.

Traditionally, a Mastiff would use its body to bring down its target, then grab and hold. Today, a goodly number would be unable to heave their bodies in the air to bring down a victim. They are too weak behind and out of condition.

The undershot mouth helped Mastiffs to hold without ripping or tearing. In former days, the undershot bite was cultivated in the breed as a very desirable trait. A scissors bite is unquestionably more attractive to judges, but I wonder if it is fully appreciated how difficult it is to obtain the broad, truncated muzzle the standard calls for combined with a scissors bite? It will most likely not be politic for me to say I consider the bite to be a purely cosmetic feature. It is wrong to fault an otherwise excellent Mastiff for being undershot, particularly as the bite is an inherent feature in the breed. Although breeders do want to improve bites, the task is thankless since the recessive undershot keeps showing up with predictable regularity. The breed would have greater benefit if we breeders concentrate our efforts on improving structure. It would also help if judges would not condemn Mastiffs based on an acceptable inherent trait.

Ch. Banyon Swainmote Murphy Brown. Sire: Ch. Lionsire Grizz; Dam: Banyon's Amelia Bedelia. Note the kindly and tolerant expression on the face of Murphy while being examined by the judge.

The standard finally addresses Mastiff temperament in greater detail. Although judges are now advised not to place a premium on showiness, I cannot see that such instruction has made a whit of difference in the show ring. As I stated in the temperament portion of the book, the Mastiff is not supposed to be a social butterfly. The Mastiff is not trained to be a guard dog. This is his legacy. He is born to be a guardian. Guard dogs do not slobber all over strangers with friendliness and, if they do, they do not possess the proper temperament of the breed, regardless how pleasing and delightful such a disposition may be to one and all. The Mastiff should be dignified rather than gay. Mastiffs in the show ring continue to be faulted inasmuch as the animal that shows excessive animation will generally get more favorable attention than one who stands quietly accepting but not necessarily enjoying the attention. Mastiffs are good and obedient animals and, to please their masters, they can become great show dogs. In truth, every time a Mastiff is set up to be examined by a stranger, the judge, the animal is being asked to submit to a circumstance somewhat foreign to his true nature. I cannot help but believe, in the mind of the Mastiff, he is probably thinking he should be examining the judge—for this would be more in line with his inherent duty!

CHAPTER 9
MASTIFFS IN THE SHOW RING

Some people believe dog shows are only beauty contests so the first thing I want to debunk is why we show in conformation classes. Showing dogs is a sport, and humans, since the beginning of time, have enjoyed different types of competition. We show our dogs as a sport. In the course of showing, we develop friendships that last a lifetime. Many breeders attend shows and exhibit to be in the company of persons who share the same interest—the hobby of dogs. Breed specialty shows, in particular, are occasions when we gather to renew and develop new friendships, often the one time a year when friends can meet each other and see the newest crop of puppies, in Sweepstakes and Futurities.

There are lots of other motivations for showing. Breeders exhibit their best animals to prove the animals are good enough to win over quality competition under respected judges. They want to prove the animals are good representatives of the breed. Breeders try to justify the animals being included in a breeding program. When the animals are bred, it is hoped they will produce quality progeny to carry forward the good qualities to future generations. Just because an animal is a champion does not necessarily mean he will produce better, or even good, progeny. But it is a starting place and it shows the breeder had enough faith in his own breeding program to invest the time and money required to show.

Many animals earn championships and never show again. Not all animals enjoy showing, and this is especially true with Mastiffs. Remember our standard which tells judges that "a premium should not be placed on showiness?" I am personally familiar with this characteristic—at each end of the spectrum. I bred a bitch who finished in a week and won BOS at a Specialty. She was born to show, she adored the attention she got. I own her great-great-great granddaughter, an exceptionally beautiful bitch, and showing her was not only perceived as punishment by her, it was equally painful for me. I finally made a deal with this bitch that if she would just go in the ring, stand still and let herself be examined in order to earn her championship, I would never take her to another show. She did, and I will not. The moral to this story is that here is a bitch who is a beautiful specimen, but she does not have it in her to be a show animal. She hated every minute on display to the public.

Luckily for the breed, now and then an animal of such exceptional quality is produced, combined with an outgoing temperament and winning personality, that the specimen clearly stands out from all the rest and practically begs to be shown. When this occurs, provided the owner enjoys competition and is willing to support the endeavor financially and emotionally, such an animal will embark on a show career.

For those of you unfamiliar with show language, "special" is the slang terminology used to refer to a champion who is being campaigned on a more-or-less regular basis with the goal of becoming the Number 1 show contender in his/her breed. Based on the number of dogs and bitches competed against and won over, his/her position in the rankings is determined. Hence, the higher the number of animals in competition, the greater the points accrued by the winner in Best of Opposite Sex, Best of Breed, in Group and in Best In Show.

As each show animal collects a record of wins, or points, so does he collect fans and supporters. Unfortunately, at the same time, top show animals collect critics. It is the critics I wish to address. It is easy to criticize owners and animals who are in the spotlight. The fact they are in the spotlight draws our attention to them so they become the subject of discussions. Campaigning an animal in today's world is a very expensive venture not only in terms of money, but also in the time taken away from families, employment or other interests. People who commit to campaigning a special deserve a lot of praise and support from every breeder of the same type of animal being shown. They do not deserve our derision. They do not deserve to have their animals ridiculed by their peers. If you have a better animal than the one being shown, put yours out there and compete in the only place it counts—the show ring. Otherwise, be a good sport and back the winning dog who is representing every single animal of the same breed.

Not so long ago Mastiffs were overlooked in group in favor of showier, more eloquent, better-moving breeds. The situation improved only due to the dedication of owners and breeders who changed things. I remember when whichever Mastiff won breed was taken home when judging was done, skipping group competition. When I asked why a dog was absent, I was told, with a very self-defeating attitude, there was no sense showing as Mastiffs are overlooked. I made a commitment when I campaigned Sherman that every time he qualified he would go in group, win or lose. It was uphill all the way. I felt then, and still feel, it is insulting to the judge who awards breed and to the judge left waiting in group to walk away.

Unfortunately for my poor Sherman, he regularly competed against the great Bullmastiff, Waldo, and the incomparable Dane, Special K. Sherman probably still holds the record for Group 5. Even so, he managed to get a few placements and helped pave the way for Mastiffs that followed. Thor came along and quickly garnered an unprecedented eight group placements. Remo showed up and won a prestigious BIS, followed by William's nine BIS achievement. Next came Tyson, followed by Jackson who bested Willie's record. We have two Mastiffs right now, Butler in the East and Otis in the West, who are BISS and BIS winners.

What needs to be recognized is that without the dedication and perseverance of the owners of these great show dogs, Mastiffs would have stayed behind in the dark ages. Instead of nitpicking because you may not like a certain champion, think about what the dog accomplished not only for himself, but for the breed. Mastiffs being shown might not be the ones you would select for your own breeding program, that is a personal decision, but they deserve our support, our praise and our gratitude because they are opening doors for future Mastiffs (which might be our own) and they are breaking new ground. My own opinion is there are no bad Mastiffs and there are no bad show dogs. There is neither room nor appropriateness for petty jealousies and envy. We owe breeders, owners, handlers and, most especially, the show animals our admiration, support and respect. Next time you lose in the breed, try to stay around for group and cheer on the Mastiff of the day. It will make you feel good to support your breed.

In 1939, Boyce of Altnacraig won Group 4 and, to my knowledge, no Mastiff placed in group again until 1955 when Marie Moore's Ch. Meps Berenice won Group 4. In 1959, Marie's Ch.

Mooreleigh Moby Dick won Group 3 and Group 4. In 1963, a Mastiff won Group 4; in 1964 two Mastiffs won, Group 3 and Group 4, respectively. In 1965, a Mastiff won Group 4. Ten years later, in 1975, circumstances had not improved much when a Mastiff was honored with Group 3. Two very significant things occurred: In 1981 gait was added to the standard, and in 1983, some 15 breeds were removed from Working and put in Herding.

In 1985, Mastiffs won 43 group placements, of which total four won the Working Group and a total of 7,749 all-breed dogs were defeated by Mastiffs. By 1995, the Mastiff had arrived! They had a long way to come and they made it. Today, the Mastiff can no longer be ignored in the Working Group. **They can compete!** Our beautifully headed, longer bodied, powerfully moving, ground-covering Mastiffs won 172 group placements in 1995. The Group was won 22 times by Mastiffs and 32,748 all-breed dogs were beaten by Mastiffs, not including additional dogs defeated when Mastiffs went Best In Show three times. Not only has the breed got a Best in Show bitch to its credit, for the first time in the history of the breed, a brindle dog won Best in Show.

The following pages contain pictures of some of the great Mastiff show dogs.

Ch. Foxglove Seize the Moment. Sire: Ch. Beowulf of Wheeler's Knoll, CD; Dam: Ch. Foxglove Singular Sensation; Breeder: L. & D. Hagey & S. Fox; Owner: Laura & David Hagey. "Ivy" won Best of Winners, Award of Merit, and was the Grand Futurity Winner at the 1995 Mastiff Specialty.

Ch. Mastiff Cove Tullysu V Himmel. Sire: Ch. Semper Fi Groppetti Gargoyle; Dam: Ch. Burdette's Sweet Maggie May; Breeder: Mark & Delwin Burdette; Owner: Karen Karably.

Ch. Axtell Meyer's Andromeda. Sire: Ch. Oak Ridges Janus; Dam: Ch. Peersleigh Bridgewood Blair; Breeder: Susan Axtell Robbins; Owner: Kelly Meyer & Susan Robbins.

Ch. Meyer's Aurora. Sire: Ch. Manatee of Axtell's Pride; Dam: Ch. Meyer's Medusa; Breeder/ Owner: Kelly & Don Meyer.

BISS Ch. Old Schools' Ursa Major. Sire: Deer Run Florister Rufus; Dam: Old School's Trouble; Breeder/Owner: John & Donna Bahlman. Ursa won BISS at the 1983 Mastiff Specialty, the first Independent Specialty Show—and she was owner/handled.

BIS & BISS Ch. Ridgewood Otis. Sire: Ch. Iron Hills Orpheus; Dam: Kayla Bradee; Breeder: Brian Moegling & Scott Barclay; Owner: Joe & Carla Sanchez. Otis has two All-Breed BIS wins and he is the only Mastiff ever to win BIS on the West Coast. He was No. 1 Breed and No. 3 Group Mastiff in 1995, Top Mastiff All Categories 1996, and he won BISS at the 1996 Mastiff Specialty.

BOSS Ch. Royal Oaks Celtic Maggie T. Sire: Storm Gruffudd of Royal Oak; Dam: Ch. Royal Oaks Celtic Mercedes; Breeder/Owner: Barb & Keith Avise & Carol Mathews. Maggie was owner/handled to win Best of Opposite Sex at the 1991 Mastiff Specialty.

Ch. Southports Prime Time. Sire: Ch. Iron Hills Warwagon; Dam: Ch. Southports Bailey Quarters; Breeder/Owner: Joe & Carla Sanchez. "Pete" was No. 13 Breed Dog 1992, No. 2 Breed & No. 4 Group 1994. He won Awards of Merit at three Mastiff Specialties.

BIS & BISS Ch. Iron Hills Into The Night is the only brindle Mastiff ever to win All-Breed Best In Shows.

Ch. Gulph Mills Moonshine. Sire: Ch. Goldleaf Montana; Dam: Ch. Gulph Mills Legacy; Breeder: Michael Gensburger; Owner: Bob Goldblatt. Moonshine was #3 Mastiff in 1994.

BIS & BOSS Ch. Pinehollow Caledonia Jackson. Sire: Ch. Pinehollows War Gator; Dam: Caledonia Cameron Pinehollow; Breeder: Nancy Hempel & Susie Farber; Owner: Nancy Hempel. Jackson holds the record as the All Time Top Winning Mastiff in the history of Mastiff's with 10 All-Breed BIS wins. He was No. 1 Breed and No. 2 Group Mastiff 1993, Top Mastiff All Categories 1994, No. 1 Breed and No. 1 Group 1995, and ranked in Top 10 Working Dogs and No. 6 Group Mastiff 1996.

BIS & BISS Ch. Iron Hills Into The Night. Sire: Ch. Iron Hills Paint Your Wagon; Dam: Kara Stonehage; Breeder: Scott Phoebus; Owner: M. & G. Capelle. "Butler" has two All-Breed BIS wins and he is the only brindle Mastiff to ever win BIS. He was No. 7 Breed Dog and No. 2 Group Mastiff 1996, and he won BISS at the 1997 Mastiff Specialty.

BIS & BISS Ch. Ridgewoods Otis is the only Mastiff to ever win BISs on the West Coast. Owners: Joe & Carla Sanchez.

Ch. Deer Run Groppetti Fawn Loni. Sire: Ch. Deer Run Wycliff; Dam: Deer Run Sophie; Breeder: Laila Stellman; Owner: Patty Groppetti.

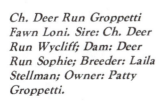

Ch. Avalon's Tucson Warrior. Sire: Ch. Iron Hills Warwagon; Dam: Ch. Niniane The Enchantress; Breeder: Cat Angus; Owner: Randy Harper. Tucson was No. 7 Group Dog 1992, No. 8 Breed Dog and No. 7 Group Dog 1993, No. 6 Breed Dog and No. 7 Group Dog 1994, No. 4 Breed Dog and No. 9 Group Dog 1995, No. 4 and No. 13 Group Dog 1996 and he is an Award of Merit Mastiff Specialty Winner.

Ch. Greiner Hall Jedadiah. Sire: Ch. Greiner Hall Chadwick; Dam: Greiner Hall Isnor; Breeder: Stephen & Leah Napotnik. Jed was No. 5 Breed Dog and No. 14 Group Dog 1992, No. 2 Breed Dog and No. 4 Group 1993, No. 4 Breed and No. 3 Group 1994, No. 8 Breed dog and No. 7 Group Dog in 1995.

BISS Ch. I-Guards T & T's Magic Moment. Sire: Ch. Lionsire Cantankerous Earl; Dam: Ch. I. Guards Tinker Belle; Breeder/ Owner: Sandra Wells. This Mastiff was No. 1 Breed, No. 3 Group, No. 4 Best of Opposite Sex Bitch 1995 and No. 8 Group Bitch 1996.

BOSS Ch. Southports Iron Maiden. Sire: Ch. Iron Hills Warwagon; Dam: Ch. Southports Bailey Quarters; Breeder/Owner: Joe & Carla Sanchez. "Maddie" is the All Time Top Winning Mastiff Bitch in Breed Points, No. 2 Breed Bitch, No. 3 Best of Opposite Sex Bitch and No. 1 Group Bitch 1992, No. 1 Breed Bitch, No. 2 Best of Opposite Sex Bitch and No. 2 Group Bitch 1993. She won an Award of Merit at the 1992 Mastiff Specialty and BOSS at the 1993 Mastiff Specialty.

Ch. Mystic Duke of Wellington. Sire: Ch. Southports Richelieu The Red; Dam: Ch. Stablemates Lady Scarlett; Breeder/Owner: Bob & Catherine Huling. "Wellie" was No. 4 Breed Dog 1993, No. 5 Breed and No. 17 Group Dog 1994 and No. 14 Breed Dog 1995—and he was always owner/handled.

Above: Am. Can. Int. Ch. Coltons Beauregard. Sire: Ch. Deer Run Sinder; Dam: Barnes Sweetpea Kirk; Breeder: Nancy Barnes; Owner: Tamara & David Kuhn. Colton was No. 12 Breed Dog and No. 4 Group Dog 1993, No. 9 Breed Dog and No. 10 Group Dog 1994, No. 3 Breed Dog and No. 6 Group Dog 1995, No. 11 Group Dog 1996 and he won BIS Veteran twice in addition to having the distinction of being the top-pointed Mastiff in CKC history, as well as winning BISS at the 1995 Canadian Mastiff Specialty—and he is always owner handled. Left: Ch. Obstagartens Lilly of Lamars. Sire: Ch. Viceroys M Cromwell of Kent; Dam: Ch. Lamars Little Erica Jill; Breeder: Margo Lauritsen; Owner: Deanna Warkentin & Margo Lauritsen.

Ch. Blu Ridge Goldleaf of Blk Pt. Sire: Ch. Goldleaf Montana; Dam: Ch. Southports Jez of Blu Ridge; Breeder: Sheldon & Susan Giventer. "Daisy" is shown here with her three owners (left to right: Joe Chambart, Diane Collings and Bob Goldblatt). This gorgeous bitch earned her championship at 9 months of age and went on to be the #1 Mastiff Bitch in 1991 and 1992 and #2 Mastiff in 1992.

Ch. Acorn Hills Silent Knight. Sire: Ch. Acorn Hill Uther Pendragon; Dam: Ch. Lionsire Indigo of Pax River; Breeder/Handler: Mary-Louise Owens. He is shown here winning Best of Breed at the Bucks County KC Supported Entry.

Ch. Peersleigh Storm Sherman telling his best buddy and handler, Mike Bowser, I won Breed, now gimme a hug!

Ch. Storm Ta-Tanka O'Applewhaites. Sire: Ch. Peersleigh Storm Sherman; Dam: Loxley Storm Druidess; Breeder: Bjorn & dee dee Andersson; Owner: Dennis & Laura Sullivan.

Ch. Autumn River's Big Ben. Sire: Lazy Hill Luath; Dam: Ch. Lazy Hill Athena; Breeder: Ginny Bregman; Owner: Bonnie Korn. Ben is shown winning Best of Breed at the Mastiff Supported Bucks County KC Show under English Breeder/ Judge Douglas Oliff. Ben also won an Award of Merit under English Breeder/Judge Richard Thomas at a Mastiff National Specialty—note the depth of body and substance of this animal as well as the beautiful breed type, plus a hard topline.

BOSS Ch. Falmorehall Mistral of Deer Run. Sire: Eng. Ch. Hollesley Medicine Man; Dam: Farnaby Fighting Faith Falmore Hall; Breeder: Sarah Windham; Owner: Tobin Jackson. The imported Mistral won Best of Opposite Sex at the 1986 Mastiff Specialty.

BOSS Ch. Storm Babe of Lazy Hill. Sire: Lazy Hill Luath; Dam: Willowledge Meredith; Breeder: Bjorn & dee dee Andersson; Owner: dee dee Andersson & K. & T. Outten. Baby became a champion in one week and won Best of Opposite Sex at the 1985 Mastiff Specialty.

Ch. Pinewoods Cover Girl. Sire: Ch. His Majesty's Lion of Judah; Dam: Ch. Pinewoods One Day At A thyme; Breeder/Owner: Carolyn Hehir.

Am. Can. Int. Ch. Foxglove Won't Be Denied. Sire: Ch. Beowulf of Wheeler's Knoll, CD, CGC, WD; Dam: Am. Can. Ch. Gulph Mills Marjorie, CD, CGC; Breeder/Owner: Laura & David Hagey. Deny was in the Top 10 Mastiffs in 1992 and 1994.

BISS CH. Iron Hills Warwagon. Sire: Ch. Lionsire Ironhill Warleggen; Dam: Ch. Iron Hills Elbereth; Breeder: Scott Phoebus; Owner: Roger Barkley. "Dave" was Top Mastiff 1989 and 1990, BISS at the 1989 and 1990 Mastiff Specialties, Top Group Mastiff 1990 and he is the All Time Top Producing Stud Dog.

Ch. Peersleigh Storm Sherman. Sire: Ch. Odin of Dahlseide; Dam: Ch. Peersleigh Princess Carolyn; Breeder: Bruce & Jackie Guy; Owner: Bjorn & dee dee Andersson. Sherman was the No. 3 Breed and No. 6 Group Mastiff of 1984, and he won Best of Breed the day before the 1985 and the day after the 1986 Mastiff Specialties over many of the same dogs.

BISS Ch. Iron Hills Earned Interest. Sire: Ch. Iron Hills Warwagon; Dam: Ch. Britestar Lionsires Addition; Breeder: Scott Phoebus & Diane Tribby; Owner: Julia & Kevin Kriebs & Pam Phoebus. "Sidney" was No. 3 Breed Bitch, No. 2 Best of Opposite Sex Bitch and No. 4 Group Bitch 1992, No. 2 Breed Bitch and No. 3 Group Bitch 1994, and she won BISS at the 1994 Mastiff Specialty.

BIS Ch. Deer Run William The Conqueror. Sire: Ch. Deer Run Wycliff; Dam: Deer Run Jai Bee Cleopatria; Breeder: Jerry & Irene Byrne; Owner: Carl & Hilary Tunick. Willy is the second All Time Top Winning Mastiff in the history of the breed with nine All-Breed Best In Show Wins.

Ch. Creekside Nkotb Mighty Hogan. Sire: Ch. His Majesty's Lion of Judah; Dam: Fantasy's Shaula of Creekside; Breeder/ Owner: Mary Ann Keirans; Owners: Eva Gomez & George Gordon. 1993 and 1997 Award of Merit Mastiff National Specialty and Westminster Kennel Club.

Ch. Brite Stars Dual Image. Sire: Yama Bushi Shin Rae; Dam: Ch. Gentry's Brite Star Panda; Breeder: P. Duncan; Owner: Lance House. "Brogran" was No. 6 Mastiff Dog in Breed and No. 13 Mastiff Dog Group 1995, No 3 Mastiff and No. 8 Mastiff Dog Group 1996.

CHAPTER 10
THE VERSATILE MASTIFF

Part of my goal in writing this book about Mastiffs has been to demonstrate to the world that Mastiffs are quite as capable of doing everything that any member of any other breed can do, with the possible exception only of racing head-to-head against a Greyhound. Mastiffs are starring in movies; they are becoming valued as therapy dogs; they are performing in search-and-rescue operations; several have earned tracking titles; some are achieving the most difficult levels of obedience titles; they are showing aptitude at carting activities; and we have had the first Mastiff successfully compete in the novice agility arena.

When writing about the Mastiff temperament, you will recall I talked about how a single harsh word could crush a Mastiff. Because they are so gentle and sensitive, always craving the approval of their owners, it is important for the owner to approach obedience with this unique temperament uppermost in mind. While I, personally, do not pursue obedience with my own Mastiffs, I have nevertheless learned one thing from them—if they are bored, the lesson is over—no matter what is being taught. Training should be upbeat and fun and all efforts need to be made to keep the dog's interest. Never try to force a Mastiff, instead instill a desire to do whatever it is you are asking of him.

Mastiffs are not particularly remarked upon for high scores in obedience, but they are extremely trainable as evidenced by the long list of titled Mastiffs in this chapter. Because Mastiffs are a "soft" breed and easily upset by corrections, they respond very well to the motivational methods utilized by many modern-day trainers. Including the use of food and play in training sessions will help keep enthusiasm high and make obedience training an anticipated part of the day for handler and dog.

The more experienced obedience trainers in our breed highly recommend training of youngsters, beginning as early as eight weeks of age. Short sessions that are fun, using food as motivation, help teach the puppy to sit, come, down and stay on command. After your puppy is fully inoculated against diseases, he should be enrolled

Ch. Miyaka Misha UDT, WDX (CGC, TT, TDI). Sire: Petrosec Muy Grande Houston; Dam: Princess. "Misha" is shown here with owner Candee Teitel. She has the distinction of being the most-titled Mastiff in history ranked #1 obedience Mastiff for three years; High in Trial at 1992 Specialty Show; multiple collar award winner for High Scoring Mastiff; #1 in Schuman points with a total of 6 collars; AKC winner three consecutive years for #1 Mastiff in Delaney points and #1 in Shuman points; one of three Mastiffs in history with utility title and one of three with tracking title.

Ch. Landmark's Ashley Cooper, CDX. Sire: Ch. Willowledge Big City Ben; Dam: Ch. Willowledge Marya, CD; Breeder/Owner: Ronald & Donna Gearns.

in puppy kindergarten, around four to six months of age. If these classes are made enjoyable for the puppy, it will promote a positive influence on his future attitude towards obedience. Puppy classes offer great benefits, such as socialization with people and other animals, and the puppy will learn basic commands with distractions, interaction with strangers, and confidence-building exercises, such as negotiating a tunnel similar to an agility tunnel or going through an obstacle course.

When the puppy reaches six months old, you may choose to continue the obedience lessons in a basic obedience class or your puppy may require a private instructor. There are pros and cons to each alternative. Group classes offer the puppy continued socialization and interaction, so necessary for the Mastiff breed. On the other hand, if the animal is very high spirited or difficult to control in a group environment, one-on-one, or individual, attention may be more beneficial and the animal may thrive on the personal training that would be geared to his particular needs. As I pointed out in the temperament chapter, remember to be very careful and selective about who helps you to train your Mastiff because this breed does not fare well if strong-arm tactics are utilized. There is nothing more sinful or heartbreaking than a beautiful Mastiff with a broken spirit. It is a good idea to try to find an instructor who has titled his own dog, at least through the advanced level. An instructor with a positive attitude is important, as well as someone who is flexible about changing methods, as indicated, with different dogs.

Basic obedience lessons will include heeling, stay, stand and come, usually off lead, and generally requires no more than 15 minutes each day. These workout sessions can be done in various places such as at a shopping center, school or park, thereby exposing the animal to different environments.

Many owners enjoy the rapport they have established with their Mastiffs through the obedience activities and, upon graduation from basic class, wish to continue into more difficult levels. Advanced obedience classes offer an opportunity to train the animal to commands off lead. Upon completion at this level, the owner and animal may wish to participate in formal competition at obedience trials in order to demonstrate what they have accomplished together and to earn titles.

The AKC offers three levels of obedience at sponsored events and any registered Mastiff, six months or older, including spayed and neutered animals, is eligible to compete. The first level is Companion Dog (CD) in which the animal must heel on and off lead, stand for examination, perform a one-minute sit/stay and a three-minute down/stay in the company of other competing dogs, and do a recall off lead. To earn a CD title, the animal must successfully perform all these exercises under three different judges and earn a qualifying score of 170 or better out of a possible 200 points.

The next level obedience title is a Companion Dog Excellent (CDX) and the animal must heel off lead, drop on recall, retrieve on the flat and over a jump, a broadjump and a three-minute group sit and a five-minute down with the handler out of sight. These exercises are considerably more difficult than Novice work because the animal must leave his handler's side for nearly all of these exercises and work independently. After qualifying three times, the dog earns the CDX title.

The most advanced obedience level earns the Utility Dog (UD) title and this is accomplished by completing the commands through hand signals, scent discrimination, directed retrieve, directed jumping and a stand/stay while in motion. Other obedience titles that may be earned are Utility Dog Excellent (UDX) which means qualifying in both open and utility at 10 shows and the Obedience Trial Champion (OTCH) which is the highest obedience honor that can be earned by a dog.

The first Mastiff to earn a Companion Dog title was Sir Belden Burn, CD, in 1944, owned by R. Belden Burn. The first advanced title earned by a Mastiff was Valiant Dazzler, CDX, in 1952, owned by Marlin Ashby. Approximately 25 Mastiffs a year earn CD titles and about two advanced titles are earned per year. The low percentage of advance titles is believed to be the result of difficult jump heights in proportion to the size and weight of the Mastiff. Jump heights were determined to be one time the height of the shoulder of the dog, or about 32 inches for a mature male Mastiff weighing about 200 pounds. There was an extremely high rate of injuries in the breed due to these regulations. In 1995, the Mastiff Club Obedience Committee, comprised of Mary Louise Owens, Nicki Camerra, Candee Teitel and Dr. Bill Newman, AKC delegate for Mastiffs, spearheaded an effort to gain AKC approval to lower heights for the Mastiff breed to three-quarters of the height at the shoulder. To the greatest benefit of our breed, this committee achieved its hard-earned goal and, effective March 1, 1997, Mastiffs jumped at the newly approved level. In the future many more Mastiffs should successfully compete for CDX and UD titles without risk of injury.

Ch. Acorn Hills Hogan, CDX, CGC, DD, WD. Sire: Ch. Iron Hills Warwagon; Dam: Arrabelle of Acorn Hill, CD; Breeder/Owner: Mary-Louise Owens.

Mastiff scores in obedience work continue to rise, many Mastiffs now scoring in the 190-point range. In recent years, the Mastiff Club instituted year-end obedience awards to pay tribute to highest scoring Mastiffs. This recognition was expanded to include a separate award for Highest Scoring Dog and Bitch in Novice and Highest Scoring Dog and Bitch in Open and/or Utility. In 1989, the first Obedience Trials were held in conjunction with the annual Mastiff National Specialty Show and 20 Mastiffs were entered in competition and by last year the entry approached 50. Winning High In Trial in obedience at the National Specialty is the equivalent of winning Best of Breed in conformation. This is a very big deal! The list of winners to date:

1989 CH. JG'S MR T, UD, Jane & Greg Gadbury

1990 CH. GULPH MILLS FOXGLOVE SAVANNAH, CD, Laura & David Hagey

1991 SOUTHERNS ROYAL SAMSON, CD, David May

1992 LIONSIRE SIR NIGEL BEWARE, CD, Lisa Robbins

1993 CH. MIYAKA MISHA, UDT, Candee Teitel & Merle Paule

1994 FOXGLOVE HOPE'S JUST IN TIME, CD, C Teitel & L & D Hagey

1995 CH. POLARIS TJ MASTERCARD MAX, CD, Nicki Camerra

1996 POLARIS OAKLANE ELOISE, CD, N Camerra, T & V Hix & L Brown

1997 CH. WANNABE RUNS SIR WINSTON KANE, CD, Melinda Gillespie

Other Mastiffs that have had notable accomplishments in the obedience ring are: Ch. Goodtimes Charly's Angel, CD, TD, the first Mastiff to earn both obedience and tracking titles, owner Ada Childs and Alane Gomez; Ch. Miyaka Misha, UDT, the most titled performance dog in the history of the breed with championship, tracking and utility titles—also the top obedience Mastiff in 1991, 1992 and 1993, owner Candee Teitel and Merle Paule; Ch. Krazy K's Stormy Knight, CD was the first Mastiff to win an all-breed High In Trial, owner L M & B E Parnell; Foxglove Hope's Just In Time, CD, the only Mastiff to win multiple High In Trial Awards at all-breed shows and he won High In Trial at the 1994 Mastiff Specialty. "Justin" finished his CD with a 196 average to become the first

Foxglove Hope's Just in Time, CD, CGC, TT, WD. Sire: Ch. Meza's Hulk Hogan; Dam: Am. Can. Ch. Foxglove Poetry In Motion, CGC; Breeder: David & Laura Hagey; Owner: D. & L. Hagey & C. Teitel & M. Paule.

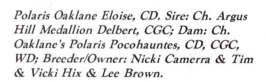

Ch. Polaris TJ Mastercard Max, CD, WD. Sire: Ch. Gold Coasts Polaris Titan, CDX, CGC, TT, TDI; Dam: Gold Coasts Polaris Carri On, CD, CGC; Breeder: Nicki Camerra & L. & P. Nicolello; Owner: Nicki Camerra. "Max" is shown winning Highest Scoring Dog at the 1995 Mastiff National Specialty.

Polaris Oaklane Eloise, CD. Sire: Ch. Argus Hill Medallion Delbert, CGC; Dam: Ch. Oaklane's Polaris Pocohauntes, CD, CGC, WD; Breeder/Owner: Nicki Camerra & Tim & Vicki Hix & Lee Brown.

Mastiff to qualify for the Gaines Regional and Classic Obedience competition, and he held a record in Novice with a 197 score, owner Candee Teitel and Laura and David Hagey; Polaris Oaklane Eloise, CD, was the second Mastiff to qualify for the Gaines Regional and Classic Obedience competition and she won High In Trial at the 1996 Mastiff Specialty. Eloise finished her CD with a 196.16 average, and scored a 197.5 in Novice, a new record for the breed. She is owned by breeder Nicki Camerra and Tim and Vicki Hix and Lucy Brown.

The breed of Mastiffs is very lucky to have a lady named Gladys Cutter Tangen as its devoted benefactor. Gladys took the Mastiff to her heart years ago and she worked hard on behalf of the breed to get new and different recognition for them. She had the idea of developing a Working Dog title which would pay tribute to Mastiffs that were able to demonstrate their ability in various endeavors. In 1992, the Mastiff Club formed a committee to further her concept. Mastiff Club President Joe Margraf described the Working Dog (WD) title as an encouragement to members to show the world that the Mastiff is still truly a working breed.

In 1994, the committee developed the test currently used for the carting or Draft Dog (DD) title. Mary Louise Owens explained that since many Mastiff owners were already using their dogs to pull carts and wagons for fun at public demonstrations and parades, it was decided to incorporate this skill and make it a working dog event. She said it was very important to understand the difference between the carting skill and a competitive weight-pulling contest. The carting skill is an exhibition event that consists of obedience both in and out of harness, an obstacle course performed while hitched to the cart, and a long haul in which the maximum weight allowed is 40 pounds. A competitive weight-pulling contest, on the other hand, allows dogs to pull up to 2,000 pounds over a short distance and the Mastiff Club does not recognize this endeavor for purposes of earning a Working Dog title.

The first Draft Dog test was held at the 1996 Mastiff Specialty Show and the first five Mastiffs to earn the Draft Dog title were:

CH. ACORN HILLS ETHAN, CD, CGC, DD, WD

CH. ACORN HILLS HOGAN, CDX, CGC, DD, WD

CH. CREEKVIEWS MAJOR MONTGOMERY, CD, CGC, DD, WD

BEOWULF PRINCE OF BROWNSHAVN, CDX, DD

HALCYON GALETEA, CD, DD

To achieve the Working Dog title, 100 points in at least three categories must be earned. The advanced achievement of Working Dog Excellent requires 200 points. The four categories are:

1: OBEDIENCE
Companion Dog (25 pts)
Companion Dog Excellent (25 pts)
Utility (50 pts)

3: TRACKING
Tracking Dog (50 pts)
Tracking Dog Excellent (50 pts)

2: TEMPERAMENT
Temperament Test OR
AKC Canine Good Citizen
(25 pts)

4: SPECIALTY
Champion (25 pts)
Agility (25 pts)
Carting/Draft (25 pts)
Search/Rescue (25 pts)
Therapy Dog (25 pts)
Canine Ambassador (25 pts)
Other (please call for acceptable items)

These Mastiffs are winners of Obedience Collar Awards from the Mastiff Club of America in the following categories:

1987 HIGHEST AVERAGE SCORE - CH. GOLDCOAST'S POLARIS TITAN, CDX

1987 TOP SHUMAN POINTS - CH. CLASSIC'S RUBILEE O'FOURELLS, UD

1988 HIGHEST AVERAGE SCORE - CH. WILSON'S FAWN FLEW-ZEE, CD

1988 TOP SHUMAN POINTS - CH. CLASSIC'S RUBILEE O'FOURELLS, UD

1989 HIGHEST AVERAGE SCORE - CH. JG'S MR T, UD

1989 TOP SHUMAN POINTS - CH. JG'S MR T, UD

1990 HIGHEST AVERAGE SCORE DOG - CH. JG'S MR T, UD

1990 HIGHEST AVERAGE SCORE BITCH - ACORN HILLS HOOF LAKE ECHO, CD

Gladys Tangen is shown here with Ch. Avalon's Lord Cearbhallain, CD, CGC, TDI, WD owned by Cat Angus.

Ch. Creekviews Major Montgomery, CD, CGC, DD, WD. Sire: Am. Can. Ch. Matts Joshua-Dogwood Knoll; Dam: Ch. Old School Creekview Major K; Breeder/Owner: Kay Routten.

A great family portrait of 4 generations: Am. Can. Ch. Medallion Mischief, CGC (No. 2 in 1990 Best of Opposite Sex points) is Dixie's daughter; Ch. Argushill Medallion Po Tater (son of Mischief); Medallion Zekiah Kayle (Tater's daughter); in front: Ch. Monty's Dixie Derby, CD, TT, TDI, WD.

1990 TOP SHUMAN POINTS DOG - CH. JG'S MR T, UD

1991 HIGHEST AVERAGE SCORE DOG - CH. ELDORADO REBEL W OUT A PAUSE, CD

1991 HIGHEST AVERAGE SCORE BITCH - CH. MIYAKA MISHA, CDX, TD

1991 TOP SHUMAN POINTS DOG - LORD TENNYSON OF OLD SCHOOL, CDX

1991 TOP SHUMAN POINTS - CH. MIYAKA MISHA, CDX, TD

1992 HIGHEST AVERAGE SCORE DOG - CH. ACORN HILLS HOGAN, CD

1992 HIGHEST AVERAGE SCORE BITCH - CH. MIYAKA MISHA, CDX, TD

1992 TOP SHUMAN POINTS - CH. MIYAKA MISHA, CDX, TD

1993 HIGHEST AVERAGE SCORE DOG - CH. MERIWETHERS MAGNUM CHASE, CDX

1993 HIGHEST AVERAGE SCORE BITCH - CH. MIYAKA MISHA, UDT

1993 TOP SHUMAN POINTS DOG - CH. MERIWETHERS MAGNUM CHASE, CDX

1993 TOP SHUMAN POINTS BITCH - CH. MIYAKA MISHA, UDT

1994 HIGHEST AVERAGE SCORE DOG - FOXGLOVE HOPE'S JUST IN TIME, CD

1994 HIGHEST AVERAGE SCORE BITCH - TUDORLANE DADDY'S DE-LIGHT

1994 TOP SHUMAN POINTS DOG - CH. ACORN HILLS HOGAN, CD

1995 HIGHEST AVERAGE SCORE DOG - CH. POLARIS TJ MASTERCARD MAX, CD

1995 HIGHEST AVERAGE SCORE BITCH - HALCYON GALATEA, CD

1995 HIGHEST AVERAGE SCORE OPEN/UTILITY - CH. RR LADY CAS-SIOPEIA, CDX

1996 HIGHEST AVERAGE SCORE DOG - MRWTHR TO LEGIT TO QUIT BLKHVN, CD

1996 HIGHEST AVERAGE SCORE BITCH - CH. MISTY MEADOWS M'LADY CASSANDRA, CD

Ch. Oaklane Polaris Pocohauntes, CD, CGC, WD; Ch. Oaklane Old School Stardust, CGC, TDI; Ch. Oaklane Rose Bay Isis, CD, CGC, TDI, WD.

1996 HIGHEST AVERAGE SCORE OPEN/UTILITY - BEOWULF PRINCE OF BROWNSHAVN, CDX

The following Mastiffs earned Working Dog Titles:

1994

Ch. Goldcoast's Polaris Titan, CDX, TT

Ch. Oaklane Polaris Pocahontas, CD, CGC

Ch. Monty's Dixie Derby, CD, CGC, TT, TDI

Ch. Beowulf of Wheelers Knoll, CD

Ch. Ironhills Sudden Justice, CD; TT, TDI

Ch. Creekviews Major Montgomery, CD, CGC, TDI

Ch. Old Schools Creekview Major K, CD, CGC, TDI

Ch. Tejas Sonrise Dakota, CD, CGC, TT, TDI

Ch. Rosebay Oaklane Jennifer, CD, CGC, TDI

Lord Tenneyson of Old School, CDX, CGC, TDI

Ch. Meriwethers Magnum Chase, CDX, CGC

Ch. RR's Cambridge of Silver Reef, CD, CGC, TDI

Ch. Acorn Hills Hogan, CDX, CGC

Ch. Legendary Fanny Flaunts It, CD, CGC, TT

Ch. Eldorado Murphy's Law, CD, CGC, TT

Ch. Avalon's Lord Cearbhallain, CD, CGC, TDI

Ch. Sidetrack's Sassie Sadie, CD, CGC, TDI

Ch. Willow's CharlieScrub Buckt, CD, CGC, TDI, TT

Ch. Plantation Roll With It Baby, CD, CGC, TDI

Ch. Miyaka Misha, UDT, CGC
   CH. MIYAKA MISHA, UDT, CGC, TT, TDI, was awarded the first Working Dog Excellent (WDE) title.

1995

Ch. Acorn Hills Ethan, CD, CGC, DD

Ch. Brite Stars Mariah of Wannabe, CD, CGC, TDI

Ch. Creekview Plantation Boo Bear, CD, CGC, TDI

Ch. Deer Run Glory to God, CD

Ch. Megamillions Sturgis of Pimlico, CD

Ch. Oaklane Rose Bay Isis, CD, CGC, TDI

Ch. Polaris TJ Mastercard Max, CD

Ch. RR Lady Cassiopeia, CDX

Ch. Westwinds Middangeards Chance, CD, CGC, TDI

Am. Can. Ch. Tippets Victoria, Am.Can.CD, CGC, TDI

1996

Beowulf Prince of Brownhavn, CDX, CGC, DD

Halcyon Galatea, CD, CGC, DD

Ch. Monarch's Orion Shall Rise, CD, CGC, TDI

Goldcoasts Polaris Carri On, CD, CGC, TDI

Ch. Niko Grossman, CD, CGC, TDI

Ch. Misty Meadows M'Lady Cassandra, CD, CGC

Companion Dog (CD) Titled Mastiffs

ACORN HILLS ENCORE', CH.

ACORN HILLS ETHAN, CH.

ACORN HILLS HOGAN

ACORN HILLS HOOF LAKE ECHO

ACORN HILLS JULIP, NA

AL CABONE

ALEXANDER OF ACORN HILL

ALDRIDGE'S SHAWN ROAR'N RUMBLE

APPLE CREEKS EBONY ONYX, CH.

APPLEWHAITES ADAM

ARCINIEGA LEGENDARY CENTAUR, CH.

ARRABELLE OF ACORN HILL

ASGARD'S CLASSACT

ASGARD'S EASTER THOR, CH.

AVALON'S LORD CEARBHALLAIN, CH.

BAILEY

BACCHUS SYMBOL OF KINGS

BARON OF WEY ACRES TARS

BEAR CLAWS OF TARTEN FARMS

BEAUREGARD BUGLEBOY

BEDFORD'S GOLIATH

BELLA DONNA

BEOWULF OF WHEELER'S KNOLL, CH.

BEOWULF PRINCE OF BROWNSHAVN

BERNGARTH BODICEA

BERNGARTH HEREWARD, CH.

BIG BLOCK AURORA OF LANDMARK

BLACKCREEK'S DESPERADO, CH.

BLACKCREEK'S DAKOTA LIGHTFOOT, CH.

BLACKHAVEN'S ADVOCATE, CH.

BLACKHAVEN'S WILLIE B, CH.

BLACKNIGHT'S COURT ASSIN

BLACKNIGHT'S PANAMA JACK

BLKHAVEN ANX LUCRESHA MCEVIL

BRITE STAR MOSES OF WANNABE, CH.

BRITE STAR'S MARIAHOFWANNABE, CH.

BRITE STARS RR JUSTA DREAM, CH.

BRITE STAR TRISTAN

BROWN VALLEY GOLDEN MIST

BUBBA'S BUCK RUN

BUFFNELL DE FINNELL

BULLCALF

BULL VALLEY DUDLEY OF NAVANOD, CH.

BUSTERS SOLO LEGACY, CH.

CAESAR OF SEATTLE

CAESAR'S DELIGHTFUL MATEUS

CALEDONIA DIAMOND TOOK C

CALEDONIA HEIFER

CALISTO OF REDGAP, CH.

CALISTO'S APPLAUSE AP-PLAUSE, CH.

CAMEO II

CASEY'S CREEK

CASTLEGATES LOCK

CASTLE KEEPSQUEEN BESS, CH.

CASTLEMIST BALOO BAYOU, CH.

CASTLEMIST FIRSTLIGHTOF DAWN

CENTURIAN MIGHTY THOR

CENTURY FARMS CHAMBER MAID

CHARMED I'M SURE, CH.

CHETAKAS TIABI V BEACON HILL

CHETAKA BROKEN ARROW, CH.

CHM CREEK COPE'S COMRADE K

CHRISTINA'S NOBLE TITAN

CLASSIC'S BRENDA BIGSTAR, CH.

CLASSIC'S DARING DAY-DREAM

CLASSIC'S RUBILEE O'FOURELLS

COBURNGORE ELIZA OF NOBLE HALL

CONDESA DE CARMELITA

CORNHAYE DANIEL, CH.

CRAIG'S DEER RUN ZUES, CH.

CREEKVIEW PLANTATION BOOBEAR, CH.

CREEKVIEW'S MAJOR ANNABELLE

CROSSBOW SHOW BIZ BECKET

CROSSBOW SHOW BIZ SHAMEE

DAHLSEIDE LORD MAYOR

DALMAS LUCKY GAMBLE, CH.

DARKLADY ROXANNE

DAWNTREADER'S BARAK BEN DAVID

DEAN'S GRIZZLEY BEARSHEBA

DEER RUN ARTEMIS

DEER RUN BOB'S SAYONARA, CH.

DEER RUN CASHELMARA OF TRENT

DEER RUN CASTLEKEEP LEGEND

DEER RUN GLORY TO GOD, CH.

DEER RUN MAYER'S LOYAL GIANT, CH.

DEER RUN MAX-ANNE

DEER RUN MISTRES THISTLEHAIR, CH.

DEER RUN MY ANGEL GABRIEL

DEER RUN SEMPER FI EBONY

DEER RUN SEMPER FI KERRA

DEER RUN SEMPER FI THOR

DEER RUN WORCHESTER, CH.

DEER RUN ZEN, CH.

DEOLINS PHANTOM OF THE OPERA

DIABLO'S JOLLY GIANT

DIABLO'S SULTAN

DUKE OF THE ROCKIES

DUTCHESS

DUTCHESS ELSA

DYAMO'S AMBITIOUS MIS-CHIEF

EICHLERS ARWEN EVEN STAR

ELDORADO LEGENDARY'S LEGACY, CH.

ELDORADO MURPHY'S LAW

ELDORADO REBEL W/OUT A PAUSE, CH.

ELDORADO WRIGHTOUS KILLIAN

ELIZABETH EVE OF TIDEWATER

ELK RIDGE JOHN OF GAUNT

ENGLISH HILDEBRANDT

FAIRHOPE KISKA KID

FAUSTUS FAVORITE SON

FLINTS MARTA, CH.

FOXGLOVE AVENEL ONE FOR ALL, CH.

FOXGLOVE HALES WE'VE A DREAM, CH.

FOXGLOVE HOPE'S JUST IN TIME

FOXGLOVE MASS APPEAL

FOXGLOVE SHINY SIX-PENCE

GARTH HULK HOGAN

G G'S MAGNIFICENT PERCIVALE, CH.

G G'S MAGNIFICENT SIR ANDREW, CH.

G G'S MAJESTIC LADY ABIGAIL

GOLD COAST'S LADY DIVA

GOLD COASTS POLARIS CARRI ON

GOLD COASTS POLARIS TITAN, CH.

GOLD COASTS SHEBA

GOLIATH OF NORTH HILL, CH.

GOODTIME CHARLY'S ANGEL, CH.

GREENBRANCH HELOUISE

GREENBRANCH JENNY G, CH.

GREENBRANCH WARWICK

GREINER HALL ATHELNEY HANNAH

GREINER HALL CHANCELLOR GROPPETTI BUZSAW, CH.

GULPH MILLS FOXGLOVE CAELIN

GULPH MILLS FOXGLOVE SAVANNAH, CH.

GULPH MILLS HERR OTTO, CH.

GULPH MILLS JABBERWOCKY

GULPH MILLS LEGENDARY CAESAR

GULPH MILLS MARJORIE, CH.

GULPH MILLS MR BEAR TO YOU

GULPH MILLS TUPPENCE, CH.

HALCYON GALATEA

HALF MOON LITTLE ALEX

HANNIBALS BIG MONTANA

HAYDEN'S GULLIVER, CH.

HERCULES OF DUCHESS FARM

HONEY-DO'S TUFFY

HONEY OF MINE

HONEY'S GREAT RELUCTANCE

HORCADO RANCH MONUMEN-TAL MADAM

King David The Psalmist, CD. Sire: Coburngore Stealth; Dam: Coburngore Ceildah; Breeder: J. Redman; Owner: R. T. Berman.

HUACHUCA MTN SAMPSON, CH.

HURRY UP BIG BERTHA

HURRY UP HERCULES, CH.

HURRY UP MAKE A BIG SPLASH

IEDA'S THOR, CH.

INDIAN RAID'S BLACK ONYX

INDIAN RAID'S EMILY DICKENSON

INDIAN RAID'S RUNNING BEAR

INDIAN RAID'S WESTAMYX PINTO

IRON HILLS BRANDI WINE

IRON HILLS SUDDEN JUSTICE, CH.

JAI BEE LOYAL PRISSY MISSY

JAI-BEE MAYER'S LOYAL LADY

JAMADEER RUN SAKI

JG'S MR T

JG' TARZAN

JOLLY DUKE OF LITTLE POND

JOPAU'S ATTILA THE HUN

KAIULANI OF RODGERS ISLE, CH.

KING DAVID THE PSALMIST BONNIE BELLE

KINGSBOROUGH DUKE'S VALHALLA, CH.

KINGSBOROUGH'S HONEY BEE, CH.

KING'S UNDER COVER ANGEL

KIRRMAN'S GOLDEN NUGGETT

KLASSY CRITTERS MISS PEACH

KLINE'S MAD MAX REVENGE

KRAZY K'S STORMY KNIGHT, CH.

LADY CAMELOT OF HALE, CH.

LADY UNA OF BEACON HILL

LAETANS NANA

LAMBAY BATHSHEBA ATHENA

LAMBAY'S CHIP OFF THE OL ROCK

LAMBAY'S IMAGE OF BEOWULF

LAMBAY'S LEAN ON ME

LANDMARK'S ASHLEY COOPER, CH.

LARRY'S MAGNIFICENT MAGGIE

LAWLESS'S KING MANCHESTER

LEGENDARY FANNIE FLAUNTS IT, CH.

LEGENDARY LADY LONDON, CH.

LIGHTNING LADY ROXANNE

LIONHEARTED DOUBLE D MARLENA, CH.

LIONSIRE KYA'S ANGEL

LIONSIRE MYA OF WINDY KNOB

LIONSIRE SIR NIGEL BEWARE

LITTLE ACRES TIFFANY

LITTLE BABE OF NAVONOD

LORD BYRON OF BERYSTEDE

LORD TENNEYSON OF OLD SCHOOL

LOXLEY LADY SINDER O'KING

LOXLEY LYNSPRIDE LADY DESTINY

Greiner Hall Athelney Hannah, CD. Sire: Bulliff Yermak; Dam: Greiner Hall Bronwen; Breeder: Stephen & Leah Napotnik; Owner: Fiona Zahnke.

LYON'S LAIR MAX-A-MILLION

MAGGIE OF THE MEADOWS

MAGNOLIAS LADY VALENTINE

MAGNO'S HONORABLE HATCHET MAN, CH.

MALBRANCH TRUDY

MANGOOLA JORDAN, AUST. CH.

MARSHALL MACK VAY

MARSH'S DUKE OF WISTORIA

MAXIMILIAN DE CANUTILLO

MEADOWLARK'S LADY FERGIE, CH.

M CREEK COPES COMRADE CAIN, CH.

MEDALLION MISS INNOCENCE, CH.

MEGAMILLION MAXIMILLION I M O T, CH.

MEGAMILLIONS KAHLUA N CREAM

MEGAMILLIONS STURGIS OF PIMLICO, CH.

MEGAMILLIONS TUFF E NUFF, CH.

MERIWETHER'S MAGNUM CHASE, CH.

MISS ROSE OF AZUREDEE

MISTRESS CHEWIE OF WARDSWOOD

MISTY ARROW OF THE ROCKIES, CH.

MISTY MEADOWS M'LADY CASSANDRA, CH.

MIYAKA MISHA

MONARCH'S APOLLO MYKANN

MONARCH'S ORION SHALL RISE, CH.

MONTAUK MASTIFF MANDEE

MOONSHADOW'S BRIDGET A WOLL

MONTY'S DIXIE DERBY, CH.

MQH MAK O MAK DANDE ROCKWOOD

MRWTHR TO LEGIT TO QUIT BLKH

MS OMEGA DE PURDUE

NACHTMUSIK AVALON LADY ANNWN

NATASHA OF TINGLEY MANOR

NAVONOD'S FULLERTON, CH.

NEWBREED'S STOMPER WILLOW

NIGHT STALKER MYSTIC LADY, CH.

NIKO GROSSMAN, CH.

OAK LANE ROSE BAY ISIS, CH.

OAK LANE'S LUCAS, CH.

OAKLANE POLARIS POCOHAUNTES, CH.

ODIN LEVIATHAN PARKHILL, CH.

OLD SCHOOL CREEKVIEW MAJOR K, CH.

OLD SCHOOL DOCTOR WATSON, CH.

OMEGA'S EAZY MAGIC

OSCARTIGH BRUIN BY THE BOG

OZARK'S MISTY, CH.

PANDORA'S BLACK MAGIC

PEACH FARM GENGHIS KHAN

PEACH FARM TASSO

PEERSLEIGH ZEPORAH

PERIPATETIC ORIONS DIANA

PLANTATION ROLL WITH IT BABY, CH.

POLARIS OAKLANE ELOISE

POLARIS' REEF BY POCOMAX

POLARIS TJ MASTERCARD MAX

PORKY'S SIMBA OF TINGLEY, CH.

PRINCE'S BRAN MUFFIN

PRINCESS SADI OF FORESTWOOD

PUFFERS B PUPPY

RAMBLEWOOD'S BIG MISS PRISS, CH.

RAMBLEWOOD'S VICTORIAN IMAGE, CH.

RAPSCALLION URSA MINOR

REMARKE OF SIR BUCKSHOT WW

REYEM'S BRENDA

RIECK'S CALLIDA

R KIMS BAM BAM OF PERIGEN

ROCKY HILL GREYSTONE GENESIS, CH.

ROCO'S BRUTE OF WASILLA, CH.

RONDAR'S MELISSA, CH.

ROSE BAY OAK LANE JENNIFER, CH.

ROYAL COURT OF THE SOUTHWIND

ROYALCOURT MAJESTIC JESTER

ROYAL SAMSOM OF SWEETBRIAR

RR LADY CASSIOPEIA, CH.

RR KR'S LADY DIANA, CH.

RR'S CAMBRIDGE OF SILVER REEF

RR SILVER REEF WINDRIVER ELI

RUMBLIN EKO'S THOJHILD, CH.

RUSTIC MANOR'S ISABELLE

SALT RIVER ZIP OF QUAIL HILL, CH.

SARA DAWN OF HERCULES, CH.

SELENE SUE

SHADOWFAX DAISY

SHERVIRARES CAPTAIN SHANE

SHIRE'S DELTA LADY

SIDETRACKS SASSY SADIE, CH.

SILVER SHADOW'S ROCKY

SIR BELDEN BURN

SIR CEDRICK, CH.

SIR MARCUS OF MAPLE CREEK, CH.

SOUTHERN GENTLEMAN, CH.
SOUTHERNS ROYAL SAMSON II
SPICE HILL'S MEMORY OF JEREMY
ST JOHN'S GLEN HUMPREY B, CH.
ST JOHN'S GLEN MONUMENTALLIL, CH.
STABLEMATE DEVON OF SUNIGLEN
STARSHINE JUNO
STONEHAVEN PEPPERMINT SWIRL
STORM ECHO O'PEERSLEIGH
STORM LANDMARK'S USA TESS, CH.
STORM QUIET REBELLION OF BH, CH.
STORM'S SWEDISH LEJON, CH.
STUBBLEFIELD'S VICTORIA
SUGARFOOT'S SHOT IN THE DARK
SUN BELLE'S S HEBA
SWEET BABY JANE
TAMARACK ODESSA
TEJAS SONRISE DAKOTA, CH.
TENNYSON'S MISTY, CH.
TESS TRUE HEART
THE BLACK PRINCE
TIPPETS VICTORIA, CH.
TRAYMATT DARCI KAKI, CH.
TREENAS ZEUS THE LION-HEARTED
TROWE AETHELWEARD OF HUDSON, CH.
TUDORLANE DADDY'S DE-LIGHT
UNICORN KNOLL'S PHOENIX
VALIANT DAZZLER

VALLEY VIEW KANGA
VALLEY VIEW KIA, CH.
VISCOUNT OF THE SOUTHWIND
VON DINKELS GINGERS RE-VENGE, CH.
WANNABE RUNS SIR WINSTON KANE, CH.
WATER'EM'S MOSES
WEE MUFFIN'S MS SARAH LOVE, CH.
WERENHOLD EDWINA
WESTERN'S SOVEREIGN SUDIE
WESTWIND MIDDANGEARDS CHANCE, CH.
WILLOWLEDGE FREDERICK
WILLOWLEDGE J.D.'S SAMANTHA
WILLOWLEDGE MARYA, CH.
WILLOWLEDGE PILIKUS PUTNAM
WILLOWLEDGE RECON SNIPER
WILLOWLEDGE SINKILLER SMITH, CH.
WILLOWLEDGE TALK OF THE TOWN, CH.
WILLOW RUN BODY BY JAKE
WILLOWS CHARLIES SCRUB BUCKT, CH.
WILSONS FAWN FLEWS-ZEE, CH.
WINDSOR'S GENTLE BEN
WINSOME'S BEAUTIFUL BABE
WRIGHTOUS WIDE BODY TANKER, CH.
YETI'S NEMESIS
ZEUS KING OF THE GODS, CH.

Companion Dog Excellent (CDX) Titled Mastiffs

ACORN HILLS HOGAN, CH.
ACORN HILLHOOF LAKE ECHO

BARON OF WEY ACRES TARS
BEOWULF PRINCE OF BROWNSHAVN

BELLA DONNA

BULLCALF
CALEDONIA HEIFER
CASTLEGATES LOKI
CHRISTINA'S NOBLE TITAN

CLASSIC'S BRENDA BIGSTAR

CLASSIC'S RUBILEE O
DALMAS LUCKY GAMBLE, CH.
DARKLADY ROXANNE
FAUSTUS FAVORITE SON

FLINTS MARTA, CH.
GOLD COASTS POLARIS
TITAN, CH.
JGMT T, CH.
LANDMARKASHLEY
COOPER, CH.
LORD TENNEYSON OF OLD
SCHOOL
MIYAKA MISHA, CH.
PANDORABLACK MAGIC
PEACH FARM GENGHIS KHAN
RAPSCALLION URSA MINOR

RR LADY CASSIOPEIA, CH.

SOUTHERN GENTLEMAN, CH.
TESS TRUEHEART
VALIANT DAZZLER
WILLOWLEDGE TALK OF
THE TOWN, CH.

Utility Dog (UD) Titled Mastiffs

SPICE HILLS MEMORY OF JEREMY (1976), owned by Leroy Pilarski
CLASSICRUBILEE O, CH. (1988), owned by Elaine & Tomas Gomez
JGMR T, CH. (1989), owned by Jane & Greg Gadbury
MIYAKA MISHA, CH., TD (1993), owned by Candee Teitel & Merle Paule

Tracking Dog (TD) Titled Mastiffs

GOODTIME CHARLY'SANGEL, CH.
KRAZY K'S STORMY KNIGHT, CH., CD
MIYAKA MISHA, CH., CDX

Novice Agility

ACORN HILLS JULIP, CD

Ch. Misty Arrow of the Rockies, CD. Sire: Greco's Daniel; Dam: Greco's Hollesley Lenora. Breeder: Mrs. Frank Greco; Owner: Tom & Lynn Nellessen.

CHAPTER 11
THE GROWING MASTIFF

I would not presume to tell someone else how to raise or feed a Mastiff. I will say in my opinion over-supplementation or over feeding in a deliberate effort to rush or force Mastiff growth can have quite disastrous results. Too many novices acquire their first Mastiffs and want to own big dogs today—unwilling to wait for the poor animals to get there on their own tomorrow. Tragically, eagerness, lack of breed information or inexperience has led to the structural destruction of many a potentially good Mastiff. The breed needs at least two full years in which to grow and should be given the opportunity to do so slowly and correctly.

Puppy buyers often ask about the correct weight for a puppy. I advise them not to pay too much attention to the actual weight in terms of exact poundage. So long as the puppy's nutritional needs are being met, the exact weight is unimportant. I also advise them to ignore charts of ideal or average Mastiff weights published in other publications. If the puppy does not have the bone and structure to support those recommended weights and you try to beef your puppy up to conform to those recommendations, you may irreparably harm the puppy. When a puppy is standing still his ribs should not be seen, but when the puppy is trotting, you should be able to see the outline of the rib cage as his skin ripples across the ribs. If the puppy can pass these optical tests, he is probably at an individually good weight. You would never want to deprive a puppy of the nutrition needed to grow correctly, but neither should he be forced to carry excess weight on the still-developing frame.

It would be better for the growing Mastiff puppy to be slightly underweight rather than a single pound overweight. Generally, to be competitive in the show ring, an animal must be in what is called show weight. Certainly a puppy in solid weight makes a better impression on everyone. However, one must consider the long-term damage that could be done. Excess weight on a fragile puppy frame may ultimately stress the entire structure and damage might not be discernible until maturity is reached and the topline sags, or the hocks and pasterns are weakened, or growth diseases have taken a toll.

This 5-month-old puppy was diagnosed as suffering from Rickets—note the roached topline.

A saying among experienced breeders is the larger the dog, the slower the growth. We use this thought to remind ourselves to give these giant dogs the time required to reach adulthood without having compromised soundness along the way. A teenage Mastiff standing 33 inches takes considerably longer to develop appropriate body substance than would a 30-inch youngster. An overweight puppy is not necessarily more muscled than his leaner counterpart, but rather he is simply carrying too much body fat. Muscle should be developing slowly commensurate with bone growth.

Nor should Mastiff puppies be over exercised. I am often asked how far is it safe to walk a Mastiff puppy? The answer is no further a distance than you are prepared to carry him home. Any tired puppy will lie down and refuse to move. A Mastiff puppy that tires will lie down and become dead weight and believe me, when you lift him in your arms it will feel like his weight has doubled. A growing Mastiff should not be permitted to run, romp or play on slippery surfaces such as wood or tile. These surfaces encourage him to slip and slide, recklessly banging into doorways, walls and furniture and thereby increasing the risk of injuring long bones, shoulders, elbows, hips and knees. You must keep in mind a Mastiff baby is clumsier than a smaller-breed puppy.

Mastiff puppies should not have unlimited access to stairs. Owners especially need to restrict a young Mastiff from unnecessary trips downstairs since the weight load is shifted to the front of the dog and he is pounding downwards on his shoulders. All Mastiffs wish to sleep in the owner's bedroom, often located upstairs, and this is easily managed by using baby gates to restrict the trip upstairs to once at night and downstairs once in the morning. Mastiff puppies need to be taught to go up and downstairs under strict supervision.

Some have a tendency to stand at the top of the stairs and leap off believing they can safely reach the bottom this way. Collar your puppy and use a leash to keep his head close to your left knee. Go down slowly and carefully, helping him put a foot on each stair as you go along. Even more control can be had by having a second person back down the stairs just in front of the puppy, thus blocking any attempt he makes to leap forward. If this procedure is repeated several times, he will learn to navigate stairs safely.

A common mistake owners make is to allow young Mastiffs to play with older, larger animals. Your puppy has great heart and he will do his utmost to keep up with the older animals. The strain may be too great. All puppy play should be strictly supervised in order to protect the puppy from injury and from taking on more than he can handle.

Mastiffs go through growth spurts, resulting in being temporarily out of balance. The hindquarters might grow higher than the front. If the back end is higher than the front, the weight load necessarily shifts abnormally to the front and he may put his front feet down incorrectly during this time to compensate for the out-of-balance weight distribution. He is then more vulnerable to injury. You need not be anxious because the puppy is suddenly out of balance, but common sense should be exercised and all vigorous play should be curtailed until he has leveled off once more and is back in balance. A growth pattern many young Mastiffs follow is the rear shoots up, the shoulders catch up soon afterwards and then the head grows, then the pattern begins all over again. Just like children, young Mastiffs need a lot of rest during these stressful growth periods.

Occasionally, a young puppy cutting teeth will have unexplained bouts of diarrhea, just like human babies. Or, they may drop down on pasterns or hocks. When this happens, veterinarians sometimes recommend calcium supplementation. The danger is too much or too little calcium can result in bone abnormalities. When our puppies show a tendency to this structural weakness in stressful growth periods, we have found it far better to feed equal amounts of kelp and alfalfa, which help him use calcium already in the body. Vitamin C is very helpful in these cases. Cooked rice can be added to his diet for a few days to eliminate any tendency towards loose stools. Naturally, if the diarrhea persists the owner needs to be concerned about the presence of some other condition and all efforts should be taken immediately to avoid dehydration. In these instances, he should be examined by a veterinarian at once.

Musculosketal Disorders: by Jeffrey Klemm, DVM (Mastiff Owner)

Osteoarthritis. This is frequently seen in dogs and is characterized by proliferative and degenerative changes in the affected joint. Degenerative changes in joints, or osteoarthritis, can occur for many different reasons, including nutrition, autoimmune problems, trauma, aging and obesity. The symptoms range from subtle lameness, to total non-weight bearing of the affected limb, to everything in between. Treatment is usually supportive (anti-inflamatories), although, if money is no object, surgery can be performed to replace a hip or anklosis, the fusing together of a very painful joint. Osteoarthritis is usually progressive. However, this progression occurs at a slow rate, so with proper medication, these animals will do well in most cases. The key to prevention consists of good nutrition and sound breeding practices.

Canine Hip Dysplasia. Canine Hip Dysplasia (CHD) is a disease common in giant breeds. Dys means abnormal and plasia means formation; hence, dysplasia means an abnormal formation. The coxofemoral joint is a ball and socket joint comprised of a femoral head (the ball) and the acetabulum (the socket). Puppies are not born with hip dysplasia. The earliest development in the puppy's life is the crucial period. The first 60 days is when soft tissue structure develops. If the growth rate is so fast muscles and tissues are not growing at the same rate as bone, the muscles may no longer hold the ball in the socket and instability sets in, or the femoral head no longer fits snugly into the acetabulum. When this happens the two joints begin growing apart and eventually cause wear on the coxofemoral joint resulting in an osteoarthritic condition.

The cause or causes of CHD are not known, and there is no cure. Its mode of inheritance depends upon interaction of numerous genes. It is considered both genetic and environmental, thought to be a polygenic trait with low to moderate heritability influenced by improper nutrition as well as the manner in which the puppy is raised. Physical signs of CHD may occur as early as two months of age, but more often surface between five and nine months of age. The animal may drag its rear when getting up, or be reluctant to go up and down stairs. In an effort to shift weight off the hindquarters because of discomfort, muscle loss in the rear may become more noticeable and increased muscles in the front could develop. The dog may have a swaying gait, or a bunny-hopping movement, and these signs may be particularly noticeable following exercise. Keep in mind that puppies have an awkward gait normally. Surgery can be very helpful on these dogs, especially if their problems started early in life. There are many different procedures, from total hip replacement to cutting the pectinius muscle. Talk to your veterinarian about what procedure best suits your animal. The best prevention is good nutrition and appropriate exercise. Do not over supplement.

The use of Vitamin C for the prevention or treatment of CHD is controversial. There is no definitive scientific study that confirms the use of Vitamin C with CHD. However, there are some studies that support its benefit. The most interesting argument justifying the use of Vitamin C is by Wendell O. Belfield, D.V.M., who compared damage from scurvy in humans to damage from CHD in dogs. Using dogs with CHD or who had produced offspring with CHD, he did trial breedings. A CHD dam was given 2,000 milligrams while gestating. Eight puppies were given 50 to 100 milligrams liquid Vitamin C at birth and 550 milligrams of powdered Vitamin C at weaning until four months, then 1,000 milligrams, then on to 2,000, until 18 to 24 months when they were diagnosed free of CHD. The bitch was bred three times, and there was no CHD in 30 puppies. Dr. Belfield is president of Orthomolecular Specialties, San Jose, California, FAX (408) 227-2732, telephone (408) 227-9334. Drops designed for puppies from birth to weaning are available as well as Mega C Plus for the older dogs from Orthomolecular Specialties.

Do Mastiffs need more Vitamin C than can be obtained from nutritionally balanced dog food? Possibly. They crave various fruits, particularly apples and oranges. They also seem to enjoy raw and cooked vegetables and the juice from cooked vegetables. None of these foods will harm them, and, indeed, they may actually be beneficial to them.

Some breeders use Glyco-Flex in Mastiff daily diets which is a product made from pure, freeze-dried perna canaliculus, an edible shellfish composed of a high concentration of vital lubricating agents called mucopolysaccharides, in addition to containing a broad spectrum of naturally chelated minerals, numerous enzymes, amino acids, vitamins and nucleic acids. Glyco-Flex helps in the management and treatment of connective tissue problems and degenerative joint disease. For those unfortunate Mastiffs diagnosed with CHD, Adequan (Polysulfated Glycosaminoglycan) (PSGAG) is being used experimentally to provide relief. Adequan has been used successfully in horses for years, but recently some veterinarians have been prescribing it for canines.

Elbow Dysplasia. This is a term for an elbow disorder that presents with acute pain and leads to chronic degeneration joint disease. This disorder is caused by several different etiologies: 1) Ununited Anconeal Process; 2) OCD of the medial condyle of the distal humerus and fragmentation of the medial coronoid. All three of these lesions are thought to be secondary to anatomical abnormalities in the developing elbow joint. The earliest symptoms of elbow dysplasia can occur as soon as four months of age with intermittent limping on the front legs. Sometimes the legs will tend to bow out from the body; that is, the elbows are held out and away from the body. Another symptom is the front feet can toe out from the body, although this toeing out can also be caused by overloading in the shoulders. When trotting, the dog will limp off and on, and occasionally when trotting, a limb will wing out and away, rather than in a normal forward, straight line.

Ununited Anconeal Process (Fragmented Coronoid Process), Osteochondrosis (Elbow Dysplasia). This is a developmental problem in the elbow caused by a faulty connection of the anconeal process, that is, one of the elbow bones, with the ulna. The projection at the end of the forearm separates, so that there is loose bone debris in the joint which prevents smooth articulation of the hinged mechanism. The debris serves to irritate the joint and will lead to arthritis in the elbow. It is thought that in order for the bone to separate, it never developed normally to begin with and failed to fuse to the remainder of the ulna. This condition is thought to be hereditary.

Osteochrondritis Dissecans (OCD). This lesion can occur in any joint in the body, but usually occurs in the elbow, shoulder, and hock. OCD is a problem in the joint in which an area of cartilage becomes loose. This flap of cartilage exposes nerve roots from the underlying bone and is very painful. Symptoms can occur anywhere from four months to one year of age. The signs are usually stiffness in the affected leg, more pronounced in the morning after exercise. These flaps can spontaneously resolve, but usually surgery is required. Surgery consists of removing the dead cartilage and allowing the bone to form a bandage (scar tissue) over the exposed nerves. For these animals, it is usually good if surgery is done before arthritic changes start developing. Heredity plays a role in this process; however, environment, stress, and nutrition can play roles also. Weight control, good nutrition, and minimizing any hard play during the first eight months to one year can help to prevent this disease.

Fragmented Medial Coronoid. The process of this disease is similar to the two previously mentioned. The only difference regarding this particular disease is its location on the inside of the elbow.

Hypertrophic Osteodystrophy (HOD). This is another developmental disease that has been linked to Vitamin C deficiency since the disease resembles scurvy. HOD affects long bones at the wrist and hock joints that become swollen and sensitive, causing lameness. In severe cases, dogs are reluctant to stand or move and bone deformity can occur. Although many dogs recover spontaneously, permanent bone changes and physical deformities may develop. There is no specific treatment for HOD. The best treatment seems to be to feed in moderation to avoid this condition—no high protein, no high calories, no over supplementation of vitamins and minerals.

Panosteitis. Panosteitis is an inflammatory disease of the long bones (i.e., femur, humerus). This disease is usually self-limiting and is more common in males puppies (i.e., 80 percent male, 20 percent female). Sometimes panosteitis is referred to as growing pains because of the similarities to the disease in humans. Dogs commonly present with acute onset of lameness with no history of trauma. The lameness may resolve on its own within a few days only to reappear in another limb later (i.e., shifting leg lameness). This usually occurs in dogs between the ages of five to twelve months but can occur as early as two months and as late as seven years. The cause of the disease is unknown. Many theories are being studied but none as yet proven. Treatment is supportive with analagesics and antiflammatories as needed. Also, limiting activity during this period is important. There is no way to prevent this disease, but prognosis is excellent.

Cruciate Knee Rupture. Cruciate injuries, unfortunately, are a fairly common injury among Mastiffs. For large animals, they are very agile and love to play hard, turning, twisting and jumping, predisposing them to knee injuries. The knee along with the external support (i.e., collateral leg) has two ligaments inside the joint that help prevent forward movement (i.e., cruciate). They form a cross inside the knee; hence the name cruciate. This ligament can rupture with stress and cause a very unstable knee joint. The animal becomes acutely lame in the affected limb, usually to the point of non-weight bearing. Repair can range from strict confinement to surgical fixation. The confinement can work if the ligament is not totally torn but strained. If it is a total rupture, surgery is the only option if you want to prevent arthritis in the joint later in life. The AKC used to bar animals from the show ring after cruciate repair, stating it was a hereditary condition. But thanks to people like dee dee, who wrote the AKC, they reversed the position on showing these dogs.

This Mastiff has undergone surgery to repair a severely injured anterior cruciate ligament.

Mastiffs love to play and know how to have a good time. I do not feel it is hereditary, but a situation in which they just want to do more than the knee was built to withstand. This is why it is so important to keep these animals in good condition and do not allow them to get overweight. Prognosis is very good if the knee is stabilized quickly. Again, it is very important to minimize activity during recovery because the good limb is supporting twice the weight it normally does. Remember this is good for any orthopedic recovery—you want to keep the healthy leg healthy.

(Author's note: The Mastiff temperament may render him vulnerable to knee injuries. Our giant breed cannot stop and turn on a dime, the type of activity typical of herding breeds. But, for heaven's sake, do not tell this to a Mastiff! They execute short, quick bursts of speed, turn and spin in the air, with their great weight, and, lo and behold, the knee is subjected to trauma. Mastiffs simply do not comprehend what goes up must come down. It was not at all unusual for one of our large dogs to fly by our kitchen window, at our eye level, with a garbage can lid in his mouth. When he injured his knee, it came as no surprise to us. My opinion is Mastiffs should have moderate angulation and either exaggeration, too straight or over angulated, creates a vulnerability for injury.)

Popping Hocks. This condition is exactly what it sounds like; that is, the hock pops out of place. One may notice an abnormal gait, especially when the dog is driving, or trying to drive, from the rear quarters.

Caudal Cervical Spondylomyelopathy (Wobblers Syndrome). This condition is an instability of the neck/spine. It is caused by spinal cord compression due to malformation of bony or ligamentous structures. Since the compression is at the neck, all four limbs can be involved, which causes a unique gait. Sometimes the front legs cross over one another and the animal trips, and often the tops of the front paws are scuffed because the hair is worn away due to the animal turning the feet under and trying to walk on the top of the feet. The rear legs splay out away from the body. In severe cases, the animal loses balance and will fall down. Generally, the animal with Wobblers Syndrome is unable to maintain any balance when backing up. The veterinarian will usually want to perform a myelogram to determine the location and type of cord compression.

Spondylosis. This is a degeneration of the vertebrae in the lumbar region of the spine. It can especially develop in aging Mastiffs and is confirmed by radiograph. One may be totally unaware the condition exists unless it is aggravated by injury.

Canine Gastric-Dilatation Volvulus (Bloat). This insidious condition is a vicious killer. It has no conscience and is totally without mercy. Bloat occurs suddenly, without warning, and if action is not taken immediately the animal can be lost within hours. What happens is that gas builds up rapidly in the stomach and cannot escape. The stomach becomes distended and twists in on itself, cutting off blood and oxygen supply to other vital organs. There is great abdominal discomfort that is obvious even if one has never witnessed bloat before. Sometimes the animal's abdominal area will become swollen until it is totally out of proportion to the rest of the body and the animal's sides become very hardened. Sometimes there is minimal swelling of the stomach. The bloating animal is in obvious distress and may whine or pace and refuse to sit or lay down. At the first onset of any of these symptoms, get your dog to the veterinary clinic at once! The clock is ticking, the situation is critical, and you do not have very much time in which to save the animal's life.

Nobody knows precisely what causes bloat. We do know vigorous exercise before or after drinking or eating can contribute to its onset. Feeding a giant meal a day rather than dividing the daily ration into several smaller meals may contribute. Bloat can also occur as a secondary reaction to another existing condition, such as a serious infection, cancer or severe parasite infestation. Gastroplexy, that is, surgery to affix the stomach permanently to the wall of the body is now the treatment of choice, and we are hearing of many successful recoveries from bloat. Once this surgical procedure is done the animal may attempt to bloat again; rather, the stomach may enlarge with gas buildup, but the stomach can no longer twist or torsion so the dog's life is not as immediately endangered as previously.

(Author's note: I owned a stud dog and have personal knowledge of at least four other stud dogs that died of bloat while living with bitches in heat that they were not being allowed to breed. My dog had not been drinking water nor eating when he bloated, but we had a bitch on her 17th day of a heat we were skipping. There is no doubt in my mind the bloat in this case was brought on strictly by emotional stress. Now, when bitches are in season and we are not breeding, we mildly sedate the stud dogs until the stress has concluded.)

Ocular Disorders: by Steven J. Dugan, DVM, MS, American College of Veterinary Opthalmologists Diplomate and Susan Barden, BS, Eye Specialists for Animals

Some eye abnormalities, verified via examination by a board certified veterinary ophthalmologist, prevent Mastiffs being certified by Canine Eye Registration Foundation (CERF), a nonprofit organization that works with the American College of Veterinary Ophthalmologists (ACVO) to maintain registries of purebred dogs not affected by major heritable eye diseases and a data base to identify trends in eye disorders and breed susceptibility, with a goal of eliminating heritable eye diseases. Although some eye irregularities may receive certification, CERF recommends animals with one or more major heritable ocular abnormalities not be used in a breeding program. Animals, of all ages, must be examined yearly to receive a valid certification number.

Entropion is a conformational defect where an eyelid margin inverts, or rolls inward, toward the eye causing eyelashes and hair to rub against the cornea resulting in ocular irritation and possibly corneal ulcerations. Entropion is usually a consequence of excessive facial skin of the forehead and periocular regions and related to the dog's skull conformation. Genetic expression is likely polygenic. Mastiffs sometimes develop a variation of entropion called "pagoda" eyelids which consists of an ectropion, or rolling outward of one portion of the eyelid margin, combined with an entropion, or rolling inward, of another portion of the same eyelid margin. These eyelid abnormalities can be severe, painful, and potentially vision threatening and may require surgical intervention. Animals exhibiting entropion or "pagoda" eyelids should not be bred.

The male puppy's eyes (on the left) react normally to a camera's flash while the two-year-old female's eyes are confirmed with Progressive Retinal Dystrophy and her eyes show an abnormal reaction to the camera's flash.

A cataract, partial or complete opacification of an eye lens or capsule, prevents eye certification. Extent of opacification determines if vision is subtly compromised or completely absent, and surgical correction may be necessary. Cataracts may be caused by trauma, inflammation in an eye, diabetes mellitus and other metabolic diseases, persistent pupillary membranes, nutritional deficiencies and aging, however when both eyes of healthy, young dogs are affected, it is usually hereditary and breeding affected animals is not recommended.

Persistent pupillary membranes (PPM), fetal blood vessels in the front chamber of eyes that do not atrophy or dissolve, which they should do by three months of age, also prevents certification of Mastiffs. Tissue strands, in Mastiffs, most often extend from iris to cornea, but can bridge the pupil, i.e., extend from iris to iris, from iris to lens surface, or form sheets of strands in the front chamber of the eye. Membranes may cause areas of corneal or lens opacification causing vision impairment or blindness therefore breeding affected or related animals is discouraged.

Progressive retinal atrophy (PRA) is a group of diseases resulting in a gradual, painless degeneration of retinas of both eyes. Clinical signs begin with night blindness (nyctalopia) and eventually (usually takes 18 to 24 months) advance to complete loss of vision. Before symptoms develop, PRA can be confirmed or ruled out by electroretinogram (ERG), an electro-physiologic diagnostic procedure that tests the health, or lack thereof, of the retinas. This disease process is usually recessively inherited and no treatment exists. No animal diagnosed with PRA, including parents and littermates, should be bred.

Mastiffs are known to have other abnormal ocular conditions that do not prevent eye certification despite them being heritable and potentially transmitted to offspring. Ectropion, an eversion, or rolling outward, of an eyelid margin, is a conformation defect resulting from excessive amounts of facial skin and skull shape. As it does not usually result in significant ocular disease, it is considered a problem which can ethically be present in breeding stock, although effort should be made to eliminate all undesirable hereditary conditions.

Macroblepharon, an abnormally large eyelid opening, another heritable ocular defect which Mastiffs may develop, does not prevent certification. It rarely creates significant manifestations, but can, in some cases, result in ongoing ocular irritation so affected dogs should not be bred.

Congenital retinal dysplasia, one or multiple abnormal folds in the retina, may be diagnosed in a puppy, but are not usually identifiable in adults. When no other ocular abnormality exists, functional vision does not appear to be affected so breeding affected Mastiffs is ethical. No relationship is established between insignificant retinal folds in Mastiffs and a more severe form that can lead to blindness in other breeds.

CHAPTER 12
BREEDING MASTIFFS

Principles of Breeding

In 1971, Brint Edwards, a top Doberman breeder, wrote that nothing was "basically wrong with inbreeding" unless hidden faults surfaced. He cited Egyptian Pharaohs who created one of the finest human lines ever known. Kinship further away than second cousins was legally forbidden, punished by death, so through inbreeding they forged a nearly faultless lineage that endured three thousand years, producing "more rulers, priests, doctors, educators and law-makers than any other family."

When used properly, experimental inbreeding assists breeders to uncover faults hidden in the line. If inbreeding is done by an experienced and knowledgeable breeder, the result can be superior offspring. Inbreeding can fix the gene pool for a line thus ensuring continuation of sought-after quality in future generations. Inbreeding is only detrimental if used casually or improperly (when inferior animals are used). Inbreeding doubles up virtues and faults so the hidden trap is not to set the gene pool to intensify faults.

These two Mastiffs, Ch. Storm Drudwenna of Swede Road and her sire Ch. Storm Hammer of Royal Oak, display excellent breed type and consistency in a breeding program.

I consider bitches the backbone of my own breeding program and I will, consequently, have more to say about them. I think of bitches as the gene carriers and attribute far more importance to their individual breed characteristics, structure, virtues, faults and temperament than to the stud dog when planning breedings. When I study a prospective breeding, I like six superior bitches (preferably related) in the first three generations of the pedigree of the bitch to be bred. Stud dogs are certainly important, too, but I would forgive a mediocre dog in a pedigree before discounting an average bitch. I always suspected my theory to be diametrically opposed to the opinions of my peers based on many discussions over the years with breeders and the importance others place in their careful selection of stud dogs. Rarely do I hear talk about the merits of bitches, however breeders expend great energy and long hours evaluating finer points or obvious faults of the stud dogs.

If you stand outside a show ring and listen to breeders talking about the dogs being shown, sooner or later you will certainly hear somebody say that "King" sired that one, and the good or undesirable points they discern are attributed solely to the sire. You will almost never hear anyone say that one is out of "Queen." No matter the outstanding traits or most unforgivable faults, the stud dog gets the credit or blame. It is as if the dam never participated in the genetic makeup of the offspring. If an average bitch is bred to a great stud dog and the litter produces only slightly better than average offspring you can bet the poor quality of the litter is laid at the door of the unfortunate stud dog. Our Sherman, with an outcross bitch, sired a puppy with a harelip and corkscrew tail (like a pig). The bitch's owners blamed poor Sherman because they decided he was exclusively at fault for the flaws. I must admit I took a perverse pleasure when, a year later, the same bitch produced the same flaws in a puppy sired by another stud dog.

When I plan a breeding, I study my bitch at great length, from all angles, standing and moving. I fantasize about how I would like a daughter of hers for myself and try to decide what I would change in the daughter. Perhaps I want a better head, or more bone or substance. Should there be improvement in the front or could the rear be better? Maybe a little length of body would help or the topline could be harder. If there were a better bend of stifle or more layback of shoulder perhaps overall movement would be enhanced. Once I visualize the imagined daughter and the parts of the dam I would change, if I could, then I have a better blueprint for what I need and am ready to look around for a stud dog who may be able to provide whatever it is I am trying to improve. I never ask too much of any stud dog, regardless of how wonderful he is or how prepotent he may be for passing along his best traits, because he can only correct so many faults.

Before considering breeding any bitch, all blinders need to be removed. With a critical eye really look at the bitch to determine if she merits being bred. The world does not need more dogs, it needs better ones. As a breeder, I believe balance is everything. If the standard for size is met, the bitch is structurally sound, typey and a good representative, if her temperament is correct for her breed, then the most important requirement for me is whether she is balanced. I want everything in proportion to everything else, the head, bone and body, front and rear should all go together to make up a pleasing, whole package. Next, study the bitch pedigree over and over and over. Serious breeders will familiarize themselves with good characteristics and undesirable faults traveling in their line. Even though she may not display the more well-known faults of her ancestors, those faults are nevertheless lurking in the genes ready to surface quickly enough if she is bred incorrectly.

The bitch selected for mating must be healthy, neither too young nor too old, and of correct weight. A bitch carrying too much weight will more likely not conceive and if she does, it will be much harder on her to deliver the pups naturally. She should be well exercised, well fed and in good condition, healthy in body and happy in spirit. Her annual shots should be up to date and she should have

Hollesley Lord Ralegh. Sire: Eng. Ch. Hollesley Medicine Man; Dam: Eng. Ch. Hollesley Rowella; Breeder: Mrs. Day; Owner: Fiona Zahnke. "Saxon" is from a full brother-sister breeding and he has had a tremendous influence on the breed in America.

a current brucellosis blood test performed to verify she is clear. She should be free of external and internal parasites.

Breeding should never be done spontaneously or casually. Enough unexpected things will occur with the onset of heat, so all plans should be laid well ahead of time. Every eventuality should be explored. Are you experienced enough to whelp the puppies on your own and, if not, will your veterinarian be on call for you, or is there an experienced breeder who will help? Is your veterinarian familiar enough with your breed to perform a cesarean section if an emergency develops? Do you have the funds necessary for such surgery? Do you work outside the home full time and, if so, can you take the time off from work to raise the litter?

It is not uncommon for a Mastiff bitch to develop complications and then puppies must be raised by hand which means bottle feeding around the clock, every two to four hours until they are weaned, at about three weeks of age. Have you the proper facilities in which to raise the puppies? A whelping box large enough to accommodate the bitch and her whelps is required and for her peace of mind it must be located in an area private enough to preclude interruptions and disturbing noises. Puppies need to be kept warm and free from draft. Cleanliness is essential. Once puppies are of an age to be placed, do you have enough homes waiting for your puppies? If not, are you prepared to keep the puppies, feeding them, socializing and training them, until homes can be found? Have you advertised the litter to generate interest and attract the best homes? Provided you have given all contingencies great thought and are prepared to meet every obligation to the dam and litter, then you can begin to search for the right stud dog.

My best puppies have come from line breeding, or breeding to a dog that is related, if only distantly, to my bitch. If that is not possible, or if the time is right to outcross for new blood and vigor or to correct a particular fault, then I want to choose a dog as similar in type as possible to my bitch, and at the same time preferably I want a dog who is himself tightly linebred or inbred. Years ago, we owned a beautifully structured bitch, but her head was not her fortune. When planning to breed, we knew we needed to improve heads on her offspring. The bitch was granddaughter to a father/daughter breeding, great-granddaughter to a son/mother breeding, and two generations further she went to a half-brother/half-sister breeding. The pedigree was so concentrated with tight breeding that she needed to be bred in such a way that her pedigree would not overwhelm the stud. We eventually chose a beautifully headed unrelated dog who, best of all, came from a full brother/sister breeding. Not all heads in the resulting puppies were what we wanted, but every head was better than the dam. We kept the best bitch and bred her to an unrelated dog for more head improvement, then linebred back with this generation to produce a consistent litter with good heads.

Ch. Lionsire Ironhill Warleggen.
Sire: Ch. Deer Run Ezekiel; Dam:
Ch. Farleys Eledwhen Steelsheen;
Breeder/Owner: Scott Phoebus.
Warleggen is shown here with
Mike Hoffman.

The same care and thought given to the pedigree of the bitch should be given to the pedigree of the stud dog. He, too, is only as good as all the dogs behind him. I want a masculine stud dog, he should be neither bitchy nor refined. The best criteria for selection of any stud dog, aside from his pedigree, is the offspring he has already produced. If he has sired litters with different bitches, so much the better. Did he put his stamp on any of his children, or better yet, all of them? If the stud has sired several litters out of different bitches, do the related offspring resemble each other? A really good-quality stud dog who also has the ability to reproduce himself, or consistently pass along his best qualities, and is proven to be a prepotent stud dog, is truly worth his weight in gold. If I am trying to improve head type, I search for a stud with an exaggerated head, plus all the desirable traits mentioned. If I want to increase bone, I search for a stud with excessive bone. If a trait is overdone or exaggerated, it is more likely to be passed along to the offspring. Naturally, this applies to faults, too. It is conceivable that an otherwise average stud dog can earn a reputation for consistently passing along a particularly good characteristic—which is why a close look at offspring is a good idea.

Difficulties of Breeding

Members of the Mastiff Club agree to adhere to a strict code of ethics that prohibits a bitch from being bred before the age of 22 months or after her seventh birthday nor, except in special circumstances, can a bitch be bred more than once a year. These guidelines were established for the welfare of the bitches being bred. Hence, the breeding life of a bitch is somewhat limited and it is important the stud dog be prolific and proficient at his job. I prefer a veteran stud that understands exactly what he is doing and who requires mini-

Tracy Bregman with her Jack Russell Terrier "Daisy" and Lazy Hill Louie.

mal human interference. An experienced stud is especially desirable when breeding a nervous, virgin bitch. The veteran does not take much time for courting or flirtation, but mates quickly and efficiently. With this kind of dog, the breeding is generally accomplished before the bitch has time to become overly frightened. When breeding a skittish, maiden bitch, a breeding rack equipped with seat belts or similar restraints is especially desirable because it will help to hold the bitch in place thus giving humans more control over the situation and reducing the risk of injury to either animal.

Some Mastiff bitches will decide for themselves the dog they wish to mate with and when this occurs there is no reasoning with the bitch about your selection of a different dog. In these cases, the breeding rack is absolutely essential. Even if the bitch and dog are willing to breed with each other, a rack should still be used. There can be a marked difference in the sizes of Mastiff dogs and bitches and the rack supports the bitch for the duration of the breeding.

Years ago, we decided to do an uncle/niece breeding with two of our Mastiffs. The bitch lived with the stud and adored him. They would play and sleep together, and were affectionate to each other. As her breeding time neared, we noticed she was giving rather a lot of attention to another male we owned. On the day of breeding it quickly became apparent she did not wish to mate her uncle and we had a major struggle on our hands. We accomplished the breeding of our choice, but when the litter was born the bitch did not have a drop of milk for her puppies, nor would she pay them the least bit of attention. I had to raise the litter with no assistance from her, beginning at birth. If a puppy from the litter went near the dam, she would growl. Her attitude towards me was very superior and condescending. She seemed to say: "You wanted them, you take care of them." The litter was as good as we had hoped. The next year we opted to breed the bitch to her choice, the stud she wanted the first time, and what a completely different situation! When his interest waned after several good breedings, she remained amorous and tried to entice his further interest. She adored the litter that resulted, almost refusing to leave the whelping box to see to her own needs and she nursed that litter through their five-week birthday.

In the 1930s, Hobart Titus wrote that one of his bitches had refused three different studs during two seasons before accepting a stud of her own choosing. One thing Mastiff owners learn is Mastiff bitches can be opinionated and stubborn, they are very particular about which dogs they choose to be mated with, as well as which ones may become their friends. After reading an earlier article I wrote, a lady from New Zealand called to get the blueprint of our breeding rack. She had a Mastiff dog and bitch she wished to breed together but every time the bitch was in season she would set her heart on breeding a Rottweiler that lived down the road. The bitch would not allow the poor Mastiff near. I was pleased to send her directions so she could build her own breeding rack and a year later the breeder called to say that with the help of her husband, veterinarian and the rack they had successful breedings and had whelped a beautiful litter of Mastiff puppies.

Understanding the Stud Dog

Young males will try to practice breeding on whatever bitches are handy, no matter if they are in season or not. Even if it is sometimes annoying, try never to tell them no. The word "no" can come back to haunt a breeder at exactly the wrong time. For the most part, let the males make pests of themselves with the bitches. If one of our dogs becomes too fresh with one of our girls, I have adopted the command "quit it" or "leave her alone." If the young dog becomes overly rude with a bitch, she will eventually put him back in his place and he generally forgives her immediately.

On the other hand, if you continually discourage the youngster and say no to him, he will begin to understand he is doing something wrong. Since the Mastiff wants to please his owners, he may not recognize the difference when the time arrives and you want him to breed a bitch. He will not wish to attempt the breeding for fear of your displeasure. Even while he is young and showing stud-dog tendencies, let him be a dog. If you do not plan to breed him, have him neutered. Otherwise, let him develop into what nature planned for him to be. It is a pleasure for any breeder to be able to work with a trained, sexually aggressive and confident stud. In Mastiffs, you encounter a goodly number of reluctant stud dogs. I have always thought this problem stems from the sensitive temperament of the Mastiff. Most of them are so lovable it is easy to pamper them and turn them into big, overgrown spoilt babies at home. This is as it should be, but it, perhaps, makes some of the breedings more difficult.

The last thing you or your bitch needs when you travel to effect a mating is the frustration and disappointment of an inexperienced dog who will not become the least bit amorous. When you are setting up a breeding, one of the first questions you should ask is whether the dog is proven, that is, has he been bred before and did he produce puppies? If so, did he breed naturally? Many of today's breeders find it easier to artificially inseminate their bitches or surgically implant fresh chilled or frozen sperm directly into the uterus. If the stud lives too far away and you choose not to send your bitch to him, then shipping sperm is the ideal solution. On the other hand, if you can deliver your bitch to the stud, it is still the best way. I think too much artificial breeding occurs and I believe some vigor in the breed may be lost as a result, and the fact is the Mastiff breed as a whole can ill afford to lose vigor when it comes to breeding.

If every breed of dogs has a major inherent problem, then in Mastiffs I am completely convinced that problem is reproduction. If the dogs were allowed to be dogs in the most natural sense they would, by choice, be pack animals. In the pack, a hesitant stud dog would not get a chance to breed a bitch. He would be weeded out at once so his tendencies, or lack thereof, would cease with him. Only the strongest, most driven and virile stud dogs would be chosen by bitches in the wild for breeding. My own opinion is reluctant stud dogs should probably not be used for breeding and in the natural order of things the tendency would disappear.

Breeding Environment

The environment where the actual breeding is to take place is very important. Breeding dogs is absolutely not a spectator sport and only those persons necessary to accomplish the breeding should be present. The dog to be used at stud should not be fed just before or just after a breeding. We allow a minimum of five hours to lapse after eating before attempting to breed a dog. Nor would we offer food for several hours following a breeding, although one of our males loved the tiny bowl of vanilla ice cream he always received following a successful breeding, after which he would sleep for hours.

The act of mating is probably the most stressful and exhaustive activity any dog will ever undertake. There is no other time in the life of a stud dog when he is more prone to fainting, collapse, heat prostration or bloat. In summer, breedings should only occur in early morning before it gets too hot or in late evening after it has cooled. In hot weather, Mastiffs should never be bred in direct sunshine, and this is particularly true if one of the animals being mated is of brindled color which tends to draw the sun and heat. The stud should not be permitted to gulp water after breeding. A little water or, preferably, crushed ice or ice cubes is better for him. If it is extremely hot, wet him down with cold water from the hose and then find a quiet, cool place for him to rest undisturbed.

If you own stud dogs that live with bitches coming and going in heat and you are not planning to breed, you need to take steps to protect the stud dogs. One of our stud dogs bloated and died while a bitch of ours was on her 17th day of heat and we were skipping the heat. This dog had no food and little water in him, he bloated purely from stress. I have heard of four other Mastiff stud dogs that bloated while living with bitches in heat they were not allowed to breed. When our girls are in standing breeding heat now, our dogs are mildly sedated to protect them from bloat.

Most stud dogs have a tendency to lose weight when they live with girls in heat. Some studs will lose weight even if the bitches do not live with them, but instead are brought to them for service. Each stud dog, naturally, develops his own unique habits. A stud dog that lives in close proximity with bitches coming and going in heat will eventually become accustomed to the smells that identify the different stages of heat and this type of stud will usually continue to eat right up to the time when the bitch enters standing/breeding cycle. At that time, the majority of stud dogs will turn away from food and lose weight. When the heat passes or the breedings are ended, the stud dogs return to their food and regain the lost weight. Force feeding a stud dog during this time, perhaps to keep him in show weight, is not a good idea. Nature dictates to him that he needs to lose the weight in order to get him into condition to perform the breeding. If one goes against nature and force feeds the stud dog, he may be placed in harms way and become even more vulnerable to bloat.

Training the Stud Dog and the Mechanics of Breeding

The breeding rack should be placed in an area with no traffic (human or otherwise) and all other dogs and bitches except the two being bred should be out of sight. If a male is being introduced to stud for the first time, the ideal bitch for mating is one the dog lives with and knows well because he will trust her and be more confident. If the bitch is unknown to the male it is imperative she be of a tolerant disposition. The first breeding should be made as pleasant as possible for the fledgling stud dog. Once the bitch has been secured on the rack the breeding can commence. If there is any doubt about how the bitch will receive the dog's attentions, then she should be muzzled at least until a tie is accomplished and the dog turned away from her. One person should always be at the head of the bitch ready to intercept if she becomes aggressive.

An inexperienced male may try to mount the front of the bitch just as quickly as the rear. Do not be discouraged or impatient with him, with your help he will figure things out. We train dogs to mount the rear of the bitch by having one person stand at the left of the bitch and one person at her right. If the dog tries to mount the head, one or the other person backs up and blocks his way. Same thing for side mounting. The idea is to make it difficult for him to get on the bitch in a place you do not want him mounting. We do not distract the dog by talking while he is trying to get around us, we just block his access. He will eventually realize his only option is to mount at the rear, because that is the only accessible area. Once the dog proceeds in that direction and mounts, we quietly praise him.

Now that the dog is in the proper position to breed the bitch, you need to kneel down at the side of the bitch's rear and ascertain if he is hitting in the right place. If he is probing too high or too low, take the dog away while you make the needed adjustment to the breeding rack with the idea of accommodating him. When the stud is back in place, you can assist him by cupping the bitch's vulva to help his aim. When the male enters the bitch, have someone at his rear give a quick push. Or you can take your thumb and forefinger and apply pressure just behind the bulb and the dog will thrust into the bitch on his own. The object is to get an inside tie, that is, the bulb of the penis will be swollen inside of the bitch so that the stud cannot withdraw from her.

One of the most frustrating mistakes the human deals with when breeding dogs is the outside tie. If you understand why they happen and how to handle them once they have occurred, then they can be eliminated altogether. The stud dog must rely on what he feels because he cannot see what is happening, consequently if he feels his penis is encircled he concludes he is inside the bitch and swells fully in order to achieve the tie. If humans would be more careful about handling the stud-dog's penis there would be fewer outside ties. When the stud needs intervention, try to help him by guiding the bitch to him rather than the reverse or with your open palm placed on the underside of the penis he can be guided in the right direction.

Once an outside tie has occurred, you are faced with several choices. The stud dog can be held in place, tight to the bitch, so the sperm is not simply lost on the ground. Or, you could back away from the stud dog, leaving him atop the bitch and wait a few minutes for him to comprehend the bulb of his penis is not in the bitch where he thought it was. We have lifted the stud back up on the bitch and left him hanging there until he figures this out. Most dogs will prod and thrust several times at this stage, before coming to understand something is not right. As soon as the stud realizes he is not where he was supposed to be he will abort the outside tie. When the penis is back up in the sheath he is ready to begin all over again. Some breeders use the theory of a bird in the hand being better than two loose in the bush, and they prefer to hold the dog and bitch together for the duration of the outside tie rather than risk losing the breeding effort altogether.

Due to the greater likelihood of conception from the inside tie we prefer to let the stud dog pull up and begin again. In addition to using a breeding rack, we use a breeding bench. One of our best stud dogs suffered a knee injury, so to avoid having to turn him on his good leg while crossing the injured leg over the bitch back, or vice versa, we built a bench that could be slipped into place under the belly of the bitch once the animals were tied. The stud dog's front feet would be carefully positioned on the bench with one foot on either side of the bitch so that he could support his own weight for the duration of the breeding, thereby taking his weight off the back of the bitch. The bench would be invaluable for the outside tie, too, since the stud dog cannot be turned away from the bitch.

When an inside tie is confirmed, help the male down off the bitch so he is standing to one side of her. After a minute or so, bring his hind leg from the opposite side across the bitch's back, carefully moving him around into position until the two animals are standing rear to rear. Turning the male puts some tension on the organs and starts a muscle action along the length of the bitch's genital tract which helps launch the sperm toward the eggs. Once the animals stand tail to tail, try not to allow the stud dog to pull too far away from the bitch. Some tension is good, but too much and he could break the tie too early and either animal is at risk for injury.

Caring for the Stud Dog and Bitch After Breeding

When the breeding is completed, the penis will reduce enough in size to allow separation from the bitch. The penis may still be partially swollen and the stud dog should be monitored until he has completely drawn the penis back up into the sheath. When he is able, take him away from the bitch and walk him until he has relieved his bladder before putting him in his quiet place.

If there was an inside tie, the bitch may be taken off the rack and put up. If an outside tie was held together, leave the bitch on the rack for a few minutes. With an outside tie, you might want to unstrap the seat belts or undo the restraints and leave her front in place on the rack and elevate her hindquarters for, perhaps, 10 minutes to encourage the sperm to set deeply in the bitch. Then, put her away without allowing her to urinate.

There is no fixed time limit once the animals are tied together. While waiting for a tie to conclude the animals can become restless and agitated. The people attending the breeding should speak quietly to them, praising and reassuring them so they may be kept calm. Breedings can range from three to forty-five minutes, or even longer. Some breeders say the bitch controls the time of the tie and others say it is the dog. I don't know which is correct, all I know is you have no choice but to wait it out. Anything can happen, really, during this time of the tie. One of our stud dogs, when he sensed a tie was nearing its conclusion, would do his utmost to get away from us in order to turn around and remount the bitch. One of our bitches howled for a solid 20 minutes during her tie, all the while wagging happily at us. She did not fight us, the stud or being restrained on the rack, she simply howled and nothing we were able to say or do would stop her. Fortunately, the stud dog was not the least bit put off by her behavior.

Another bitch of ours that had flirted and encouraged the stud, a dog she lived with and adored, decided after being tied with him that she no longer wanted to participate in the breeding. She fought with all her considerable strength to displace the stud dog, who had already been turned around. In those days, we had no seat belts or restraints on the breeding rack and after vigorous thrashing and struggling she managed to roll onto her side and off of the rack. We literally caught her midair and were able to hold her by all four legs, upside down, until the breeding reached its conclusion which, thankfully, was not very long. I have often thought we must have appeared totally ridiculous during that breeding, hanging on to that bitch with her in a position similar to that of deer when hunters bring them in suspended from poles. By the way, both of the above mentioned bitches went on to whelp litters from those breedings.

Missed Pregnancies

Ideally, breedings take place every other day until the stud dog is no longer interested. Despite the fact that many matings of Mastiffs are textbook breedings, for some inexplicable reason the bitches just do not conceive. Most often the reason is that breedings are being done on the wrong days, either too early or too late. Blood tests have gone a long way towards eliminating misses, but there are still too many missed pregnancies in Mastiffs even when the blood

What do ya mean, you didn't want 15 children? (Can. Ch. Storm Drudwen of Lazy Hill & Can. Ch. Northwood Earl of Locxley).

work dictated the best days to breed. A nervous, high-strung bitch may be more successfully bred in her own environment rather than having to travel to the home of the stud dog.

When the Mastiff bitch is in heat, her vulva becomes very distended and swollen. Every time she squats to urinate she can drag unwanted debris back up inside of her that could result in a low-grade infection that may not be noticed or may not even be detectable. Even the most minor of infections can interfere with conception. If a bitch of mine is well bred and misses more than once, she is put on a regimen of low amounts of Amoxicillin or a similar antibiotic prescribed by the veterinarian for the duration of her next season and bitches that were not conceiving have gone on to have successful pregnancies.

Responsibilities of Bitch Owners

Bitch owners have responsibilities to stud-dog owners. As already mentioned, breedings need to be planned in advance. Even with this precaution, sometimes the services of the stud dog are so much in demand he is promised to several bitches who need to be bred at the same time and a conflict occurs. It is, therefore, wise for the bitch's owner to have a second choice of stud dog in mind if a conflict happens and the first choice stud dog is not available when needed, or the bitch's owner may want to be prepared to call off breeding until the next season. The owner of the bitch should contact the owner of the stud dog at the onset of heat to ascertain the breeding can go forth. If for some reason the bitch cannot keep the breeding appointment, the bitch's owner needs to contact the stud dog owner immediately and release the stud dog from the obligation so he can accommodate another bitch that may have been set aside for your bitch.

When we accept a bitch for breeding to one of our stud dogs, we always want to know whether the bitch is a house pet or accustomed to being kenneled. It would be traumatic to take a house pet, already somewhat nervous due to being in heat and in strange surroundings, and house her in our kennel. We try to make the bitch as comfortable as possible under the circumstances because we understand her mental state is important and may help her to conceive.

One of the most important responsibilities of the bitch's owner, to my mind, is the bitch not come to us with fleas. Fleas can take hold in the home and kennel and spread like wild fire. This has happened to us on several occasions. Unfortunately, the time and money necessary to remedy the problem is not reimbursable. For this reason, we now require a statement from the bitch's veterinarian that she is free of fleas (they are not in the best interests of the bitch anyway).

The bitch should be accompanied by enough of her own food to see her through her stay. While we would not mind feeding the visiting bitch, we may not use the food she is accustomed to eating and a change might cause diarrhea which would not be pleasant for anyone, most especially the bitch. If she has a favorite toy, bone or blanket, these items should come with her too. Remember, the purpose is to make her feel at home for the duration of her stay.

It is not at all uncommon for a bitch to be blood tested, pronounced ready to breed and conceive, and sent along to the stud dog, yet upon arrival at her destination and upon presentation to the stud dog the bitch is no longer in breeding heat and the dog may show only casual interest in her, but he will not attempt breeding. What happened is that while the bitch was en route she set back in her heat, literally she went backwards. If this occurs, within a few days the bitch will usually catch back up to where she had been and the stud's interest increases daily so that within a few days the breeding will proceed normally.

When the bitch returns home after the breeding, she needs to be kept away from all other dogs for at least a week. You will not wish for another dog to have access to the bitch, possibly even manage a breeding with her, and thus call into question the parentage of the resulting litter. Even though DNA testing is available and can now be sought to determine positive parentage through blood work, it is much easier and safer to confine her until she is well and truly out of heat.

Years ago, one of our dogs was committed to service a bitch from several states away. Once heat commenced, she was closely monitored by her veterinarian and when the time was considered right the owner brought the bitch to us. A breeding was easily accomplished, one day was skipped, and she was bred again after which the stud dog totally lost interest. The owner and bitch returned home to prepare for a litter. A week went by and the owner called to say the bitch was beginning to stand again and was flagging anew for a dog the bitch lived with. Not completely understanding what was happening, as we were all convinced the bitch had ended her breeding heat, it was agreed the bitch should be taken back to her veterinarian. Much to the surprise of all of us the veterinarian confirmed the bitch had rolled back into heat and was at exactly the same stage of heat she had been in when she came to us previously for breeding. The owner immediately returned the bitch to our stud dog and we had one more breeding between the animals. Interestingly enough that bitch eventually delivered a lovely litter, exactly 61 days from the first breeding.

Care of and Changes in the Pregnant Bitch

Caution should always be exercised when a bred bitch is reintroduced to her canine friends because the rapid hormonal changes taking place may affect her temperament and she could become testy or show aggression to a dog or bitch that, under normal circumstances, is her best friend. Most bitches go through slight personality changes while pregnant. They are extremely affectionate during pregnancy and towards the end of gestation they will not want their owners out of sight.

We begin our bitches on two pet tabs a day from the day of breeding and midway through the pregnancy increase to four pet tabs a day which she will stay on until puppies are weaned. It is essential a pregnant bitch be well nourished to enable her to meet the extra demands put on her by the developing puppies. Failure to meet nutritional requirements can have an adverse effect on muscle mass, liver, spleen and pituitary function and may even result in ineffectual nursers. In the last stage of pregnancy this deprivation could cause stunted growth of the fetus.

Many breeders automatically switch their bred bitches from adult to puppy food. Studies show a protein level of 25 percent to 30 percent is adequate, combined with a maximum fat content of 9 percent which should be made up of at least 25 percent linoleic acid. If the fat level goes above 13 percent there is evidence of a decrease in average birth weight and a higher rate of death during the first 24 hours. There are no sure signs early on to detect pregnancy, but there are some clues you can watch for. Sometimes my bred bitches sleep deeply for an entire week following being bred when previous to the breeding they would have been off playing. Sometimes they throw up food which is only partially digested, or yellow bile or a mixture of bile and grass. When canines feel uncertain in their stomachs they will graze on grass. Between the third and fourth week after being bred, bitches may go off their food for a day or two, and stay off for upwards of two weeks, picking at and nibbling their food but not really eating with their former appetite.

If the bitch is not already receiving two meals a day, halfway through the gestation period you will want to begin feeding her twice a day. Towards the end of gestation, if the bitch has become very uncomfortable, feed smaller amounts spread over three or four feedings. I have never had a pregnant bitch ingest double her normal amount of food, which often is the recommendation during pregnancy and whelping. Generally, we feed about three-quarters of the normal daily intake in the morning and the same amount again in the evening. If the bitch cleans up these two meals and looks about hopefully for more, we add a little more in both feedings. With Mastiffs, one needs to keep in mind if the bitch gains a lot of weight, and the pregnancy turns out to be false, then you must go about cutting back the food to reduce her weight.

Around five weeks along, pregnancy can become obvious unless there are only one or two puppies and then pregnancy may not be detected until the last moment. As the last two weeks of gestation are approached, the bitch's appetite may lessen or disappear altogether. Pregnant bitches are so uncomfortable at this stage of gestation, particularly if they are heavy in whelp, that you really must pamper and cater to them. Cooked hamburger or chicken mixed with rice and a little of their normal dog food may whet the appetite.

It is not at all uncommon for a Mastiff heavy in whelp to lose bladder control near the end, so please, please don't scold them for they can not help such accidents. They feel so much pressure on their bladders that before they can communicate to you they need to be let out, they have already urinated. A bitch of ours, carrying 14 puppies, not only had no time to warn us, she was not forewarned herself. As she walked across the room she would loose a stream of urine, never even having had time to squat. If the bitch is carrying a particularly large litter, she could even experience restricted breathing due to the pressure on her diaphragm. I have heard of Mastiff bitches who have contracted pneumonia because of this complication.

Exercise during the latter stage of pregnancy needs to be strictly monitored. The bitch certainly needs exercise, but she should not be permitted to run, jump or play at this time. If the bitch is high spirited, controlled walking on leash would be in her best interests.

Pseudo-Pregnancy (False Pregnancy)

Sadly, sometimes a bitch can be well and truly bred and for no apparent reason does not conceive. She may demonstrate all the symptoms of normal pregnancy when, in fact, she has no puppies inside her. She either did not conceive a litter or, perhaps, she resorbed the litter that had begun to develop. Unless the bitch is confirmed pregnant by palpation or sonogram you will not know which condition actually applies. She might maintain an appearance of healthy pregnancy right up to the last few weeks of the gestation period, reckoned to be 59 to 65 days. My personal knowledge with this condition is that during the last two weeks before puppies are due, the bitch that has missed being pregnant will lose interest in food and may appear a bit depressed.

In most cases, the mammary development consistent with a true pregnancy will start to dissipate and the abdomen will shrink back to its former size, unless the bitch was so well nourished to accommodate the false litter that she gained excess weight. This condition is called a false pregnancy, or pseudopregnancy. It is a fallacy to believe a bitch must be bred to experience a false pregnancy. Mastiffs can have perfectly normal heat cycles, be confined the duration of their season, so one is positive they are not bred, yet the bitch will increase and show all the behavior patterns of the bitch that was bred.

I had a bitch in a motel room while we were attending out-of-state dog shows and she began to demonstrate bizarre behavior that was alarming. She had minor mammary enlargement, but otherwise looked to be in good weight and health. The evening began with her alternating between frequent solid bowel movements and diarrhea. In between these bouts of diarrhea, she was purging herself by emptying her stomach of all food. I never travel without a supply of Kaopectic for the dogs, so she was doctored immediately and we brought the initial problem under control. As the night progressed, her temperature dropped so much she was cold to my touch and she began trembling, showing marked attention to her hindquarters, which was eventually followed by licking of her vulva. It finally dawned on me she was whelping an imaginary litter. A quick telephone call home to check the calendar confirmed my theory. I felt so sorry for her, and understanding how much stress she was under, we packed up and left for home immediately, skipping the shows. In her next season we bred her, she conceived and delivered gorgeous whelps.

Whether bred or not complications can develop with a false pregnancy and the bitch needs to be monitored. Some will have so much mammary development they begin milk production which can, in turn, lead to infection that requires treatment with an antibiotic.

Pyometritis (Pyometra)

Pyometra is a life-threatening condition that is widely recognized as one of the most serious and dreaded infections that can occur in a valuable breeding bitch. "Pyo" means pus, "metra" means uterus, hence, it is defined as pus in the uterus. As recently as 15 years ago, when a bitch was confirmed with pyometra the only immediate and satisfactory resolution in order to save the bitch's life was to institute antibiotic and fluid therapies in order to stabilize and strengthen the bitch and then surgery was performed to remove the ovaries and uterus, a procedure called ovariohysterectomy, more commonly known as spaying. There are two types of pyometra, open and closed. *Neither type should be taken lightly. At the onset of any symptom or upon the first suspicion of pyometra, the bitch should be taken to the veterinarian at once.*

Of the two forms, open pyometra is the least severe because the cervix is open and allows drainage of the pus. In some open pyometra cases the condition has been mistakenly diagnosed as an aberrant heat. The abnormal vaginal discharge is foul smelling, of creamy consistency and is tomato-soup colored. The closed form has no avenue of drainage, since the cervix is not open, consequently the pus builds up inside the uterus, intensifying and spreading the infection until the bitch's life is in jeopardy. In the case of closed pyometra, because the uterus enlarges due to an accumulation of pus, there will be a pronounced swelling of the abdomen. Other signs of this infection are a noticeably increased thirst, increased urination, fever, extreme lethargy and overall weakness. When clinical blood work is performed it will reveal an elevated white blood cell count.

The condition has often been blamed on hormonal imbalances. It was once thought to occur only in older bitches who had irregular heat cycles, although mismate shots administered to abort ill-conceived litters are also known to have resulted in pyometra. The infection will most often develop within weeks of going out of heat, whelping a litter, or after being bred and missing conception. The earlier pyometra is diagnosed and appropriate therapy begun, the better the chance of preserving the bitch's uterus.

In 1981, there was a hallmark case of pyometra in Mastiffs when Ch. Peersleigh Princess Carolyn, owned by Dr. Roscoe and Jacqueline Guy, was diagnosed with closed pyometra. Carolyn was considered a most worthy representative of the breed, having won three coveted Working Group placements before that group was reduced by nearly half from 34 breeds. Carolyn, a maiden bitch, was a product of father/daughter breeding and a granddaughter of mother/son breeding, so when she was accidentally caught in season by her sire, a mismate shot was administered to preclude a litter being conceived. It was believed the injection caused closed pyometra. Carolyn was in dire condition and underwent a new and radical treatment at a well-known and highly respected university veterinary hospital. The treatment was successful, Carolyn was pronounced well and released. Once home, she relapsed back into the former condition and underwent the treatment a second time. Over the next two years, Carolyn produced two litters containing 15 puppies, including my dear Sherman, and 11 puppies including my Samantha.

Veterinarians, through advanced knowledge and modern medicine, are now able to save many valuable bitches for future breedings. In 1996, one of my favorite bitches underwent successful therapy for open pyometra and she went on to whelp puppies. The treatment of choice is difficult for the bitch. My bitch was treated with high dosages of antibiotic and received two daily injections of prostaglandins for more than a week. The shots, which sting, are intended to cause hard uterine contractions to squeeze pus out of the uterus. Immediately after the shots are administered, the bitch is walked for at least 30 minutes, as this helps her endure the treatment with less discomfort. The treatment causes vomiting, and it can cause diarrhea.

CHAPTER 13
WHELPING AND PUPPIES

Gestation, Whelping, Brood Bitch and Lactating

Gestation is the period during which the bitch is pregnant and carrying her puppies. It is generally accepted that puppies will be whelped 63 days, or 9 weeks, from conception. It is perfectly normal for a bitch to whelp anywhere from 58 to 65 days of gestation, but if puppies are born before 57 days it is more likely they are too young to survive.

Whelping is the act of birthing puppies and newborn puppies are often referred to as whelps. There is no way to know in advance how much time it will take to whelp a litter as it depends on the health and physical condition of each individual bitch, the environment in which the whelping will take place and how many puppies must be delivered by the bitch.

A female canine who is a maiden is referred to simply as a bitch and after giving birth to a litter of puppies she is labeled a brood bitch. Lactation refers to the secretion or production of milk and a lactating bitch is one who is producing milk and nursing her puppies.

The author's bitch "Cookie" pregnant with 14 puppies.

The Whelping Box and Supplies for Natural Whelping

As mentioned, a private area free of noise and distractions should already be selected for the whelping box. Approximately two weeks before the litter is due, the whelping box should be assembled. Some breeders use a sheet of linoleum to cover the floor of the box. Others put a sheet of plastic under the box to protect from any fluid leakage. If the box is new it should be clean. If the whelping box was used to raise a litter previously, it will need to be scrubbed completely clean before being put together. You will not want to run the risk of germs from a former litter transferring to or contaminating a new litter. An easy method of cleaning the used box is to fill a spray bottle with half bleach and water, spraying and scrubbing as you go with a hard bristle scrub brush until all surfaces are sanitary. The well-rinsed pieces of the box should be left in the sun to dry and air for a few days. After setting up the whelping box, layer it with newspapers, old sheets or blankets, keeping in mind everything, including the sheets and blankets, may be shredded. If the dam is a first timer, she should be encouraged to sleep in the box a week or two before the due date.

Birthing puppies is a messy affair. You will want to remove soiled material after the final puppy is born. Other supplies you will want on hand are plenty of clean towels, hot water bottles or electric heating pads, a heat lamp with infrared bulb, clock, rectal thermometer, several clean or new cardboard boxes, dental floss, iodine, sterile scissors (3 to 5 minutes in boiling water), notepad and pencil, flashlight, and phone numbers to reach your veterinarian in an emergency.

When the dam is ready to settle down with her litter, and the soiled material she used to whelp in the box is removed, you will

Tia, Can. Ch. Storm Brudwen of Lazy Hill, pregnant with 15 puppies.

need to cover the floor of the whelping box with something to offer both warmth and secure footing to the puppies. Whatever you decide to use, choose something that can be easily changed and washed. Rubber-backed bathroom carpeting is ideal, and depending on the size of your whelping box may possibly be purchased to fit its dimensions. I use 6' x 5' carpets that work nicely in our whelping box, and I lay clean towels over the entire area. As the bitch cleans her puppies and dampens small areas, individual towels can be replaced as needed. Every other day or so I change the carpet so the surface stays warm and dry for the puppies. Crawling newborns get excellent traction on layered surfaces. I use the carpet and towel system in the box until puppies are well up on their feet and weaned. When weaned, one end of the box is layered with newspapers, covered by additional shredded newspaper, and the other end of the box remains carpeted. The importance of keeping puppies warm, dry and clean cannot be over emphasized.

The Bitch in Labor

We are closing in on the long awaited event, the birth of puppies, and the most important advice you will ever get is stay with your bitch. Do not leave her alone at this critical time. If this is her first litter she is scared, nervous, apprehensive and most likely does not understand what is happening. She will have felt sensations and changes going on inside long before you can detect any overt signs of labor and by staying at her side, you can calm and reassure her. She needs to be soothed and only someone she trusts can restore her confidence. This is definitely not the time for company to drop by, particularly if the people are unknown to your bitch. Believe it or not, she is in charge of her body and she has the ability to call off or suspend her labor if she feels the least bit threatened. If she does this, it could endanger the puppies if it is, indeed, their time to be born.

There are many different signs whelping is imminent. Your bitch may display a single sign, all of them, or absolutely none. There are no rules. Each bitch is uniquely different and approaches birthing in her own way. Mastiffs are so strong and stoic you may see no sign at all prior to the first puppy entering the world. In addition to refusing all food, the earliest sign that whelping is beginning are slight panting, restlessness and shivering.

A week before the due date you should begin taking the bitch's rectal temperature twice a day, both to establish her normal body temperature and to begin watching for a drop in temperature. Her temperature may decline in small increments until it is around the 100-degree mark and it may stabilize here for a day or more. This, in and of itself, is not abnormal. It explains why the bitch intermittently shivers and should not concern you. However, when the temperature dips to 99 degrees and below, it is generally an important indication whelping is near and you may anticipate labor will begin within 12 to 24 hours. This significant change in the bitch's body temperature is nature's way of reducing the body temperature the puppies maintained while they were safely harbored inside the uterus. Nature is helping prepare the whelps so they are able to withstand the shock of a greatly reduced temperature out in the world into which they are about to be thrust.

The bitch may start to nest, she will circle and move papers and blankets around in the whelping box several days before the event, or only minutes before. Some bitches become quite frantic to dig and tear at whatever material is in the whelping box. As labor progresses, she may pant harder than she did earlier and you may observe her arching her back or see some rippling of muscles in her back. She may vomit one time, or several times during whelping, or not at all. Her eyes may take on a dilated or glossy appearance. She may begin to look anxiously toward her rear and start licking her vulva. Some bitches brace themselves against the whelping box as they strain, others may stay on their feet and hunker down while they labor to push out a puppy.

You might be able to observe actual labor, when the uterus hardens or tenses with a contraction and then, as the contraction passes, the uterus relaxes again. Some Mastiffs will deliver a puppy, to all appearances, absolutely effortlessly without you seeing anything. Often a bitch will feel what she believes is a strong urge to have a bowel movement and she may communicate to you a desperation to go outside. Go with the bitch just in case she is confused and instead is preparing to deliver the first whelp. At night, be sure to use your flashlight and do not let her out of your sight. Walking her on leash is prudent and it would be wise to take along a towel since puppies are very slippery and you need to get the puppy into the warmed-up room quickly.

If you recall the bitch I described who entertained us by howling nonstop when she was bred, you will enjoy hearing about her special method of whelping. As each puppy was pushed into the world, she screamed its arrival to everyone within a 10-block radius. After producing nine healthy, strong puppies she settled down to nurse them. I was positive she was done, based on her attitude and contentment to lay and feed the puppies. Almost eight hours after the last puppy was born, I gave her a shot to clean her out. My husband took her outside on leash so that whatever she produced wouldn't mess up our already tidy area inside. As I stood in the doorway watching them walk, the bitch squatted and screamed, at the same time my husband yelled she was having a puppy, and simultaneously that poor little guy went rolling down our mountain side! My poor husband was calling out to me for direction, and my poor bitch was nearly strangling herself on the leash trying to get away and follow her baby, when I yelled to let her off leash because she knew what to do. The puppy turned out fine, the bitch was fine and my husband survived, too. Yet another bitch of ours gave no sign whatsoever of labor. She would sit down in a lovely obedience sit, roll over on a hip and out would slide a puppy. She was the most nonchalant whelper I've ever known.

The Puppies Being Born

Each puppy is contained in an intricately designed double-layered sac. The first sac to emerge is the water bag. If it ruptures being forced out it produces a fluid ranging from a yellowish-straw hue to a greenish-tinted black color. As it pushes along the birth canal it can burst and thus lubricate the passage in preparation for the following puppy. The puppy should be in yet another sac, a thin, transparent membrane which is filled with a gelatinous amniotic fluid that served to protect the whelp and umbilical cord. The cord links the puppy to the placenta which is how the puppy was nourished and able to receive oxygen from the dam. Once the amniotic sac containing the puppy detaches from the uterine wall all connection to the dam to receive nourishment and oxygen is interrupted. This is why is so important to break open the sac immediately and enable the puppy to get air.

It is instinctual for the dam to tear the sac open and encourage the puppy to take its first breath. Sometimes, with first-time mothers and firstborn puppies, there is a delay and the dam does not do her job quickly enough. If this happens, you must intercede at once, tear the sac open at the end that contains the puppy's head and get the puppy breathing, otherwise the puppy is liable to drown in its own amniotic fluid. The object is to interfere with the dam as little as possible, yet at the same time you need to make certain the puppy is not in any immediate distress.

I have heard horror stories about bitches who whelped their puppies and simply walked away. One breeder I know stayed up with her bitch for three days and nights and, finally, in total exhaustion the breeder took a short nap. When she awakened, four whelps were strewn around the room, still encased in their sacs, completely cold and well beyond resuscitation. This is why it is so important to stay with the bitch, and if you must rest, have another family member stand in for you.

Each puppy should be followed by its own placenta. Bitches are inclined to eat the placenta. Ingesting one or two should not affect her. If she eats more than a couple, it may make her nauseous and could cause her to have messy bowel movements, but otherwise it should not harm her. If the afterbirth (placenta) doesn't appear with the next contraction, right behind the puppy, you may still be able to facilitate its removal by tugging very gently downwards on the cord and, thus, getting it from out of her. It is important to count the placentas because if even one stays inside the bitch it can cause serious complications.

If the dam is clever and doing her job properly, she will shred the umbilical cord with her teeth. Since Mastiffs can have an underbite you should be sure the bitch's bite won't hinder this activity. If she has to work hard at severing the cord she might cause an umbilical hernia to the puppy. If she is badly undershot you will need to sever the cord for her. Before breaking the connection of the umbilical cord that extends between the puppy and placenta pinch the cord one and a half to two inches away from the puppy's abdomen with the thumb and forefinger of one hand and with your other hand gently stroke or milk upwards on the cord towards the puppy. What you are doing is pushing placental blood in the cord towards the puppy so there will be less bleeding when the cord is separated and, more importantly, this is the last nutrition the whelp receives

First puppy is born and all cleaned up.

Dam is cleaning the first puppy while the second awaits her attention. Note the umbilical cord is still attached to the puppy and the placenta, which is yet to appear.

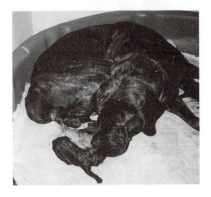

Dam is now attending to the second puppy.

While three puppies nurse, the fourth puppy is arriving—you can clearly see the puppy's front leg and head visible through the membrane.

Newborn Mastiff puppies by Ch. Peersleigh Storm Sherman out of Loxley Storm Druidess.

through the umbilical cord and it may be just enough to help the puppy through the trauma of being born. After this is done, sever the cord in the same spot where you previously pinched it by tearing with your fingers or cutting with sterile scissors. This cord is remarkably resilient and extremely slippery and the area where you pinched the cord may have dried out a bit thereby creating a weak area in which to tear. If you tear the cord, be very careful you do not pull away from the puppy because the strain could cause an umbilical hernia to the puppy. Always work towards the puppy.

If the bitch's instincts are on target she will begin vigorously cleaning the puppy. Aside from the actual birth of the puppy, this is the most important step in the birth process. Not only is the dam bonding to her whelp, her energetic licking and cleaning is actually nature's way of getting the puppy's systems stimulated. She is simultaneously warming and drying her puppy and removing any birthing fluid remaining in the puppy that may interfere with breathing. She is stimulating the puppy to ensure the contents of the bowels are removed. The first bowel movement from the puppy is called meconium and consists partly of debris from mucous membranes lining the intestines and partly of bile which was secreted by the liver. Until the puppy gets this meconium out of its system, proper digestion can not take place.

If the dam is indifferent or hesitant about working the puppy, you will need to place the puppy in a towel, preferably a warm towel, and energetically rub the puppy yourself. This requires some elbow grease on your part so do not be overly gentle. Rub fairly briskly to get the circulation in the puppy going. You will want to hear the puppy cry out or squeak as this assures you the whelp is sucking in deep breaths of air. When the puppy is breathing, you need to clear up any lingering sound of congestion. Being quite sure that you have a firm grip of the puppy wrapped in a towel, one hand securely wound around the back of the body supporting the whelp's spine, and one hand tightly cupping the head supporting the whelp's neck, you can give a quick swing in a downward arc to expel fluid from the mouth and nose.

Once the puppy is breathing clearly, you can tie off the umbilical cord about one half inch away from the puppy's abdomen with dental floss. When the cord is neatly tied off and the job complete, apply a tiny amount of iodine to the stump of the cord. The cord should dry up quickly and fall off the puppy in a day or two.

If the bitch is not already laboring to deliver the next puppy, have her lie down in the box and encourage the puppy to nurse on her teat. It takes very little encouragement on your part, only hold the baby to the teat, squeeze a drop out and let the whelp get a taste, he should do the rest. As soon as the bitch begins to show signs of restlessness or preparations for the next puppy, remove the live whelp from her and place it in the cardboard box that you have set up in one corner of the whelping box so she sees and knows exactly where her puppy is. Never take the puppy away from her as this can distress her. If she frets or is distracted, it may take her mind off of what she needs to be doing.

The cardboard box should already be waiting for the puppies with a heating pad set on low, or hot water bottles, covered with toweling so puppies will not be burned. The heat lamp should not be directly aimed at the cardboard box, but rather hung some two to three feet above the whelping box so the general area is kept warm. Another towel should be laid across the top of the cardboard box so the warmth in the box is self-contained and a type of incubator is created. With each new puppy, repeat this process until the whelping is finished. When you believe the bitch has finished delivering all her puppies, encourage her to lie down with them to be nursed and cleaned.

Try to find time between delivery of each puppy to make notations in your note pad. This is a good way to keep count of the placenta for each puppy. Note the exact time of birth and if you are using a baby scale, weigh each newborn and record the weight, sex, color and any unusual markings. Should events get very hectic you can refer back to your notes and it will tell you exactly how much time lapsed between birthings. This is important information, especially if you need to consult your veterinarian who will want to have as much information as possible in order to advise you. The bitch should deliver her whelps about every 30 minutes to two hours. I tend to become concerned if three hours lapse between births.

X-Raying Before or After Whelping
Except when a bitch is so heavy in whelp you are uncertain

whether she will need a cesarean section in order to get all the whelps
out alive, or when there is some doubt as to whether the bitch has
only one or two puppies and such a small litter may not be a sufficient amount of puppies to promote natural labor, there is no justification for radiographing a pregnant Mastiff. Puppy skeletons do
not start to calcify until around 40 to 45 days and, generally, they
will not show clearly on radiograph until about 55 days of gestation,
or later, by which time the bitch is nearing her time to whelp. Any
woman ever x-rayed at a dentist's office knows the first question
asked is whether she is pregnant. If she is unsure of her condition
or confirms pregnancy, her abdomen is covered by a leaded apron
to protect the unborn fetus from harmful effects of radiation. Therefore, I cannot rationalize why bitches are put through the emotional
turmoil in advanced and cumbersome pregnancy, of being taken to
a veterinarian, lifted up on a table (in the case of a pregnant Mastiff
it takes three or four people to safely lift) to x-ray.

What possible difference does it make knowing how many
whelps are there? One learns in due time, anyway. Often a radiograph does not provide an exact whelp count. I suspect most radio-
graphs taken in the last days of gestation are done to satisfy owner
curiosity. Putting a bitch through additional stress is, to my mind,
counterproductive. I do strongly recommend radiographing within
24 hours of birth of the last puppy to be certain the dam has delivered all puppies. If a whelp remains in the bitch or if a placenta is
retained, the veterinarian will wish to give a shot to force the uterus
to contract and expel whatever was not delivered naturally during
the birthing process.

Whelping Complications in Mastiffs

While I do not mean to alarm the reader whose Mastiff is
due to whelp puppies, it is no great secret Mastiff bitches are prone
to whelping problems. The more information you have, the better
armed you will be and, thus, more able to help your beloved bitch
and ensure the safety of her puppies. I have heard, or read, the average size of Mastiff litters range from five to eight puppies. What
one needs to understand is to arrive at these averages there are
countless litters of 12 to 16 puppies offset by an equal amount of
litters containing only a whelp or two. With four to ten puppies, the

Mastiff bitch usually does nicely on her own with only your assistance.

Whelping complications tend to occur with very small and overly large litters. These big girls just do not do well in either extreme. If the dam has only a puppy or two she may fail to produce an adequate amount of hormonal oxytocin, generated from the pituitary gland, to prompt labor which means the only solution is to perform a cesarean section to remove the litter or it will not be born on time and instead stay inside the bitch and eventually drown in amniotic fluid. Not only have puppies been senselessly lost, but if dead puppies stay in the uterus and decompose, it is certain the integrity of the uterus will be compromised and a serious infection could result in the bitch needing to be spayed to save her life. If the dam has a very large litter, she may deliver half her puppies and when the second half should be born she is too exhausted to continue laboring. There have been instances in which Mastiffs were so tired they gave no detectable response to injections administered to force continued labor. If this happens surgery must be performed to remove remaining whelps.

Uterine inertia, the failure for various reasons to labor, must be considered if a Mastiff exceeds by several days her due date to whelp, has too few whelps to promote labor or has too many puppies and stops labor midway through with no sign of finishing delivery of the litter. Possible causes of uterine inertia: a puppy too large to deliver naturally; a puppy may have already died in the uterus and interrupted hormone balance; the bitch is overweight and lacks the fortitude to labor; there is too abundant an amount of amniotic fluid; or, a bitch may be emotionally upset due to environmental stress.

You must be alert for danger signs and upon appearance of any of these conditions contact the veterinarian at once. If you misinterpret a sign, it is preferable to disturb the veterinarian and suffer mild embarrassment for being wrong than to overlook something serious. To sit back and do nothing to help the bitch, hoping things will improve on their own, would be wrong and unconscionable. The earlier a problem is dealt with, the greater the chance of safe resolution.

The most obvious sign something is wrong is when the bitch has had strong labor contractions for more than two hours with no puppy appearing. If the first puppy in line to be born is too big and cannot pass, all remaining whelps are in jeopardy. Other symptoms of trouble: the water bag has broken and after two hours no puppy is produced; the bitch is well along in delivering puppies and stops labor; before labor has begun, a dark greenish discharge appears which could indicate a puppy is detached from the uterine wall and its oxygen supply from the dam is severed. If three hours between delivery of whelps has passed, one must assume something is wrong. A bitch of ours, 57 days along in pregnancy from a single breeding tie, quite heavy with puppies, began with one of the danger signals, a small amount of a dark green vaginal discharge. The veterinarian prescribed a mild antibiotic that would not harm the puppies and might protect her uterus. We waited to see if the discharge increased. The bitch was so full of puppies and they were so young, we were trying to buy time. On the 59th day, the discharge increased greatly in volume and a cesarean section was performed. As suspected, one whelp had died and was just beginning to slip out of the amniotic sac, so our timing was excellent and 13 healthy puppies survived. Had we waited even one day longer, the deceased puppy could have begun to contaminate the remaining whelps.

Cesarean Sections and Anesthesia

Knowing in advance a cesarean section may be necessary, because of the nature of the breed and the possibility of too few or too many whelps, I must now caution that far too many Mastiffs and puppies are lost while under the influence of anesthesia. Pregnant Mastiffs are particularly vulnerable and so are the babies during a cesarean section, possibly because anesthesia is administered based on weight. Whole litters can die due to poor management or because anesthetic crossed the placental barrier and depressed puppies to such an extent they could not manage that all important first breath.

Litters are lost because of inexperience and a lack of farsighted planning by the bitch owner. Accept that your bitch may require a cesarean section. Do your homework ahead of time. Communicate with your veterinarian before an emergency situation develops. Explain that there is a high rate of loss in Mastiffs due to anesthesia. Find out if your veterinarian has ever performed a cesarean procedure on a Mastiff. Ask what anesthesia he uses. Contact longtime breeders and determine what anesthesia their veterinarians use. Ask your veterinarian if he is willing to contact a veterinarian with a history of successful cesarean sections on Mastiffs. Ask if your veterinarian is agreeable to changing his usual procedures to accommodate your breed and its special requirements. If your concern and requests are resented, find another veterinarian. You will want the confidence of knowing if your bitch arrives at the clinic with healthy whelps inside her, a skilled professional will send you home with live, thrifty babies and a bitch that is awake and somewhat alert.

I will state outright, and probably bring about my own demise in some veterinarian circles, that there are some circumstances that warrant a cesarean even when a bitch has sent out no real distress signal. Nobody, I repeat, nobody shares the intangible rapport, communication and understanding that the owner has with the bitch. Breeders must be guided on these rare occasions by their own innate instincts. This advice is not necessarily meant for novice pet owners, although I would be hard pressed to ignore their intuition. It is for the breeder who is able to combine knowledge with personal feelings. In other words, if everything inside of you screams do something now instead of waiting, there may be a reason and your gut feeling is sometimes best.

My foundation bitch's second litter made me believe in my instinct and the belief stayed and served me well over the years. The whelping of her first litter had a bearing on the second. The first litter was an ongoing, living nightmare. She was serviced four times and went 67 days from the last service with no indication of labor. She was closely monitored by our veterinarian and reluctantly he performed a cesarean. The first four puppies, two pounds each, were detached from the uterus, out of sacs, and drowning. The most heroic measures were insufficient to revive them. Six puppies were under a pound each, black in color and obviously premature. Mastiff puppies of double-fawn parentage often have black overlay at birth, but my puppies were solid black, but for one who had fawned out a bit. Hair that should have covered muzzles was not present, muzzles had a spongy appearance. Pads on the feet were undefined. The worst problem was labored breathing. Determined to save them, I fought for them morning and night for the next three weeks (looking back, I am still amazed they survived).

You will understand now I was prepared to expect anything when this bitch was bred again. I thought she had missed conception until 47 days when I felt a puppy kick. Pregnancy was confirmed and the doctor recommended we let her whelp naturally. Still new at this whelping business, I was all for doing it nature's way and gathered everything needed to have babies at home. When she reached 63 days from the last service something changed my mind. I cannot really describe it any better than to say I looked in her eyes that morning and knew puppies had to come out that day. There was nothing to base my feeling on, yet the instinct was so strong I was frantic. I bundled my bitch into the van and headed to the clinic. The doctor, understandably, preferred "we" let her whelp naturally. I stood my ground. I never knew why he gave in, but he did and it seemed only minutes later he shouted "Thank God you brought her in." Three puppies were in one uterine horn, the other horn empty, and her uterus had flipped over. She could never have had the puppies on her own and had she tried it could have been disastrous.

This same scenario reoccurred years later. A bitch was heavy in whelp and I planned a cesarean, lamely justified on surgery done to correct a hock injury I did not want stressed or re-injured during labor. The cesarean revealed a masculine ligament, resembling a giant piece of white seaweed, that blocked the cervix so no puppy could have been born naturally.

Assuming your bitch requires a cesarean section, you will need to make slightly different preparations. Take a supply of towels along with you for rubbing puppies and reserve at least three clean towels for the trip home. You will need a cardboard box and at least two hot water bottles. Hopefully, the clinic's staff is present to help start puppies breathing. When puppies are born at home they arrive one at a time, or on very rare occasions two may come at once. At the clinic, the doctor is removing them from the uterus as rapidly as possible, and as soon as the sacs are torn open he is handing them off to you or the staff. His immediate concern is the welfare of your bitch. He cannot see to the whelps until her abdomen is sutured and she is stabilized. So, all at once, puppies need to be rubbed, stimulated, dried and their cords tidied up and tied off. It is important to remember that at home there was a room warmed for whelping and puppies would have been getting individual attention. This does not happen at the clinic so there is ample opportunity for puppies to chill, especially when many different people are working on the puppies and you cannot monitor them.

Hypothermic (chilled) Puppies

The real danger about chilled puppies is that they are placed in your warmed-up cardboard box, or an incubator, and after a few minutes they begin to feel comfortably warm to your touch so you relax, believing they are doing fine. This scenario can be devastatingly misleading and results in what will be labeled a "fading puppy" because the chilled whelp will die in a day or so for no discernible reason. You will not be able to recognize, it is difficult to ascertain, which puppy may have chilled, or if any or all of them chilled, at any point in time between leaving the dam's uterus, through the ensuing and sometimes frantic revival process, and being placed in their warm box or incubator.

If you understand what happens to the puppy when it chills, you can take definite steps to reverse the problem before it leads to death. When a puppy's temperature dips below 94 degrees, its digestive tract becomes paralyzed. The puppy will appear weaker, or more listless, and your first inclination is to feed him to make him stronger. If this puppy is fed before being warmed up he will certainly die, perhaps not immediately, but later he will fade and die. Unfortunately, almost every veterinarian encourages the owner to put puppies on the dam to suckle while she is still at the clinic. I stopped doing this years ago and without a doubt it has saved many of my puppies. Do not feed them until each puppy is warmed. Unless warming is done in gradual increments starting with the lowest level of heat, an incubator is not sufficient. Nor is a heat lamp, heating pad or hot water bottle good enough. To warm a puppy by these methods will only surface warm him, but will not warm him internally.

Your body is the best heat conductor. Place each puppy under your clothing, against your bare chest. Gently rub them, constantly, for a minimum of 30 to 40 minutes. Now the puppy is warmed both internally and externally. If you take an otherwise healthy puppy that is chilled and lifeless and follow these directions, you will actually feel life returning to him as he starts squirming, twitching and breathing more freely. Remember, during the next few weeks, whether puppies stay with the dam or are bottle fed, they cannot regulate their body temperature so you must continue to guard against their becoming chilled.

We had a litter of 15-day-old puppies on heating pads and under a heat lamp when our electricity went out in the wee hours of a bitterly cold morning. Our alarm clock did not ring and, sleep deprived, we missed a feeding. When we awakened, the puppies had gone seven hours without nourishment (normally fed every three hours) and all puppies were cold and limp. Because they were on what had become cold, wet towels for so long, they were thoroughly chilled. Family members carried three and four puppies at once in our shirts, holding folded towels over our clothing to transfer as much warmth as possible. That was Christmas Eve, by the way, and we still have our "Noel." All babies survived the frightful ordeal. The important thing is not to panic, but set about righting the wrong in the speediest way possible.

Taking the Bitch and Litter Home

Let's return to the scene at the clinic, you have a box full of hungry newborns and a very groggy bitch who just successfully came through major surgery. Your bitch probably is placed on a blanket

The author's Maggie with her babies.

on the cold floor. Trust me when I tell you everyone at the clinic wants to see those cute babies nursing on the dam. Please do not do it. There is a notion that the bitch will bond more quickly to her puppies if she wakens to find them nursing. My opinion is she is in a twilight state, trying hard to grasp what is happening around and to her. She may hear the puppies crying and cock her ears to listen, but in reality all she hears and relates to is your safe, familiar voice. As soon as she can get to her feet and navigate, take her home. Just before you depart, ensure the water is still hot in the water bottles and that there is no leakage from the bottles around the puppies. Cover the box with two towels to keep the warmth inside the box.

Puppies and Antibiotics

If the veterinarian has confidence in you, ask for bottles of unmixed pediatric amoxicillin and cephalexin for oral suspension. Should the puppies become sick, you will only need to call for consultation and then start the puppies on the appropriate medication at once. With sick puppies, time is of the essence. The quicker treatment is begun, the better a puppy's chance for survival. If the puppies are on antibiotic therapy, you need to feed them plain yogurt containing natural cultures. Antibiotics are nondiscriminating. All bacteria present is targeted for destruction and this means good bacteria necessary in the puppy's tummy is being eliminated together with bad bacteria. Yogurt is a probiotic and can, literally, save your puppy's life by maintaining balance in the stomach. Puppies like the taste and yogurt is easy to administer with a syringe, an eyedropper or teaspoon. Before feeding it to the puppy, stir the yogurt well, warm it slightly and stir it well again. Feed it slowly into the side of the mouth. From birth to a week of age, 1cc once a day. Beginning at one week to two weeks, 3cc a day.

Warming Puppies and First Feeding on Dam

Once home, assist the dam to stretch out on her side in the whelping box. Set the cardboard box up with a heating pad on low, covered by a towel, and cover the top of the box with another towel. Warm puppies inside your shirt, one by one, and as each one is warmed, put it on the dam to nurse. Do not leave the puppies alone with the dam, you cannot completely trust her yet. Check each puppy's abdomen to be certain it is receiving nourishment. Some puppies are ineffectual nursers. They go through the motions of nursing, make smacking noises as though they are industriously getting food when in fact they are getting nothing. They eventually fall off the teat too tired to continue. If a puppy is an ineffectual nurser, you must intervene. You may have to carefully milk out some of the colostrum and feed it to the puppy. When this happens, I like to use a 3cc syringe, or an eyedropper, slipping the nourishment into the side of the mouth.

As each puppy fills and falls off the teat, stimulate its genitals to make him urinate and defecate. Remember the meconium? If the bitch had whelped the puppies naturally she would have cleaned this out, but as she is temporarily incapacitated you must perform this chore for her and the puppy. Use a cotton ball with a dab of baby oil on it. Stroke the puppy's abdomen in a downwards motion towards the genitals. So long as the puppy has the birth matter in him, the stool will appear stringy and blackish. I am never comfortable until the stool changes to a light brown to yellow color and urine goes from yellow to nearly clear. Hopefully, the dam will assume this duty in a day or two, but until she does you must clean and evacuate the puppy after every feeding. When all puppies are full and clean, put them in the cardboard box located in the whelping box beside the dam. Do not take them away from her, but do not leave them alone with her either. Stay near. She is vaguely aware of them, but has probably not made the connection they are hers. If she is a first-time dam, there could be a day or so delay before all comes together and she comprehends they came from her. On first coming home, all she wants to do is sleep off the effects of anesthesia.

Puppy Cords, Eyes, Ears, Toenails, Stools, etc.

Umbilical cords should dry and fall off in a day or two. Monitor to see that the cord dries. An umbilical infection is serious. The cord is an easy way for infection to enter the puppy. Eye lids are sealed tight at birth and puppies cannot hear. Eyes begin opening around 9 to 17 days and if the dam is not cleaning puppies, wipe the eyes with a warm damp cloth daily, especially from day nine

Ch. Niniane The Enchantress with her litter by Ch. Iron Hills Warwagon.

until opened. Puppies begin to hear around the same time eyes start to open. Puppies cannot regulate body temperature and do not develop a shivering reflex until about a week of age. Healthy puppies cry when they are too hot, too cold or hungry. Healthy puppies yawn often and constantly twitch while asleep. They should be well hydrated with a plump appearance. Begin trimming toenails by the end of the first week. Dewclaws can cause injury when they crawl over one another, a curved nail can scratch or blind another puppy. At three weeks, take fresh stools from several puppies to the veterinarian to see if worms are present.

Caring for the Lactating Bitch

It is always best to let the dam support the litter if she has adequate milk. Puppies need to nurse every two hours around the clock. In order for the bitch to produce milk, they must take milk from her. If she is to meet the needs of growing whelps she must have fresh water and plenty of quality food. There is discomfort after a cesarean and for a few days the dam may show no interest in food. You need to help her along, establish some sort of balance to get her to take care of herself. She may accept warm broth, or perhaps chicken and rice will tempt her. Ask your veterinarian for Nutra-Cal, or a similar product, to mix in with the food your bitch is agreeable to eating. Nutra-Cal is a high calorie and vitamin supplement in low volume form. Not only will it give her energy, it stimulates the appetite. If she refuses to eat, the supplement is thick and syrupy, in toothpaste form, and can be squeezed directly into her mouth.

By the day after puppies are born, the bitch should begin showing interest. As puppies nurse, she will probably be curious and start nudging and nosing them. You will, of course, praise and encourage her. I sit in the whelping box to clean puppies so their urine and stool can be dribbled on the dam's front legs. She is quick to clean herself and often will move on and clean a puppy. Be persistent and do not give up in your efforts to involve the bitch in the care of her puppies. Take her temperature twice daily as you will want assurance no infection is setting in. Monitor the sutures that closed her abdomen, a daily wipe with alcohol will help keep her clean.

Ordinarily first milk, or colostrum, is waiting in the breast when the whelps are born and, full of vitamins and antibodies, it protects puppies until they can receive their inoculations. If an over-zealous owner constantly checks the teats, looking for milk in the last week of gestation, they can cause let down of the milk to occur prematurely. Please do not squeeze the teats until whelps have arrived and are prepared to nurse. The lactating Mastiff can be very problematic. She can inadvertently bring her milk in too early herself if very heavy in whelp because of the friction created just by her getting up and down and accidentally rubbing the breasts. Sometimes a bitch does not let down milk until a day or so after the birth, after the puppies have first used the colostrum. The bitch, ideally, will only produce as much milk as puppies require. If she makes more milk than they can use, it is not going to be turned over properly and it will in due time spoil.

Eclampsia

Eclampsia is milk fever, a deficiency in blood calcium that seems to occur when puppies nurse on the dam and apparently drain too much of her calcium. It poses a serious threat and symptoms cannot be ignored. She may whimper, pace with a stiffness of gait, or lie with legs extended. She could lose coordination, wobble or fall over. She may have rapid breathing, show anxiety and become restless and run a fever. If this is neglected and advances to a more severe stage, she could suffer convulsions, lose consciousness and she could die. In rare instances, the condition occurs before puppies are born.

Hysteria, or the Dam Eating Her Puppies

A dam eating her puppies is not as monstrous, uncommon or abnormal as it sounds. Constantly monitor a first-time mother—especially nervous, over protective, possessive or unsocialized dams. In a convoluted sense she is trying to protect her puppies. She could turn on and hurt them due to anxiety, emotional upset caused by environmental factors such as other animals nearby, or being in unfamiliar surroundings she does not trust. Over-handling of puppies, particularly by children, can upset her or she may become anxious if puppies are kept from her. Experts suggest hysteria is hypocalcemia related or due to faulty placenta-eating instincts that cause confusion, or a puppy is sickly, hypothermic or otherwise unwell, and it is a natural culling instinct.

Metritis

This bacterial infection of the uterus can follow whelping (a complication of a retained fetus or placenta), or result from miscarriage or, less frequently, can be a complication of artificial insemination. It is easily confused with other bacterial infections, therefore vaginal cultures need to be done to identify the specific bacteria. Indications of this infection are a foul-smelling abnormal vaginal discharge, fever, dehydration, anorexia or depression. She may have unsatisfactory milk production and be disinterested in puppies. If metritis persists untreated the bitch could advance into septicemia. When diagnosed, puppies should, of course, cease nursing on the dam.

Mastitis

Monitor the bitch's breasts before she whelps and check them several times daily after whelping. Mastiffs are notorious for developing mastitis. It occurs when a milk, or mammary, gland is inflamed and bacterial infection can be present. Milk in the affected breast may be discolored, yellow to brownish, stringy or lumpy in texture or possibly blood tinged. The breast may be swollen and hardened, and very painful for the bitch. She may run a high temperature, shiver or vomit. Sometimes an affected breast develops an abscess, requiring careful treatment. If mastitis sets in, the veterinarian will wish to start her on appropriate antibiotics at once.

Puppies with Mastitis

Veterinarians may recommend you tape over affected breasts and continue nursing puppies on remaining teats. You may be told to drain infected breasts until milk runs clean. I vehemently oppose any medical opinion advising Mastiff puppies nurse on a dam diagnosed with mastitis. If mastitis rears its ugly head, puppies are greatly at risk. Litters of Mastiffs have been lost to mastitis and, horribly, puppies can sicken and die all at once or be lost a day at a time. You need to understand, if your bitch has this, she is introducing bacteria to puppies through milk. Depending on how much they drink, they may be only mildly discomforted and quickly respond to antibiotic, or they may be deathly ill with severe symptoms such as projectile diarrhea, and they may not have sufficient body weight to withstand this symptom.

Mastitis can manifest itself in Mastiff babies around the head and eyes. Eyes will swell, in which case lids must be opened prematurely and treated with antibiotic if sight is not to be permanently compromised. I am convinced, based on case studies with my bitches, that Persistent Pupilary Membrane (PPM) is a direct complication of mastitis in Mastiffs. Litters I raised on dams medicated for mastitis had PPM. Repeating the same breedings and hand-raising puppies produced no PPM. There is absolutely no doubt when Mastiff puppies are subjected to any bacterial infection, it can settle in eyes and retard eye development. Mastitis-sickened puppies commonly get abscesses, or boils, around the face and neck area. Puppies with mastitis are listless and show no interest in nourishment or, indeed, in living. They may vomit and you need to watch them in case part of the vomit is inhaled into the lungs which could cause aspiration/inhalation pneumonia. Mastiff babies are fragile creatures and mastitis is a nasty complication which should be seen as a potential killer.

Drying-up the Dam's Milk

If metritis or mastitis is diagnosed, measures should be taken to dry up the dam's milk. She will get heavy with milk when puppies suddenly stop nursing. Not only is she driven to care for her puppies but, in a self-serving way, she knows she will feel better physically if they take her milk. She may get desperate to have relief from them nursing. To help dry her milk, you must completely re-verse your pattern of caring for her. Where before she was encour-aged to drink lots of water and eat plenty to make milk, you must now reduce her food intake to half her normal amount, and allow slightly restricted amounts of water. An aspirin every four to five hours for two days may help relieve discomfort. She will be very concerned about her babies so if they retained firm stools through the ordeal, hold each one for her to clean after bottle feeding and she can stay involved with them.

I know a breeder whose bitch and litter stayed at a friend's and when the bitch was sent home with mastitis, the puppies stayed behind to be bottle raised. The following day, the breeder returned home from work to find furniture turned over, papers shredded and things knocked off tables. The dam upset an urn containing ashes of a former favorite Mastiff. I defended the naughty bitch and ex-plained her behavior as being caused by being taken away from her babies. The ashes were mostly recovered but the breeder felt awful having to vacuum up the rest. We look back at the incident and laugh, but it was not funny at the time.

How to Raise Puppies by Hand

Try to get the first milk, or colostrum, in puppies before be-ginning alternate feeding. There are excellent products available that resemble bitch's milk, to name a few, Esbilac, GME Goat Milk For-mula Esbilac, Goat-A-Lac with Acidophilus, Just Born-Milk Re-placer and Veta-Lac. I have raised many Mastiff puppies on home-made formula and associate breeders have requested the recipe and now raise their puppies on it as well. As you will see, the best thing about this formula is it is adjustable to suit individual puppies:

> 1-2/3 Cup Sterile Water (boil 3-5 minutes)
> 1 Can Evaporated Milk
> 2 Egg Yolks (no egg whites)
> 1 Tablespoon Honey or White Syrup

Mix ingredients together and divide in baby bottles. Refrigerate until used. Heat bottle in microwave to kill yolk germs and shake well before feeding ensuring it is neither too hot nor too cold for the puppy.

Premature or weak puppies only drink small amounts at a time so they should be fed 1-1/2 hours around the clock. Adjust the formula and use 2 cups sterile water and 2 tablespoons honey or syrup. If puppies are uninterested or not thrifty enough to nurse, use an eye dropper or syringe. Insert tip at the side of the mouth and dribble slowly into mouth. Gently pat baby's back to aid digestion and stay near heat lamp as this type of puppy is very vulnerable to chilling. When the puppy is stronger and ingesting more, move to the next phase of feeding.

Prepare first three batches of formula according to original recipe for stronger, more vigorous puppies who take in more milk by bottle than if working hard to get milk from dam. Feed this type puppy every 2 hours around the clock for 2 days. The third day, as puppies become adept at drinking from the bottle, stretch feeding to every 3 hours around the clock. The third or fourth day, if puppies nurse well and are active, delete honey or syrup from recipe. At a

Bredwardine Brynhoffnant with her baby by Ch. Tamarack Aethelred. Lizzie and her puppy are owned by Bill & Diane Bearley.

week, change sterile water to tap water and now the recipe, including tap water and excluding sweetener, stays the same until weaning. At week's end puppies should be filling nicely and feedings can be stretched to four-hour intervals, but never any longer.

Puppies should be burped after every feeding or they will very likely regurgitate. Hold puppy in an upward position or lay it against your shoulder and alternately pat gently and rub upwards on the back. Even with the stronger puppy, remember you must not let the puppy chill. If the bitch does not clean the puppy, you must do it. Most puppies stop drinking when full and so should be fed as much as they want. Sometimes a puppy will overeat and when this occurs he will usually take less at the next feeding. The color of a puppy's stool is an indication of how well the puppy fares. If the feeding schedule is right, and the puppy digests what he takes in, the stool will be bright yellow and of a thick ribbon consistency. If he is not given adequate time between feedings to properly digest his intake, stools take on a tinted lime-green color and if feedings are not spaced further apart the stool will turn towards diarrhea. This is an important warning that you must stretch the time between feedings. If you miss or ignore this warning, the stool will turn white or clear and advance to projectile diarrhea.

Dehydration is a critical concern for young puppies without sufficient body weight to endure it for long. Diarrhea must be brought under control immediately. From birth to a week, give 1cc of kaopectic after every bout of diarrhea. From a week to three weeks, give 2 or 3cc after every bout. Electrolytes (found in the baby section of most super markets) are invaluable and might give the puppy strength to survive.

A single puppy in a litter presents a unique difficulty. It will not have stimulation from litter mates crawling on and over him. If you are raising a single puppy, give lots of hand rubbing all over his body before every feeding.

An aggravating problem associated with bottle feeding is puppies sucking on each other. Puppies who waken near mom automatically seek her teat. In a cardboard box, a puppy searches for the teat and finds a puppy's foot or penis. Unfortunately, the puppy being sucked quite enjoys the attention and if it continues uninterrupted medical problems such as rashes or abscesses can develop. If the behavior cannot be stopped, it may be necessary to separate puppies until weaning.

When puppies reach two weeks, assuming they are healthy and drinking vigorously on the bottle, you can safely divide feedings into five times spread out over the day and evening. You can try for a well-earned full night's sleep without getting up in the middle of the night to feed. For example, feed every 4 hours, start at 8 AM, 12 PM, 4 PM, 8 PM and end at 12 AM (then, quickly, rush off to bed!).

Weaning the Puppies

Understandably, you want to dispense with bottle feeding so the obvious question is when is it safe to wean the puppies? If you wean too early, it may not go well. As you have worked very hard to keep the whelps healthy to this point, strive for a wee bit more patience. When puppies are well up on their feet, eyes are opened and new teeth have broken through the gums, you may consider weaning. In the last week of bottle feeding, puppies can drink as much as 7 to 10 ounces per feeding. At this stage, I wonder if nutritional needs are being met and dislike putting so much liquid at one time into a puppy. However, I wait for appearance of the primary clues to tell me it is okay to wean. These clues usually show up at three weeks unless the whelps were premature or have been sickly in which case they will appear a few days later.

Weaning is a stressful proposition for puppies and only strong, healthy puppies should be weaned. Delay weaning if puppies have diarrhea until diarrhea is brought under control. If puppies are diagnosed with worms, delay weaning until worming is completed. Do not add the stress of weaning to an already compromised puppy. Begin weaning with the first morning feeding when puppies are quite hungry. A pie pan is perfect for a couple of puppies. There are wonderful puppy feeding pans with raised centers, for larger litters, to prevent puppies crawling through the pan. Regardless of the dish selected, weaning is still a messy affair.

Cereal is designed for a human baby's needs. Puppy food is designed to meet a growing puppy's needs. Most breeders have a fa-

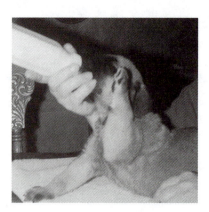

Bottle-feeding Porker.

vorite brand of dog food they already use and wean using the puppy variety of their chosen brand. I recommend putting dry puppy food in a blender to crush it to a fine grain or powder. For the first few feedings use formula to soak the food, mixing until watery and sloppy. Put the bowl down and just watch them dig in. Some puppies are slow to catch on so use a teaspoon and carefully dribble the mixture in their mouth to be sure they, too, are getting nourishment.

Be sure the room where weaning is taking place is warm because puppies will crawl in the food, lick it off one another, and they get wet and cold. Have a few towel-covered boxes waiting with heating pads on low and a pan of warm sudsy water (few drops baby shampoo). Use a wash cloth to wipe each puppy clean, towel dry and put them in the boxes. Stay nearby for within the hour they become too warm and will want back in the whelping box.

Feed three weaning meals (for instance 8 AM, 2 PM and 8 PM) then, about 11 PM bottle feed with formula. Follow this schedule for several more nights then at 11 PM, instead of bottles, fill the feeding pan with 3 cups warm water and one can of evaporated milk. It may take several times for them to lap the milk, but this soon becomes the favorite meal of the day. By the third day, stop using formula to soak the food and begin using tap water. Hot water on puppy food destroys vitamins, use room temperature tap water. Also, puppies continue to want a bottle and as they need to learn to drink water with the increase in solid food, I fill a baby bottle with fresh tap water and off and on throughout the day let each puppy drink water from the bottle. In a day or so a pan of water can remain with them.

At four weeks, put brightly colored soft buckle collars on each puppy. Tie a short colorful length of shoe string, long enough to hang down the puppy's chest but not long enough to trip the puppy, on the ring of the collar and sit back and prepare to be entertained. The puppies will leash break each other by pulling and tugging on the strings.

Coccidiosis

Coccidiosis, a protozoan disease, must be confirmed by stool sample looked at under microscope. The dam can be a carrier and pass it to her puppies or it can be caused by overcrowding, or unsanitary conditions and passed back and forth through the feces. Puppies have diarrhea, possibly blood streaked, and become disinterested in food. They may have cold symptoms, runny nose, cough, weakness. The veterinarian will prescribe sulfa drugs and antibiotics.

Canine Herpesvirus

This virus is transferred through saliva or nasal secretions. Puppies can be exposed during the trip down the birth canal so it first takes hold during birthing, or the dam may transmit it to the puppy through licking, or puppies may get it through secretions of dogs allowed to visit with them. Herpesvirus is thought to be a double-stranded DNA virus inactivated by sunlight, drying and heat. Infected puppies cry in agony due to stomach muscles cramping. They will not want nourishment, breathing is labored and bloody diarrhea develops. There is a high mortality rate. The disease shows up between one and three weeks of age and multiplies quickly due to lower puppy body temperatures. The virus is killed at elevated temperatures, 100 to 101 degrees, so the only chance of survival is for the puppies to be maintained at 100 degrees for short periods of time, supported by fluids and antibiotics. If the puppies live, it is possible liver and kidneys are damaged.

Hookworm

Hookworms are as tiny as a strand of hair and increase rapidly. They hook into the intestinal wall and suck blood, consequently puppies can become anemic quickly. Death could occur as soon as 10 to 12 days of age. They will have liquid diarrhea, possibly blood streaked, and gums become gray. Treat the same as for roundworms.

Roundworm

This is the most common parasite that infects puppies. Worms resemble 1- to 3-inch pieces of string. The dam harbors larvae in her muscles and whelps are often born infested. Severe infestations can lower puppy resistance to infection and cause diarrhea which can result in death. Puppies have a bloated appearance, as though they overate, and gums may be lighter than normal. Dewormers are administered based on individual weight.

Septicemia

This can be related to Escherichia Coli (E. Coli), Pseudomonas, Streptococci or Staphylococci. Any of these microorganisms in the bloodstream causes blood poisoning or septicemia and can kill young puppies. Sanitary, sterile conditions at birth help to avoid the infections.

Coprophagy (Stool Eating)

Young puppies, especially during weaning, will eat stools. Puppies produce bowel movements almost the moment they are done eating so you need to be there to clean them up. Keep the puppy area clean. If stool eating becomes a problem, usually occurring in the night when you sleep, start leaving food down overnight. This habit must be stopped because it is not only disgusting to humans, it is unhealthy for the puppies and can result in upset stomachs or diarrhea.

"Cookie" at six weeks—owned by the author.

CHAPTER 14
HOW TO SELECT A MASTIFF PUPPY

Picking A Breeder

You have already given careful thought to the kind of dog you want. You responsibly did your homework and narrowed the list of candidate breeds to only a couple. Then you researched your selections even further to see which breeds would best suit your family and environment. Finally, you decided you wanted a Mastiff. Excellent choice! Now you need to find a reputable breeder from whom to buy your newest family member.

Choosing a breeder is greatly a matter of personal preference. Not only do you want to obtain a healthy puppy from good parentage, but it is equally important you feel comfortable with the breeder from whom you are buying your puppy. Unfortunately, sometimes things unexpectedly happen and you want to feel the breeder of your puppy cares. You want a responsible breeder who demonstrates concern for your puppy and who will respond to you with compassion and advice.

The best place to begin your search for a breeder is to contact the Breed Clubs for a list of breeders in good standing. Membership in a Breed Club generally denotes a sincere commitment to the breed. Most clubs have Codes of Ethics to provide breeders with established guidelines for better breeding. When a breeder joins a Breed Club he agrees to abide by recommendations written for the welfare of the breed. The suggestions may, for example, state the earliest age at which a bitch could safely be bred or a specific age past which it would be detrimental to breed a bitch.

For the buyer, membership in a Breed Club is no guarantee breeders will honor their obligations, but it is a good starting place to learn about different breeders. Some breeders proudly list their club membership affiliations in advertisements they place in dog magazines, which is another good source to locate breeders or learn about litters.

The Mastiff Club of America, Inc. is the parent club for Mastiffs and a member club of the American Kennel Club. In addition, there are many regional Mastiff clubs around the country that would be pleased to refer inquiries to member breeders, as follows:

MIDWEST MASTIFF FANCIERS

SOUTHERN STATES MASTIFF FANCIERS

NORTH & EAST MASTIFF CLUB

THREE RIVERS MASTIFF CLUB

ROCKY MOUNTAIN MASTIFF FANCIERS

PACIFIC NORTHWEST MASTIFF FANCIERS

CHESAPEAKE MASTIFF CLUB

REDWOOD EMPIRE MASTIFF CLUB

A sales contract is an excellent idea, signed by breeder and buyer, as it eliminates questions later on and stipulates conditions under which puppies can be returned to breeders in the event the buyer can no longer care for a puppy. A good contract advises buyers of certain remedies they are entitled to if the puppy does not fulfill promises made by the buyer.

Some buyers acquiring a puppy from a breed they have never owned before need guidance to raise the puppy and in this case they want to find a breeder who will patiently mentor them with the developing puppy. Not all breeders are willing or have time to spend with buyers once they have relinquished puppies to new homes.

Purchase of a puppy should never be done spontaneously or on the spur of the moment. Afterwards, you can have a puppy you do not really want and even if the puppy can be taken back to the breeder, the circumstance would be unnecessarily disruptive and stressful for the puppy. Decide first you are ready to meet the myriad obligations associated with a new puppy. Then, and only then, begin to search for a breeder.

After you acquire a list of breeders, call as many as necessary until you find the breeder you feel is right for you. Visit and talk with as many breeders as possible. You and members of your family will need to meet adult members of the breed to be certain you are prepared to own a member of this giant breed. Ask questions about the breed. Ask about genetic problems and common structural faults in the breed and ask if the sire and dam are genetically tested for common hereditary conditions in the breed. If a breeder tells you he

Puppies produced by breeders Dennis & Laura Sullivan, Applewhaites' Farm.

will sell you a puppy that will never develop eye problems, or hip and elbow problems, run, do not walk, to the next breeder on your list.

If parents of the puppy are certified free of such disorders, chances are increased the puppy will not be afflicted. However, recessive genes can have an unfortunate influence and these problems can unexpectedly occur. Put your trust in the breeder who openly discusses developmental problems and trust the breeder who signs a contract giving the buyer recourse in the event a problem develops. Visit several litters of puppies before making your final selection of a new puppy. You want to learn how to care for your puppy and about his nutritional needs. Buyers should receive a record of shots given and future shots required, and a medical history on the puppy that includes a worming schedule.

Listen carefully to all answers given to you and be prepared to answer personal questions about your family and home environment. Do not be insulted if the breeder asks for references—and checks them. The breeder may want to visit your home. This should not be resented as it is an indication the breeder cares very much about the future welfare of the puppies.

Numerous articles say buyers should meet the sire and dam of puppies they are considering purchasing. It is advantageous if you can do this but very often it is not realistic. Nor should it be held against the litter. Reputable breeders are dedicated to breeding selectively to produce better puppies. This may involve long-distance travel, taking or shipping the bitch to the stud dog's home where she may live until the breeding is accomplished. Or, the bitch may be bred by use of shipped fresh chilled or frozen semen, sometimes requiring surgical implant. These methods of breeding are becoming more common and are a lot more costly and time consuming than conveniently breeding to the dog next door. Committed breeders invest time and money to do the best breeding they can and it is not always possible to meet both parents. If the breeding agreement called for giving up the pick of the litter in lieu of a fee for services of the stud dog, that puppy may be sold out of the stud owner's home in which case the dam may actually be the parent not seen. Certainly if either sire or dam are available on site with the puppies one should be able to visit with them. Buyers should see at least one parent and pictures or a video of the other parent.

Picking A Puppy

A buyer's first concern, even before viewing the litter, should be the environment in which puppies are raised. When you enter the puppy quarters does it smell clean and fresh? That is not to say a fresh stool may not be present and we all recognize that smell! But is there a sickly or sour smell? Puppies with diarrhea present a very distinctive smell. I have found puppies raised clean from birth housetrain more quickly because they actually enjoy being clean. Healthy puppies are generally clean puppies.

Now that you have met one or both of the parents of the puppies and, presuming you are suitably impressed, you have seen where puppies were raised and decided the breeder raised them with care, let us look at the babies. Do they have the "me" attitude? That is, do they have an attitude that says "look at me." A well-adjusted puppy is a totally self-involved creature, selfish by nature, the world centers around him and he thinks he deserves all the hugs, pets and kisses, and he instinctively competes and demands your attention.

Are puppies bright eyed and playful? Do they have that overall picture of good health? It is not easy to describe the look, but it is easy to see if they do not have it. A listless puppy, or one that hangs back, drops his head down, or slinks away may have something wrong. Any puppy can back away from a stranger or something new but a stable puppy comes right back because of overwhelming curiosity. Puppy coats should feel good to you. The fur may not be spotlessly clean, few puppies who play hard and run through or roll over stools are spotlessly clean, but it should feel soft. Healthy puppies are what good breeders strive for and what prospective buyers should demand. You picked this breeder to purchase your puppy from because you trusted him and like his Mastiffs. Rely on his knowledge to help you select your puppy. The breeder has spent weeks with the puppies and has a good opinion of each puppy's social skills and needs.

Claudia Dvorak's young male puppy, Duncan, bred by the author.

If a pet-quality puppy is being purchased, breeders will explain why the puppy is considered a pet. An evaluation that deemed a puppy pet quality generally implies it has a fault the breeder does not want perpetuated in progeny. The head may not be impressive, or bone is too fine, or perhaps the tail has a kink, or if male, maybe he is monorchid or cryptorchid, in which case the breeder will probably insist the puppy be neutered so he can live a long and healthy life without threat of cancer. There are many valid reasons to evaluate a puppy as pet quality, but health is not one of them. A pet should be every bit as healthy as show prospects.

Buyers have the right to reasonably expect a pet to serve its purpose and function just as a show prospect should be able to serve its purpose and function. Many of today's breeders use restricted registration for pets, a service the AKC offers. It is called "limited registration" and the ownership papers clearly state "offspring are not eligible for registration." Breeders may withhold registration papers altogether for pet-quality puppies, in which case it should be written in the sales contract. The contract may actually require neutering or spaying of the puppy.

If show/breeding quality is sought, your examination of prospects needs to be more thorough so you must be familiar with the standard and, more important, with faults common in the breed. Anyone who studies pictures of early Mastiffs repeatedly see where today's faults come from. Many Mastiffs behind our pedigrees were high in the rear, straight stifled, some had snipey heads and other looked like Danes or Bullmastiffs.

Mastiffs are considered a "head" breed, and that aside for a moment, the first thing I look for in a great puppy is balance, which is everything. If something does not fit with something else then the whole picture is out of whack. I want that perfect Mastiff head, too, but I want the head to go with the body, the body to go with the legs, the legs with the feet, the front should match the rear, and so on. The Mastiff should be rectangular. Puppies begin to show body length as soon as four to five weeks of age. If puppies are to mature into adults who move as the standard dictates, they must have length of body that will enable them to reach in front and drive from the rear.

So, now we have a balanced and rectangular puppy. We also want a puppy with good feet, well-arched toes and tight like a catfoot. The feet are the foundation of what will be a heavy-duty adult and if the foundation is not good, well, how can the whole package be good?

Watch puppies playing freely, running, trotting, sitting down and getting to their feet. Sure, they are clumsy, but try to look beyond that. Does he stand foursquare? Does he have a wide-set rear end with legs set squarely and not close together? Same thing with the front? If balance is there and structure is right, a puppy will sometimes walk into an almost perfect show stand. When the puppy is moving, do his hind feet slip right into the spot his front feet just vacated or do any of his limbs wing away from the body? Is the tail set high? The higher it is, the better, because as he grows it has nowhere to go but down. If it is low on a puppy, it will be too low at maturity. Now we have a balanced, rectangular puppy, beautiful feet and a high tail set.

What next? Probably the most important considerations when picking a Mastiff show puppy is head, bone size and overall substance. Our standard describes *a head type*. In fact, there are

Ch. Storm Timber's Maid of Swede Road. Sire: Ch. Storm Hammer of Royal Oak; Dam: Storm Besty Ross of Swede Road; Breeder: Bjorn & dee dee Andersson; Owner: Bob & Jane Gurka.

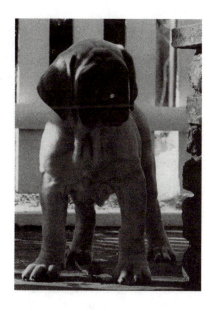

probably 10 types. The standard calls for wrinkle when at attention, so take a squeaky toy with you to get the puppy to "set up" his head. In my experience, what you see at 8 to 10 weeks is a miniature version of what you will have at two to three years. My puppies either have gorgeous heads or poor heads by 10 weeks. If heads are gorgeous, they may go long and narrow and lose some stop in growth stages, but at maturity the gorgeous head comes back. On the other hand, if the head is poor, it is not going to get any better with age. The same thing is true with bone size, either they have it or not. If he has great bone, while growing he may go to "leg" and lose some of the bone, but it returns with maturity. If he is fine boned, or "bitchy," it is not going to get better later.

A common mistake buyers make is to pick the best-headed, biggest and heaviest substanced puppy. Every lover of Mastiffs admires a good typey head, but a drop-dead gorgeous head atop an unsound body or belonging to a Mastiff who cannot get around a show ring is not much good to anybody's breeding program. Remember, the largest puppy has the greatest opportunity to fall apart before reaching maturity. Some things are hard to predict, toplines, rear angulation and overall size at maturity all fall in this category. Your best bet is to look at the parents and other dogs from the same line and gauge your chances of getting what you want. Remember, those old dogs in the pedigree jump forward and influence the puppies. Sadly, there is no great secret to help you predict level toplines. To some extent the same is true with angulation. Most puppies have good angulation and so it always comes as a big surprise and disappointment when they shoot up in the rear and go straight behind, never to return to that former bend of knee and level back.

One rule of thumb that may help is to look for good lay back of shoulder in the puppy. Chances are the adult will have angulation in the rear to match angulation in the front. If shoulders are too straight, it is a safe bet rear angulation will be straight at maturity. We have a balanced, rectangular puppy with good feet, high tail set, beautiful head that only wrinkles at attention and impressively huge bone, plus our puppy has great shoulder lay back and will keep his perfect angulation and this wonderful puppy walks into the perfect show stand. What more could we possibly want? Now we look at what I call the cosmetics—coat type and color, pigment and bites.

Timber's Murdock of Deerfield. Sire: Moonstone's Bart of Montague; Dam: Ch. Storm Besty Ross of Swede Rd; Breeder/Owner: Bob & Jane Gurka.

What are common coat faults in the breed? One type of coat is longer and silkier, with no undercoat, or longer hair that has undercoat. Surprisingly, I have had coats that were too short with no undercoat. The proper Mastiff coat is short with a thick undercoat. I have owned Mastiffs who could be bathed in the morning and were still damp at night and this is the coat called for in the standard. A puppy with long hair, tufts of hair growing out of the ears or feathering on the underbelly or tail will have a coat not to the standard. As far as color is concerned, fawn is fawn. Apricot ranges from reddish fawn to deep, dark mahogany. Brindle color varies from very light brindle to almost totally black. Coats too black, with no noticeable brindling are as incorrect as brindles more light in appearance than dark. A coat of a solid color, apricot or fawn, with little or light brindling is not correct. Proper brindle should give an overall impression of darkness, with evenly distributed brindling throughout. The darker the puppy, the better, as brindle will lighten with age. There is controversy among breeders about proper brindle color and I said it was only cosmetic.

The standard calls for black muzzles, noses and ears—also cosmetic. Often Mastiffs are born with dark ears and by the time they reach 8 to 10 weeks ears have fawned out. If facial pigment is dark or there is a rim of black around the inside of ears, it should be of no concern. By the time the Mastiff reaches maturity, ears will probably be the same color as the mask. Some breeders believe every few generations a breeding must be done with brindle to preserve pigment. I do not subscribe to this school of thought. I have owned brindles with black pigment, and they passed pigment to their children. I also owned a brindle whose mask and ears were more brindled than black and he never improved pigment in his offspring. A brindle who lacks black pigment cannot pass what he does not have, any more than could a fawn or apricot.

The standard prefers a scissors bite, but allows for an underbite so long as teeth do not show when the mouth is closed. The standard does not mention overbite and some veterinarians are confused when presented a 10-week-old Mastiff who has this type of bite. The more overshot at this young age, the better the chances are of having a scissors bite at maturity. As the skull grows and develops, bites change accordingly. If a puppy has a scissors bite at 10 weeks, the mature animal may go somewhat under. If a puppy is undershot at 10 weeks, the teeth may show at maturity.

Some Mastiff clubs require breeders keep puppies until their eight-week birthday. It really is best not to separate puppies from their dam and litter mates too early. If puppies are taken prematurely from the dam, she is deprived of the opportunity to teach them canine manners they need to survive out in the big world they are entering. If puppies are shipped by airplane to new owners, it is best not to ship them before 10 weeks of age.

Bringing the New Puppy Home

Before picking the puppy up you will want to be prepared at home. Get a bag of the same dog food he is accustomed to eating and several bottles of water from the first home. Changes in food or water can result in bothersome diarrhea, but if you are prepared in advance it is easily avoided. The changeover to your water can be done slowly and if you plan to change the puppy's diet, do it slowly over at least a week's time so that his digestion does not become upset. You will want safe toys and chew bones and you need to prepare a sleeping area. Perhaps you have already purchased a crate for this purpose. If you plan to crate train your puppy, be sure to use a rubber backed carpet for him to sleep on as when he jumps into or out of the crate there is a risk he will slide on the slippery crate bottom.

I have guided many puppy buyers to shop at yard sales for a child's playpen which can be set up beside the owner's bed. The puppy will feel close to you, yet is safely confined in a specific area. He will not wish to soil his sleeping area and will soon learn to bark to be taken outside. If you are vigilant and get up a few times in the night the puppy can be house trained in a matter of weeks. The playpen can be dismantled during the day. The first few days and nights in a new home with strangers can be a very frightening prospect for the new puppy. From his point of view he is not only insecure because he is not comfortably at home where he was confident, but he is also missing his dam and playmates and the routine to which he was accustomed. New smells, new noises, new people and new surroundings can be overwhelming for the baby. New owners will wish to make the transition from the old home to the new home as smooth as possible. Visitors should be discouraged during the first few days while the puppy adjusts. Puppies have enough new things to accept without unnecessary distractions.

Puppies make wonderful Christmas presents, especially for children, but it is a bad idea to introduce a puppy to a new home during the family celebrations when homes are full of company and other responsibilities take precedent over settling him into the family. It is far kinder for the puppy to move a week or two before the holidays or several weeks afterwards. If the puppy must make the move during this time, remember that many Christmas plants are poisonous to the puppy.

Schedule feedings to coincide with the schedule he was on before moving. Keep reminding yourself that as big as he is, he is still just a baby. You would not expect a two-month-old human baby to be potty trained, nor would you play with a human baby to the extent you would exhaust him. All babies need a lot of sleep. Your new puppy will need to be taken outside to relieve himself frequently. Some of the early signs he needs to go are whining, pacing, fretting and smelling around on the ground. Always praise him when he does what is required of him and always take him back to the same area so he will begin to recognize his own smell and associate what you expect of him with that area.

Living With Your Mastiff

Remember I said Mastiffs are not for everyone? They grow rapidly and some experience attendant medical problems. It is not inexpensive to medicate, feed and care for a growing Mastiff. Equally important is the new owner's responsibility to the developing temperament. Some Mastiffs are hereditarily shy and others have a tendency to become environmentally shy if not well socialized while young and impressionable. Mastiff puppies need to be taken out and exposed to as many situations as possible so that as adults they are confidence in all situations. This means owners must expend a lot of time and effort taking them along on expeditions away from home. The Mastiff is, perhaps, not suitable for an active family that travels often and is unable to care for a pet while they are away from home. Mastiffs can refuse nutrition or grieve when left behind. Some have stubborn or willful temperaments and new owners must be prepared to meet this challenge by being more dominant than the animal, which is all part of developing respect between animal and owner. Participation in obedience instruction is a must.

Living with a Mastiff means keeping hand towels nearby to wipe away "goobers" from his mouth and it means "slingers" must be cleaned off walls and furniture. It means hair on clothes and in carpets because, make no mistake, Mastiffs shed. Nails must be trimmed and, ideally, Mastiffs should be fed twice daily because these giant dogs cannot ingest in one feeding their daily intake without putting them in harm's way. Living with a Mastiff means having feet stepped on and being bumped around on occasion. Living with a Mastiff means nonstop entertainment for the owner, loyal companionship and endless unselfish love. It means your next door neighbor's house might be targeted by burglars, but your house will probably be skipped. It means being surrounded by crowds who have a million questions you must answer every time you and your Mastiff go for a walk. Living with a Mastiff also means that you, the owner, have superb judgment and exceptionally good taste.

Timber Symphony in Black. Sire: Moonstone's Bart of Montague; Dam: Ch. Storm Besty Ross of Swede Rd; Breeder/Owner: Bob & Jane Gurka

Sherman is waiting around to go into Group on a hot summer afternoon in Virginia. What's a guy to do? Sleep under a wet towel on a bag of ice—it works every time!

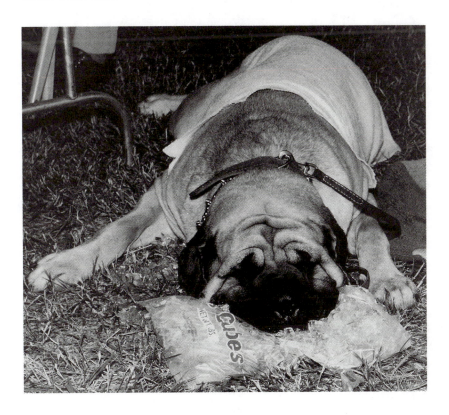

THE END.

INDEX